UNDERSTANDING AND USING

English Grammar

FIFTH EDITION

VOLUME B

Betty S. Azar
Stacy A. Hagen

Understanding and Using English Grammar, Fifth Edition
Volume B

Azar Associates: Sue Van Etten, Manager

Pearson Education, 221 River Street, Hoboken, NJ 07030

Staff credits: The people who made up the *Understanding and Using English Grammar Fifth Edition* team, representing content creation, design, manufacturing, marketing, multimedia, project management, publishing, rights management, and testing, are Pietro Alongi, Rhea Banker, Elizabeth Barker, Claire Bowers, Stephanie Bullard, Jennifer Castro, Tracey Cataldo, Dave Dickey, Warren Fischbach, Nancy Flaggman, Lester Holmes, Gosia Jaros-White, Barry Katzen, Amy McCormick, Julie Molnar, Brian Panker, Stuart Radcliffe, Jennifer Raspiller, Lindsay Richman, Robert Ruvo, Alexandra Suarez, Paula Van Ells, and Joseph Vella.

Contributing Editors: Barbara Lyons, Janice L. Baillie
Text composition: Aptara

Disclaimer: This work is produced by Pearson Education and is not endorsed by any trademark owner referenced in this publication.

Printed in the United States of America
ISBN 13: 978-0-13-427523-9
ISBN 10: 0-13-427523-3

To my beautiful grandsons,
Jude and Asa
B.S.A.

For Andy and Julianna
S.H.

Contents

Preface to the Fifth Edition

Understanding and Using English Grammar is a developmental skills text for intermediate to advanced English language learners. It functions principally as a classroom teaching text but also serves as a comprehensive reference text for students and teachers.

Understanding and Using English Grammar takes a time-tested approach that blends direct grammar instruction with carefully sequenced practice to develop all language skills. Grammar is viewed as an organizing system to help students make sense of the language they see and hear, rather than as a mere collection of rules. This perspective provides a natural, logical framework for students to make English their own.

This edition has been extensively revised to keep pace with advances in theory and practice. Every aspect of the previous edition was reviewed, including the charts, exercises, and sequencing of grammar points. We are excited to introduce significant new features and updates:

- **New as well as updated grammar charts based on corpus research** reflect current usage and highlight the differences between written and spoken English in informal and formal contexts.

- **Pretests at the start of chapters** let learners check what they already know and orient themselves to the chapter content.

- **A wide range of thematic exercises** provides opportunities for contextualized language use.

- **A variety of new readings** covers current topics, strategies for student success, study skills, and other academic and practical content.

- **More meaning-based and step-by-step practice** helps learners better grasp concepts underlying the target grammar.

- **Article use (*a, the, an*)** is now the focus of an entire chapter.

- **New guided writing activities** are supported by writing tips and editing tasks.

- **Self-study practice for gerunds and infinitives** has been added, beginning with Chapter 1, so that students can learn at their own pace.

- **A fresh design** includes a generous use of photos to add interest and serve as the basis for fluency practice.

- **A large increase in the number of exercises** supports teachers who would prefer not to supplement.

- **Three topics, absent in the Fourth Edition, are back in the Fifth Edition:** *The Subjunctive in Noun Clauses, Past Forms of Infinitives and Gerunds,* and *Using a Possessive to Modify a Gerund.*

Now more than ever, teachers will find that they can select from an extensive repertoire of presentations, activities, and tasks depending on the specific needs of their classes. To accommodate all of the new material, some Fourth Edition content has been moved to MyEnglishLab.

Components of *Understanding and Using English Grammar,* Fifth Edition:

- **Student Book with Essential Online Resources** includes the access code for audio, video, expanded practice of gerunds and infinitives, self-assessments, and teacher resources with the Student Book answer key.
- **Student Book with MyEnglishLab** includes the access code to MyEnglishLab, an easy-to-use online learning management system that delivers rich online practice to engage and motivate students.
- A comprehensive **Workbook** consists of self-study exercises for independent work.
- A **Teacher's Guide** features step-by-step teaching suggestions for each chart and notes on key grammar structures, vocabulary lists, and expansion activities.
- A revised **Test Bank** with quizzes, chapter tests, and mid-term and final exams.
- A **Chartbook,** a reference book that consists of only the grammar charts.
- *AzarGrammar.com,* a website that provides a variety of supplementary classroom materials as well as a place where teachers can support each other by sharing their knowledge and experience.

MyEnglishLab

MyEnglishLab provides a range of interactive activities that help motivate and engage students. MyEnglishLab for *Understanding and Using English Grammar,* Fifth Edition has been thoroughly revised and includes:

- Rich online practice for all skill areas: grammar, reading, writing, speaking, and listening.
- Instant feedback on incorrect answers.
- Remediation activities.
- Grammar Coach videos.
- Bonus material not included in the Student Book, including expanded practice of gerunds and infinitives.
- Robust assessments that include diagnostic tests, chapter review tests, mid- and end-of-term review tests, and final exams.
- Gradebook and diagnostic tools that allow teachers to monitor student progress and analyze data to determine steps for remediation and support.
- Student Book answer key in the Teacher Resource folder.

The Azar-Hagen Grammar Series consists of

- *Understanding and Using English Grammar* (blue cover), for upper-level students.
- *Fundamentals of English Grammar* (black), for mid-level students.
- *Basic English Grammar* (red), for lower or beginning levels.

Acknowledgments

We are indebted to the reviewers and other outstanding teachers who contributed to this edition by giving us extensive feedback on the Fourth edition and helping us shape the new Fifth edition.

In particular, we would like to thank Maureen S. Andrade, Utah Valley University; Dorothy Avondstondt, Miami Dade College; Judith Campbell, University of Montreal; Holly Cin, Houston Community College; Eileen M. Cotter, Montgomery College, MD; Andrew Donlan, International Language Institute, Washington, D.C.; Gillian L. Durham, Tidewater Community College; Jill M. Fox, University of Nebraska; William Hennessey IV, Florida International University; Clay Hindman, Sierra Community College; Sharla Jones, San Antonio College; Balynda Kelly Foster, Spring International Language Center, CO; June Ohrnberger, Suffolk County Community College, NY; Deniz Ozgorgulu, Bogazici University, Turkey; Jan Peterson, Edmonds Community College; Miriam Pollack, Grossmont College; Carol Siegel, Community College of Baltimore County; Elizabeth Marie Van Amerongen, Community College of Baltimore County; Daniela C. Wagner-Loera, University of Maryland, College Park; Kirsten Windahl, Cuyahoga Community College.

From the start, we have benefited from a first-rate management and editorial team that helped us every step of the way. Gosia Jaros-White, our publisher at Pearson, handled each stage of the process with focus, efficiency, and kindness. We were lucky to once again have Robert Ruvo, our project manager at Pearson, to keep track of a myriad of detail with schedule, production, and delivery. Barbara Lyons, our development editor, brought unparalleled skill and insight to the charts and exercises. Our longtime production editor whiz, Janice Baillie, has an encyclopedic knowledge of the series, and every page benefited from her expertise. We are grateful as always to Sue Van Etten, our steady and savvy business and website manager, for keeping the business side of things running smoothly.

We'd also like to thank the talented writers we are so fortunate to have: Geneva Tesh, Houston Community College, for the new Workbook and MyEnglishLab material; Kelly Roberts Weibel, Edmonds Community College, for the updated Test Bank, and Martha Hall, the New England School of English, for the revised Teacher's Guide.

We are grateful to the Pearson design team of Tracey Cataldo, Warren Fischbach, and Stephanie Bullard for their creativity and patience.

Our gratitude also goes to Pietro Alongi, Director of Content, and Amy McCormick, Category Manager at Pearson. They have been involved with the series for many years now, and we appreciate the dedication they bring to each new edition and their vision for the series.

Our thanks also to our illustrators Don Martinetti and Chris Pavely for their engaging artwork.

Finally, we would like to thank our families for always supporting us and cheering us on.

Betty S. Azar
Stacy A. Hagen

CHAPTER 12

Noun Clauses

EXERCISE 1 ▸ Warm-up. (Chart 12-1)

Check (✓) all the complete sentences.

1. _____ Are they triplets?

2. _____ They look almost identical.

3. _____ I don't know.

4. _____ How old you think they are?

5. _____ How old are they?

6. _____ I don't know how old they are.

7. _____ how old they are

12-1 Introduction

(a) in the park (b) on a rainy day (c) her grandparents in Turkey	Sentences contain phrases and clauses. A phrase • is a group of words. • does not contain a subject and a verb. • is not a sentence. Examples (a), (b), and (c) are phrases.
(d) He went running in the park. (e) She visited her grandparents in Turkey.	A clause • is a group of words. • contains a subject and a verb. Examples (d) and (e) are clauses.
independent clause (f) ⌐Sue lives in Tokyo.¬ *independent clause* (g) ⌐Where does Sue live?¬	Clauses can be independent or dependent. An INDEPENDENT CLAUSE • contains the main subject and verb. • is the main clause of the sentence. • may be a statement or a question. • can stand alone.
dependent clause (h) ⌐where Sue lives¬	A DEPENDENT CLAUSE • is not a complete sentence. • cannot stand alone. • must be connected to a main clause.
noun clause (i) We don't know ⌐where Sue lives.¬	Example (i) is a complete sentence. It has • a main subject (**We**). • a main verb (**know**). • a dependent clause (**where Sue lives**). The dependent clause — where Sue lives — is also a noun clause. *It is the object of the verb* **know** *and functions like a noun in the sentence.*

EXERCISE 2 ▸ Looking at grammar. (Chart 12-1)

Underline each clause in the sentences.

1. I couldn't hear what you said.

2. What did you say?

3. No one knows where Tom went.

4. Where did Tom go?

5. I'd like to know where Tom went.

6. How do you know where Tom went?

EXERCISE 3 ▸ Looking at grammar. (Chart 12-1)

Add punctuation and capitalization.

1. Where did Sara go did she go home → *Where did Sara go? Did she go home?*

2. I don't know where Sara went → *I don't know where Sara went.*

3. What does Alex need do you know

4. Do you know what Alex needs

5. We talked about what Alex needs

6. What do you need did you talk to your parents about what you need

7. My parents know what I need

EXERCISE 4 ▸ Warm-up. (Chart 12-2)
Choose the correct sentence in each.

1. Where does Brad live?
   a. I'm not sure where he lives.
   b. I'm not sure where does he live.

2. I'm looking for Brad.
   a. Could you tell me where is Brad?
   b. Could you tell me where Brad is?

12-2 Noun Clauses with Question Words

Question	Noun Clause	
wh + helping + **S** + **V** verb Where does she live? What did he say? When do they go?	*wh* + **S** + **V** (a) I don't know *where she lives*. (b) I couldn't hear *what he said*. (c) Do you know *when they went*?	Noun clauses can begin with question words. In (a): *where she lives* is a noun clause. It is the object of the verb *know*. In a noun clause, the subject precedes the verb. NOTE: Do not use question word order in a noun clause. Helping verbs *does*, *did*, and *do* are used in questions but not in noun clauses.*
S **V** Who lives there? Who is at the door?	**S** **V** (d) I don't know *who lives there*. (e) I wonder *who is at the door*.	In (d) and (e): The word order is the same in both the question and the noun clause because *who* is the subject in both.
V **S** Who are those men?	**S** **V** (f) I don't know *who those men are*.	In (f): *those men* is the subject of the question, so it is placed in front of the verb *be* in the noun clause. COMPARE: *Who is at the door?* = *who* is the subject of the question. *Who are those men?* = *those men* is the subject of the question, so *be* is plural.
What did she say? What will they do?	**S** **V** (h) *What she said* surprised me. (i) *What they will do* is obvious.	The noun clause can come at the beginning of the sentence. In (h): *What she said* is the subject of the sentence. Notice in (i): A noun clause subject takes a singular verb (e.g., *is*).

*See Appendix Chart B-2 for more information about question words and question forms.

EXERCISE 5 ▸ Looking at grammar. (Chart 12-2)
Change each question to a noun clause.

Questions from Parents

1. A: How old is your friend Paul?

   B: I don't know _____*how old he is*_____.

2. A: Where does he live?

   B: I'm not sure _____.

3. A: When does the party start?

    B: I'll check _____.

4. A: What time are you leaving?

    B: I need to ask my roommate _____.

5. A: Whose phone numbers are those?

    B: Uh, I'm not sure _____.

6. A: Who left the stove on?

    B: I wasn't the one _____.

7. A: Who are those people?

    B: I don't know _____.

8. A: What happened?

    B: I don't know _____.

9. A: Why did Anna break off her engagement with Thomas?

    B: _____ is a mystery.

10. A: Where did the car keys go?

    B: I don't have any idea _____.

11. A: What are you doing in class?

    B: It's a little confusing. It's not clear yet _____

    _____.

12. A: Do you understand what Mom and I said?

    B: No, I'm sorry but _____

    _____ is still not clear.

EXERCISE 6 ▸ Looking at grammar. (Chart 12-2)

Work with a partner. Take turns making questions with noun clauses. Begin with **Can you tell me**.

School Questions

1. How is this word pronounced? _____*Can you tell me how this word is pronounced?*_____

2. What does this mean? _____

3. What was my grade? _____

4. Who am I supposed to talk to? _____

5. When is our next assignment due? _____

6. How much time do we have for the test? _____

7. When do classes end for the year? _____

8. Where is our class going to meet? _____

9. What time does the computer lab close? _____

EXERCISE 7 ▸ Looking at grammar. (Chart 12-2)
Make questions with the given sentences. The words in parentheses are the answer to the question you make. Begin with a question word (*who, what, when, where, why*). Then change the question to a noun clause.

A Friend's Visit

1. Tom will be here (*next week*).

   QUESTION: _____*When will Tom be here?*_____

   NOUN CLAUSE: Please tell me _____*when Tom will be here.*_____

2. He is coming (*because he wants to visit his college friends*).

   QUESTION: _____

   NOUN CLAUSE: Please tell me _____

3. He'll be on flight (*645, not flight 742*).

   QUESTION: _____

   NOUN CLAUSE: Could you tell me _____

4. (*Jim Hunter*) is going to meet him at the airport.

   QUESTION: _____

   NOUN CLAUSE: Do you know _____

5. Jim Hunter is (*his former college roommate*).

   QUESTION: _____

   NOUN CLAUSE: Please tell me _____

6. He lives (*on Riverside Road near the airport*).

   QUESTION: _____

   NOUN CLAUSE: I'd like to know _____

7. Tom is (*in Chicago*) right now.

   QUESTION: _____

   NOUN CLAUSE: Please tell me _____

8. He is there (*for a conference*).

   QUESTION: _____

   NOUN CLAUSE: Do you know _____

9. He works for (*a technology company*).

   QUESTION: _____

   NOUN CLAUSE: Could you tell me _____

10. He has worked for them (*for ten years*).

    QUESTION: _____

    NOUN CLAUSE: Do you know _____

EXERCISE 8 ▸ Let's talk. (Chart 12-2)

Work with a partner. Take turns asking questions and responding with *I don't know* OR *I wonder*. Use the names of your classmates.

Example: Where is (_____)?
PARTNER A: Where is Marco?
PARTNER B: I don't know where Marco is. OR I wonder where Marco is.

PARTNER A	PARTNER B
1. Where does (_____) live?	1. How long has (_____) been married?
2. What country is (_____) from?	2. Why are we doing this exercise?
3. How long has (_____) been living here?	3. Who is looking at their phone?
4. Where are you going to eat lunch/dinner?	4. What is (_____) phone number?
5. Where is (_____) favorite restaurant?	5. Where did (_____) go after class yesterday?
6. What is (_____) favorite color?	6. Why is (_____) smiling?
7. What kind of watch does (_____) have?	7. How often does (_____) go to the library?
8. Whose book is that?	8. Why was (_____) absent yesterday?
9. How far is it to the airport from here?	9. How much did that book cost?

EXERCISE 9 ▸ Let's talk. (Chart 12-2)

Underline the noun clauses. Are these sentences true for you? Circle *yes* or *no*. Discuss your answers.

1. What my family thinks of me is very important to me.	yes	no
2. I always pay attention to what other people think of me.	yes	no
3. Where we live is exciting.	yes	no
4. How we eat is healthy.	yes	no
5. I think how most celebrities behave is admirable.	yes	no
6. I usually don't believe what I read in advertisements.	yes	no

EXERCISE 10 ▸ Looking at grammar. (Chart 12-2)

Complete each sentence with the words in parentheses. Use any appropriate verb tense. Some of the completions contain noun clauses, and some are questions.

1. A: Where (*Ruth, go*) _____*did Ruth go*_____? She's not in her room.

   B: I don't know. Ask her friend Tina. She might know where (*Ruth, go*) _____*Ruth went*_____.

2. A: Oops! I made a mistake. Where (*my eraser, be*) _____? Didn't I lend it to you?

   B: I don't have it. Ask Sally where (*it, be*) _____. I think I saw her using it.

3. A: The door isn't locked! Why (*Franco, lock, not*) _____ it before he left?*

   B: That doesn't sound like Franco. I don't know why (*he, lock, not*) _____ it. Maybe he just forgot.

---

*Word order in negative questions:
   Usual: *Why didn't you call me?* (with *did* + *not* contracted) Very formal: *Why did you not call me?*

4. A: Mr. Lee is a recent immigrant, isn't he? How long (*he, be*) _____ in this country?

   B: I have no idea, but I'll be seeing Mr. Lee this afternoon. Would you like me to ask him how long (*he, be*) _____ here?

5. A: Which road (*we, be supposed*) _____ to take? It's not on the GPS.

   B: I've never been here before. I don't know which road (*we, be supposed*) _____ to take.

EXERCISE 11 ▶ Let's talk: interview. (Chart 12-2)

Interview your classmates. Begin with **Do you know** followed by a question word (**who, what, when, where, how many, how long, how far**). If no one in the class knows the answer to a question, research the answer. Share any information you get with the rest of the class.

Trivia

Example: the shortest month of the year
SPEAKER A: Do you know *what* the shortest month of the year is?
SPEAKER B: Yes. It's February. OR No, I don't know what the shortest month is.

1. the number of minutes in 24 hours
2. the winner of the Nobel Peace Prize last year
3. the place (country) Buddha was born
4. the distance from the earth to the sun
5. the year the first man walked on the moon
6. the time it takes for the moon to rotate around the earth

EXERCISE 12 ▶ Warm-up. (Chart 12-3)

Underline the noun clauses. What words are added when a *yes/no* question is changed to a noun clause?

QUESTION: Has the mail arrived?
NOUN CLAUSE: I wonder if the mail has arrived.
               I wonder whether the mail has arrived.
               I wonder whether or not the mail has arrived.
               I wonder whether the mail has arrived or not.
               I wonder if the mail has arrived or not.

12-3 Noun Clauses with *Whether* or *If*		
Yes/No Question	**Noun Clause**	

Will she come?
 	
Does he need help?
	(a) I don't know *whether she will come.*
	    I don't know *if she will come.*
	
	(b) I wonder *whether he needs help.*
	    I wonder *if he needs help.*
		When a *yes/no* question is changed to a noun clause, **whether** or **if** is used to introduce the noun clause.
		
		NOTE: **Whether** is more common in writing and **if** is more common in speaking.

	(c) I wonder *whether or not* she will come. (d) I wonder *whether* she will come *or not.* (e) I wonder *if* she will come **or not**.	In (c), (d), and (e): Notice the patterns when **or not** is used.
	(f) *Whether she comes or not* is unimportant to me.	In (f): The noun clause can be in the subject position with **whether**.

EXERCISE 13 ▸ Looking at grammar. (Chart 12-3)
Complete the sentences by changing the questions to noun clauses.

At the Office

Let me know if ...

1. Is the financial report ready?
2. Will it be ready tomorrow?
3. Does the copy machine need paper?
4. Is someone waiting for me?
5. Do we need anything for the meeting?
6. Are you going to be there?

Please check whether ...

7. Did they get my message?
8. Is the copy machine working?
9. Is there any paper left?
10. Is this information correct?
11. Did the fax come in?
12. Are we going to have Monday off?

EXERCISE 14 ▸ Let's talk. (Chart 12-3)
Work with a partner. Take turns asking questions and restating them with *I wonder*.

Example:
PARTNER A: Does Anna need any help?
PARTNER B: I wonder whether/if Anna needs any help.

PARTNER A	PARTNER B
1. Where is Tom?	1. What causes earthquakes?
2. When is he coming?	2. When was the first book written?
3. Is he having car trouble?	3. Why did dinosaurs become extinct?
4. How long should we wait for him?	4. Is there life on other planets?
5. Did anyone call him?	5. How did life begin?
6. Did he forget?	6. Will people live on the moon someday?

EXERCISE 15 ▸ Let's talk: interview. (Chart 12-3)
Interview students in your class. Ask each one a different question. Begin with *Can/Could you tell me*. Share a few of your answers with the class.

1. Have you ever won a prize? What? → *Can/Could you tell me if you have ever won a prize? What did you win?*
2. Have you ever played a joke on someone? Describe it.
3. Have you ever stayed up all night? Why?
4. Have you ever felt embarrassed? Why?
5. Have you ever been in an earthquake? Where? When?
6. Do you have a talent like singing or dancing (*or something else*)? What?
7. Are you enjoying this interview? Why or why not?

EXERCISE 16 ▸ Let's talk: pairwork. (Charts 12-1 → 12-3)

Work with a partner to create short conversations. Partner A asks a question. Partner B answers the question beginning with the words in *italics*.

Example: When does the next bus come?
　　　　　I don't know …
PARTNER A (*book open*): When does the next bus come?
PARTNER B (*book closed*): I don't know when the next bus comes.

SITUATION 1: You're at a tourist center.

Let's ask …

1. Where is the bus station?
2. How much does the city bus cost?
3. Is there a bike rack on the bus?
4. Is this bus schedule correct?

We need to figure out …

5. How far is it from here to town?
6. How much does it cost to take a bus from here to downtown?
7. Is there free Wi-Fi anywhere?

Change roles.

SITUATION 2: You're late for work.

I don't know …

8. Where did I leave my keys?
9. Are my keys in my bag?
10. Where is my shoe?
11. What did I do with my briefcase?

SITUATION 3: You have a new neighbor.

I'll find out …

12. Is he single or married?
13. What does he do?
14. Where does he work?
15. Would he like to come to dinner?

EXERCISE 17 ▸ Let's talk. (Charts 12-1 → 12-3)

Work in small groups. What would you say in each situation? Use noun clauses.

Example: Someone asks you about the time the mail comes. You're not sure.
Possible answers: → *I'm not sure what time the mail comes.*
　　　　　　　　　→ *I don't know when the mail is supposed to be here. (Etc.)*

1. You see a restaurant. You can't tell if it's open yet. You ask a man standing outside.
2. You were absent yesterday. You want to know about homework. You ask another student.
3. Someone asks you the date. You don't know, but you tell them you'll find out.
4. Someone asks you about the weather tomorrow. Is it supposed to be sunny? You haven't heard.
5. You're at a clothing store. You're buying a coat and want to know about the return policy. How many days do you have to return it? You ask a salesperson.
6. Your friend asks you if you want to go to a movie or watch one at home. Both sound good to you. You tell your friend you don't care which you do.
7. You are planning a hiking trip with a friend. This friend wants to bring his dog and asks you if it is OK. It doesn't matter to you.
8. You have a late fee on your bill. You want to know why. You call the company and ask.

EXERCISE 18 ▶ Warm-up. (Chart 12-4)
Complete the second sentence of each pair with
to get or **to do**. Is the meaning in each pair the
same or different?

1. a. Susan doesn't know what she should do.

   b. Susan doesn't know what _____ .

2. a. She needs to figure out how she will get home.

   b. She needs to figure out how _____ home.

12-4 Question Words Followed by Infinitives

(a) I don't know *what I should do.* (b) I don't know ***what to do.*** (c) Pam can't decide *whether she should go or stay home.* (d) Pam can't decide ***whether to go or (to) stay home.*** (e) Please tell me *how I can get to the bus station.* (f) Please tell me ***how to get to the bus station.*** (g) Jim told us *where we could find it.* (h) Jim told us ***where to find it.***	Question words (***when, where, how, who, whom, whose, what, which,*** and ***whether***) may be followed by an infinitive. Each pair of sentences in the examples has the same meaning. Notice that the meaning expressed by the infinitive is either ***should*** or ***can/could.***

EXERCISE 19 ▶ Looking at grammar. (Chart 12-4)
Make sentences with the same meaning by using infinitives.

1. Sally told me when I should come. → *Sally told me when to come.*
2. The plumber told me how I could fix the leak in the sink.
3. Please tell me where I should meet you.
4. Robert had a long excuse for being late for their date, but Sandy didn't know whether she should believe him or not.
5. Jim found two shirts he liked, but he wasn't sure which one he should buy.
6. I've done everything I can think of to help Andy get his life turned around. I don't know what else I can do.

EXERCISE 20 ▶ Looking at grammar. (Chart 12-4)
Complete the sentences with your own words. Use infinitives.

1. A: I can't decide what _____*to wear*_____ to the reception.

   B: How about your green suit?

2. A: Do you know how _____ ?

   B: No, but I'd like to learn.

3. I don't know what _____ my mom for her birthday. I can't decide

   whether _____ or _____ .

4. Before you leave on your trip, read this tour book. It tells you where

   _____ and what _____ cheaply.

EXERCISE 21 ▸ Warm-up. (Chart 12-5)
Check (✓) the grammatically correct sentences.

1. __✓__ We know that the planets revolve around the sun.

2. _____ Centuries ago, people weren't aware that the planets revolved around the sun.

3. _____ That the planets revolve around the sun is now a well-known fact.

4. _____ Is clear that the planets revolve around the sun.

12-5 Noun Clauses with *That*

Verb + *That*-Clause

(a) I **think** *that Bob will come.* (b) I **think** *Bob will come.*	In (a): **that Bob will come** is a noun clause. It is used as the object of the verb **think**. The word *that* is usually omitted in speaking, as in (b). It is usually included in formal writing. See the list below for verbs commonly followed by a *that*-clause.

agree that	*feel* that	*know* that	*remember* that
believe that	*find out* that	*learn* that	*say* that
decide that	*forget* that	*notice* that	*tell* someone that
discover that	*hear* that	*promise* that	*think* that
explain that	*hope* that	*read* that	*understand* that

Person + *Be* + Adjective + *That*-Clause

(c) **Jan is happy** *(that)* *Bob called.*	*That*-clauses commonly follow certain adjectives, such as *happy* in (c), when the subject refers to a person (or persons). See the list below.

I'm *afraid* that*	Al is *certain* that	We're *happy* that	Jan is *sorry* that
I'm *amazed* that	Al is *confident* that	We're *pleased* that	Jan is *sure* that
I'm *angry* that	Al is *disappointed* that	We're *proud* that	Jan is *surprised* that
I'm *aware* that	Al is *glad* that	We're *relieved* that	Jan is *worried* that

It + *Be* + Adjective + *That*-Clause

(d) **It is clear** *(that)* *Ann likes her new job.*	*That*-clauses commonly follow adjectives in sentences that begin with *it* + *be*, as in (d). See the list below.

It's *amazing* that	It's *interesting* that	It's *obvious* that	It's *true* that
It's *clear* that	It's *likely* that	It's *possible* that	It's *undeniable* that
It's *good* that	It's *lucky* that	It's *strange* that	It's *well known* that
It's *important* that	It's *nice* that	It's *surprising* that	It's *wonderful* that

That-Clause Used as a Subject

(e) *That Ann likes her new job* is clear.	It is possible but uncommon for *that*-clauses to be used as the subject of a sentence, as in (e). The word *that* is not omitted when the *that*-clause is used as a subject.
(f) *The fact (that) Ann likes her new job* is clear. (g) *It is a fact (that) Ann likes her new job.*	More often, a *that*-clause in the subject position begins with **the fact that**, as in (f), or is introduced by **it is a fact**, as in (g).

To be afraid has two possible meanings:
    (1) It can express fear: *I'm afraid of dogs. I'm afraid that his dog will bite me.*
    (2) It often expresses a meaning similar to "to be sorry": *I'm afraid you have the wrong number.*

EXERCISE 22 ▶ Let's talk. (Chart 12-5)

Work in pairs, small groups, or as a class. Answer with *that*-clauses.

1. a. What have you recently heard on the news?
   b. What have you recently found out on social media?

2. a. What do scientists know for sure?
   b. What have scientists recently discovered?

3. a. What do parents hope for their children?
   b. What should parents promise their children?

4. a. What do many teenagers think?
   b. What do many adults believe?

EXERCISE 23 ▶ Let's talk: interview. (Chart 12-5)

Interview your classmates. Ask each one a different question. Their answers should follow this
pattern: ***I'm*** + *adjective* + *that*-clause.

Example: What is something in your life that you're glad about?
→ *I'm glad that my family is supportive of me.*

1. What is something that disappointed you in the past?
2. What is something that annoys you?
3. What is something about your friends that pleases you?
4. What is something about nature that amazes you?
5. What is something about another culture's traditions that surprises you?
6. What is something that you are afraid will happen in the future?
7. What is something about your future that you are sure of?

EXERCISE 24 ▶ Looking at grammar. (Chart 12-5)

Make noun clauses beginning with ***It*** and any appropriate word(s) in the box. Make another
sentence with the same meaning by using a *that*-clause as the subject.

apparent	a pity	surprising	unfair
clear	a shame	too bad	unfortunate
a fact	strange	true	a well-known fact
obvious			

1. The world is round.
   → *It is a fact that the world is round.*
   → *That the world is round is a fact.*
2. Tim hasn't been able to make any friends.
3. The earth revolves around the sun.
4. Exercise can reduce heart disease.
5. Drug abuse can ruin one's health.
6. Some women do not earn equal pay for equal work.
7. Irene, who is an excellent student, failed her entrance examination.
8. English is the principal language of business throughout much of the world.

EXERCISE 25 ▶ Game. (Chart 12-5)

Work in teams. Agree or disagree with the statements. If you think the statement is true, begin with **It's a fact that**. If you think the statement is false, begin with **It isn't true that**. If you're not sure, guess. Choose one person to write your team's statements. The team with the most correct statements wins.

1. _____It's a fact that_____ most spiders have eight eyes.

2. _____It isn't true that_____ some spiders have twelve legs.

3. _____ more men than women are colorblind.

4. _____ 25% of the human body is water.

5. _____ people's main source of vitamin D is fruit.

6. _____ a substance called chlorophyll makes plant leaves green.

7. _____ the World Wide Web went online in 2000.

8. _____ elephants have the longest pregnancy of any land animal.

9. _____ the first wheels were made out of stone.

10. _____ a diamond is the hardest substance found in nature.

11. _____ the Great Wall of China took more than 1,000 years to build.

EXERCISE 26 ▶ Looking at grammar. (Chart 12-5)

Restate the sentences. Begin with **The fact that**.

1. It's understandable that you feel frustrated. → *The fact that you feel frustrated is understandable.*
2. It's undeniable that traffic is getting worse every year.
3. It's unfortunate that the city has no funds for the project.
4. It's obvious that the two leaders don't respect each other.
5. It's a miracle that there were no injuries from the car accident.

EXERCISE 27 ▶ Warm-up. (Chart 12-6)

Look at the quoted speech below. Circle the quotation marks. Is the punctuation inside or outside the quotation marks? In item 3, what do you notice about the punctuation?

> Watch out! Are you OK? You look like you're going to fall off that ladder.

1. "Watch out!" Mrs. Brooks said.
2. "Are you OK?" she asked.
3. "You look like you're going to fall off that ladder," she said.

12-6 Quoted Speech

Quoted speech refers to reproducing words exactly as they were originally spoken or written.* Quotation marks ("...") are used.**

Quoting One Sentence

(a) She said, "My brother is a student."	In (a): Use a comma after **she said**. Capitalize the first word of the quoted sentence. Put the final quotation marks outside the period at the end of the sentence.
(b) "My brother is a student," she said.	In (b): Use a comma, not a period, at the end of the quoted sentence when it precedes **she said**.
(c) "My brother," she said, "is a student."	In (c): If the quoted sentence is divided by **she said**, use a comma after the first part of the quote. Do not capitalize the first word after **she said**.

Quoting More Than One Sentence

(d) "My brother is a student. He is attending a university," she said.	In (d): Quotation marks are placed at the beginning and end of the complete quote. Notice: There are no quotation marks after **student**.
(e) "My brother is a student," she said. "He is attending a university."	In (e): Since **she said** comes between two quoted sentences, the second sentence begins with quotation marks and a capital letter.

Quoting a Question or an Exclamation

(f) She asked, "When will you be here?"	In (f): The question mark is inside the closing quotation marks since it is part of the quotation.
(g) "When will you be here?" she asked.	In (g): Since a question mark is used, no comma is used before **she asked**.
(h) She said, "Watch out!"	In (h): The exclamation point is inside the closing quotation marks.
(i) "My brother is a student," said Anna. "My brother," said Anna, "is a student."	In (i): The noun subject (**Anna**) follows **said**. A noun subject often follows the verb when the subject and verb come in the middle or at the end of a quoted sentence. NOTE: A pronoun subject almost always precedes the verb. *"My brother is a student,"* **she said**. VERY RARE: *"My brother is a student,"* **said she**.
(j) "Let's leave," whispered Dave. (k) "Please help me," begged the homeless man. (l) "Well," Jack began, "it's a long story."	*Say* and *ask* are the most commonly used quote verbs. Some others: *add, agree, announce, answer, beg, begin, comment, complain, confess, continue, explain, inquire, promise, remark, reply, respond, shout, suggest, whisper.*

Quoted speech is also called "direct speech." *Reported speech* (discussed in Chart 12-7) is also called "indirect speech."

**In British English, quotation marks are called "inverted commas" and can consist of either double marks (") or a single mark ('): *She said, 'My brother is a student'.*

EXERCISE 28 ▶ Looking at grammar. (Chart 12-6)
Add punctuation and capitalization.

1. Henry said there is a phone call for you.
2. There is a phone call for you he said
3. There is said Henry a phone call for you

4. There is a phone call for you, it's your sister, said Henry.
5. There is a phone call for you, he said. it's your sister.
6. I asked him, Where is the phone?
7. Where is the phone? she asked.

EXERCISE 29 ▶ Reading and writing. (Chart 12-6)

Part I. Read the fable. (Fables are stories that teach a lesson.) Then work with a partner and look at the punctuation in each quotation. Explain why some sentences have commas and some have periods. Write the lesson or moral at the end of the story together.

The Grasshopper and the Ant

Once upon a time, there was a lazy grasshopper and an industrious ant. The grasshopper spent his summer days in the sun, chirping and hopping about. It never occurred to him to work. The ant, however, was getting ready for winter. He dragged seeds, leaves, and grains to his nest.

One day the grasshopper visited the ant. "It's such a nice day," he said. "Come out and play with me."

The ant shook his head. "I can't," he replied. "I have too much work to do. I need to get ready for the winter," he added. "You should do the same."

The grasshopper laughed and said, "I have plenty of food. And besides, winter is far away."

Winter came. The ant was snug in his nest, and the grasshopper was starving. There was no food to be found anywhere.

And the moral of the story is _____

_____

summer

winter

Part II. Write a fable that is well known in your country. Use quoted speech. Read your fable to a partner or small group.

EXERCISE 30 ▶ Warm-up. (Chart 12-7)

Look at the words in blue. Do you know why two verbs are present and one is past?

WEATHER REPORTER: "A strong storm is coming."

  a. She just said that a strong storm is coming.
  b. She has said that a strong storm is coming.
  c. She said yesterday that a strong storm was coming.

12-7 Reported Speech

Quoted speech uses a person's exact words, and it is set off by quotation marks. *Reported speech* uses a noun clause to report what someone has said. No quotation marks are used.

NOTE: This chart presents general guidelines to follow. You may encounter variations.

Quoted Speech	Reported Speech	
(a) "The world *is* round." →	She **said** (that) the world *is* round.	The present tense is used when the reported sentence deals with a general truth, as in (a). **That** is optional; it is more common in writing than speaking.
(b) "I *work* at night." →	He **says** he *works* at night. He **has said** that he *works* at night. He **will say** that he *works* at night.	When the reporting verb is simple present, present perfect, or future, the verb in the noun clause does not change.
(c) "I *work* at night." → (d) "I *am working*." → (e) "I *worked*." → (f) "I *have worked*." → (g) "I *had worked*." →	He **said** he *worked* at night. He **said** he *was working*. He **said** he *worked/had worked*. He **said** he *had worked*. He **said** he *had worked*.	If the reporting verb (e.g., *said*) is simple past, the verb in the noun clause will *usually* be in a past form. Here are some general guidelines: simple present → simple past present progressive → past progressive simple past → no change or past perfect present perfect → past perfect past perfect → no change
(h) Immediate reporting: — What did the teacher just say? I didn't hear him. — He **said** he *wants* us to read Chapter 6. (i) Later reporting: — I didn't go to class yesterday. Did Mr. Jones give any assignments? — Yes. He **said** he *wanted* us to read Chapter 6.		In spoken English, if the speaker is reporting something immediately or soon after it was said, no change is made in the noun clause verb.
(j) "*Leave*." →	She **told** me *to leave*.	In reported speech, an imperative sentence is changed to an infinitive. **Tell** is used instead of **say** as the reporting verb.* See Chart 14-4, p. 308, for other verbs followed by an infinitive that are used to report speech.

*NOTE: **Tell** is immediately followed by a (pro)noun object, but **say** is not: *He told **me** he was late.* *He said he was late.*
Also possible: *He said **to me** he was late.*

EXERCISE 31 ▸ Looking at grammar. (Chart 12-7)

Change the quoted speech to indirect speech.

Overheard in the Elevator

1. LARRY: "Jason and Liz are engaged."

   a. Larry says _____Jason and Liz are engaged_____.

   b. Larry has said _____Jason and Liz are engaged_____.

   c. Larry said _____Jason and Liz were engaged_____.

2. TEACHING ASSISTANT: "Not many in the class have a passing grade."
   a. The teaching assistant said _____ had p _____ .
   b. The teaching assistant says _____ have _____ .
   c. The teaching assistant will say _____ will have _____ .

3. SOMEONE: "There are 1,440 minutes in a day."
   a. Someone said _____ .
   b. Someone says _____ .

EXERCISE 32 ▸ Let's talk. (Chart 12-7)

Work with a partner. Take turns completing the sentences with noun clauses.

A Restaurant

1. "Your order is ready," said the waiter. → *The waiter said our order was ready.*
2. "I'm having the special," Mustafa said. → Mustafa Said he Was having the sp
3. "We went there for our anniversary," my parents said.
4. "I went to school with the chef," my dad said.
5. I talked to Noor yesterday. She said, "I'm going to join you for lunch."
6. I just talked to Noor. She said, "I'm going to join you for lunch."
7. Mustafa said, "I have never tasted such a delicious dessert."
8. A customer said, "There is a mistake on our bill."

EXERCISE 33 ▸ Looking at grammar. (Charts 12-3 and 12-7)

Change the quoted speech to reported speech.

At a Meeting

1. Talal asked Leo, "Do you want to begin?" → *Talal asked Leo if/whether he wanted to begin.*
2. Maria asked us, "Have you seen my notes?"
3. Oscar asked me, "What are you talking about?"
4. "Does the decision need to be made today?" asked David.
5. Lillian asked, "Is everyone sure this is the right decision?"
6. Ricardo asked me, "Is what you are saying true?"

EXERCISE 34 ▸ Looking at grammar. (Chart 12-7)

Complete the sentences with *said* or *told*.

A TV News Station

1. The owner _____ that he wanted a more interesting newscast.
2. He _____ the TV ratings were dropping.
3. He _____ the director needed to work hard to improve the ratings
4. The director _____ him that she felt the newscast needed more investigative reporting.
5. A reporter _____ he had just finished a report on government corruption.
6. She _____ him to do a longer series on the topic.

EXERCISE 35 ▶ Warm-up. (Chart 12-8)

Complete the description of Alicia and George's conversation.

Where are my glasses? I can't find them and I have to leave.

I know why you can't find them. They're on your head!

Alicia said she _____ find her glasses and that she _____ leave. George told her that they were on her head.

12-8 Reported Speech: Modal Verbs in Noun Clauses

(a) "I *can* go."	→ She said she *could go*.	The following modal and phrasal modal verbs change when the reporting verb is in the past:
(b) "I *may* go."	→ She said she *may/might go*.	
(c) "I *must* go."	→ She said she *had to go*.	
(d) "I *have to* go."	→ She said she *had to go*.	
(e) "I *will* go."	→ She said she *would go*.	
(f) "I *am going to* go."	→ She said she *was going to go*.	

can	→ could
may	→ may/might
must	→ had to
have to	→ had to
will	→ would
am/is/are going to	→ was/were going to

(g) "I *should* go."	→ She said she *should go*.	The following modals do not change when the reporting verb is in the past:
(h) "I *ought to* go."	→ She said she *ought to go*.	should
(i) "I *might* go."	→ She said she *might go*.	ought to } (no change)
		might

EXERCISE 36 ▶ Let's talk. (Chart 12-8)

Students A and B will have a short conversation. Your teacher will ask other students about it.

Example:
STUDENT A: What time can you go?
STUDENT B: Two-thirty.
TEACHER: What did Manuel (*Student A*) want to know?
STUDENT C: He wanted to know what time he could go.
TEACHER: What did Helen (*Student B*) say?
STUDENT D: She told him that he could go at two-thirty.

1. STUDENT A: Can you speak Arabic?
   STUDENT B: _____.
   TEACHER: What did (*Student A*) ask?
                What did (*Student B*) say?

2. STUDENT A: Where will you be tomorrow at three o'clock?
   STUDENT B: _____.
   TEACHER: What did (*Student A*) ask?
              What did (*Student B*) say?

3. STUDENT A: Will you be on time for your next class?
   STUDENT B: I may _____.
   TEACHER: What did (*Student A*) ask?
              What did (*Student B*) say?

4. STUDENT A: What might happen in the future?
   STUDENT B: _____.
   TEACHER: What did (*Student A*) want to know?
              What did (*Student B*) say?

5. STUDENT A: What should we study after Chapter 12 of this book?
   STUDENT B: _____.
   TEACHER: What did (*Student A*) want to know?
              What did (*Student B*) tell (*Student A*)?

EXERCISE 37 ▸ Looking at grammar. (Charts 12-7 and 12-8)
Complete the conversations with a past form of the verbs in parentheses.

1. A: The test is scheduled for Monday.
   B: Really? I heard it (*schedule*) _____ for Tuesday.

2. A: Mikhail can't come tonight.
   B: Are you sure? I heard he (*can*) _____ come tonight.

3. A: It's raining outside.
   B: Really? I thought it (*snow*) _____.

4. A: Tony has to get a passport.
   B: Are you sure? I heard he (*has*) _____ to get a visa.

5. A: Marita hasn't applied for a job yet.
   B: That's not what I heard. I heard she (*apply*) _____ for work at her
      uncle's company.

6. A: Ms. Alvarez is going to retire.
   B: Really? I thought she (*continue*) _____ in her sales position
      for another year.

EXERCISE 38 ▸ Listening. (Charts 12-7 and 12-8)
Listen to the sentences. Complete them using past verb forms to report the speech that you hear.

1. The speaker said that she _____ *wasn't going* _____ to the personnel meeting because she
   _____ *had to* _____ finish a report.

2. The speaker said that he _____ Marta any money because his
   wallet _____ in his coat pocket back at home.

3. The speaker said that someone in the room _____ very strong perfume and it _____ her a headache.

4. The speaker said that he _____ Emma at the coffee shop at 9:00. He said he _____ not to be late.

5. The speaker said she _____ looking for a new job and asked her friend what he _____ she _____.

6. The speaker said that they _____ late for the concert because his wife _____ a business function after work.

EXERCISE 39 ▸ Looking at grammar. (Charts 12-7 and 12-8)

Change quoted speech to reported speech. Study the example carefully and use the same pattern: **said that ... and that**.

1. "My father is a businessman. My mother is an engineer."

   He said that ____*his father was a businessman and that his mother was an engineer.*____

2. "I'm excited about my new job. I've found a nice apartment."

   I got an email from my sister yesterday. She said _____

   _____

3. "I expect you to be in class every day. Unexcused absences may affect your grades."

   Our sociology professor said _____

   _____

4. "Highway 66 will be closed for two months. Commuters should seek alternate routes."

   The newspaper said _____

   _____

5. "Every obstacle is a steppingstone to success. You should view problems in your life as opportunities to prove yourself."

   My father often told me _____

   _____

   _____

EXERCISE 40 ▸ Writing. (Charts 12-1 → 12-8)

Read each conversation and write a report about it. Your report should include an accurate idea of the speaker's words, but it doesn't have to use the exact words.

Example: JACK: I can't go to the game next week.
   TOM: Really? Why not?
   JACK: I don't have enough money for a ticket.

Possible written reports:

→ Jack told Tom that he couldn't go to the game next week because he didn't have enough money for a ticket.

→ When Tom asked Jack why he couldn't go to the game next week, Jack said he didn't have enough money for a ticket.

→ Jack said he couldn't go to the game next week. When Tom asked him why, Jack replied that he didn't have enough money for a ticket.

1. ALEX: What are you doing?
   LEA: I'm drawing a picture.

2. ASAKO: Do you want to go to a movie Sunday night?
   MARTA: I'd like to, but I have to study.

3. JOHNNY: How old are you, Mrs. Robinson?
   MRS. ROBINSON: It's not polite to ask people their age.
   JOHNNY: How much money do you make?
   MRS. ROBINSON: That's impolite too.

EXERCISE 41 ▸ Warm-up. (Chart 12-9)

Choose the correct verb in each sentence.

1. It's important that we   be / are   on time to our own wedding!

2. My brother insists that he   speak / speaks   at our wedding dinner.

12-9 The Subjunctive in Noun Clauses	
(a) The teacher *demands* that we *be* on time.	Sentences with subjunctive verbs generally *stress importance or urgency*. A subjunctive verb uses the simple form of a verb. It does not have present, past, or future forms; it is neither singular nor plural. A subjunctive verb is used in *that*-clauses with the verbs and expressions listed at the bottom of this chart.
(b) I *insisted* that he *pay* me the money.	
(c) I *recommended* that she *not go* to the concert.	
(d) *It is important* that they *be told* the truth.	
	In (a): *be* is a subjunctive verb; its subject is *we*.
	In (b): *pay* (not *pays*, not *paid*) is a subjunctive verb; it is in its simple form, even though its subject (*he*) is singular.
	Negative: *not + simple form*, as in (c).
	Passive: *simple form of be + past participle*, as in (d).
(e) I *suggested/recommended* that she *see* a doctor.	*Should* is also possible after *suggest* and *recommend*.*
(f) I *suggested/recommended* that she *should see* a doctor.	

Common verbs and expressions followed by the subjunctive in a noun clause

advise (that)	propose (that)	it is essential (that)	it is critical (that)
ask (that)	recommend (that)	it is imperative (that)	it is necessary (that)
demand (that)	request (that)	it is important (that)	it is vital (that)
insist (that)	suggest (that)		

*The subjunctive is more common in American English than British English. In British English, **should** + *simple form* is more usual than the subjunctive: *The teacher **insists** that we **should be** on time.*

EXERCISE 42 ▸ Looking at grammar. (Chart 12-9)
Complete each sentence with the correct form of the verb in parentheses.

In a Courtroom

1. The court clerk has advised that everyone (*stand up*) ___*stand up*___ when the judge enters the room.

2. It is essential that people (*turn off*) _____ their cell phones.

3. It is important that everyone (*dress*) _____ appropriately for court.

4. The clerk has asked that the witness (*tell*) _____ the truth and nothing but the truth.

5. The jury has asked that the judge (*explain*) _____ the instructions one more time.

6. The judge insisted that everyone (*be*) _____ quiet when the verdict was read.

EXERCISE 43 ▸ Looking at grammar. (Chart 12-9)
Choose the correct verb. Some are active and some are passive.

Naming a Baby

1. The hospital requested that the parents   provide / be provided   a name for the birth certificate.
2. The grandparents insisted that the baby   give / be given   a traditional name.
3. A sibling asked that the parents   choose / be chosen   a popular name.
4. A cousin suggested that the baby   name / be named   after a great-grandmother.
5. The parents requested that they   allow / be allowed   to choose a name without any outside help.

EXERCISE 44 ▸ Looking at grammar. (Chart 12-9)
Complete each sentence with the correct form of the verb. Use the words in the box. Some are active and some are passive. NOTE: *share* is used twice.

lock	share	show up	turn off	use	wear

Work Rules

1. It is important that everyone _____ for work on time.

2. It is critical that everyone _____ an ID badge while at work.

3. It is vital that employees not _____ computer passwords with other employees.

4. It is vital that computer passwords not _____ by employees.

5. It is important that the heat _____ in offices at the end of the day.

6. It is imperative that the last person out of the office _____ the door.

7. Management has requested that employees not _____ social media for personal purposes during work hours.

EXERCISE 45 ▸ Check your knowledge. (Chapter 12 Review)

Correct the errors.

1. Tell the taxi driver where do you want to go.

2. My roommate came into the room and asked me why aren't you in class? I said I am waiting for a telephone call from my family.

3. It was my first day at the university, and I am on my way to my first class. I wondered who else will be in the class. What the teacher would be like?

4. My professor asked me that what did I intend to do after I graduate?

5. What does a patient tell a doctor it is confidential.

6. What my friend and I did it was our secret. We didn't even tell our parents what did we do.

7. The doctor asked that I felt OK. I told him that I don't feel well.

8. I asked him what kind of movies does he like, he said me, I like romantic movies.

9. Is true you almost drowned? my friend asked me. Yes, I said. I'm really glad to be alive. It was really frightening.

10. It is a fact that I almost drowned makes me very careful about water safety when I go swimming.

11. I didn't know where am I supposed to get off the bus, so I asked the driver where is the science museum. She tell me the name of the street. She said she will tell me when should I get off the bus.

12. My mother did not live with us. When other children asked me where was my mother, I told them she is going to come to visit me very soon.

13. When I asked the taxi driver to drive faster, he said I will drive faster if you pay me more. At that time I didn't care how much would it cost, so I told him to go as fast as he can.

14. My parents told me is essential to know English if I want to study at an American university.

EXERCISE 46 ▸ Reading and writing. (Chapter 12 Review)

Part I. Read the passage. <u>Underline</u> the three noun clauses. Which one has the subjunctive?

Plagiarism

Simon is researching the topic of cell phone radiation for a term paper. He has found extensive information on the Internet. One paragraph in particular gives easy-to-understand information about radiation transmission. Simon is pleased that the information is very clear and pastes it into his paper. However, he changes the font so that it matches the rest of his paper.

What Simon has just done is commit plagiarism — the copying of someone else's work without citing the source. Think of it as the stealing of ideas. In the Internet age, it is very easy to copy and paste information into a paper. Colleges and universities have strict policies regarding plagiarism. In some cases, schools may fail or expel a student for plagiarism.

Generally plagiarism is explained in the student handbook. Many schools have "honor codes" that students agree to follow. It is essential that every student know the school policy regarding plagiarism.

Part II. Research information about the plagiarism policy at your school. If your school doesn't have a policy, choose a university in an English-speaking country to research. Write a paragraph summarizing the information. Use at least one noun clause with the subjunctive in your paragraph.

EXERCISE 47 ▸ Reading and writing. (Chapter 12)

Part I. Read the paragraph from a U.S. government website.*

Cell Phones and the Brain

Scientists are looking into a possible link between cell phone use and certain types of tumors. One type is called an acoustic neuroma ("ah-COOS-tik nur-OH-ma"). This type of tumor grows on the nerve that connects the ear to the brain. It doesn't cause cancer, but it may lead to other health problems, like hearing loss. Another type scientists are looking into is called a glioma ("glee-OH-ma"). This is a tumor found in the brain or central nervous system of the body.

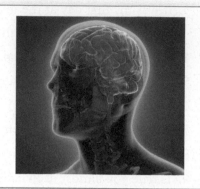

---

*Source: http://www.cdc.gov/nceh/radiation/cell_phones._FAQ.html

Part II. Now read two paraphrases of the paragraph. One way to avoid plagiarism is to paraphrase information — to express an author's ideas in your own words. What differences do you see between the two paraphrases? Which paraphrase seems most appropriate to you? Consider the following questions and discuss your opinions with your classmates:

1. In which paraphrase have the ideas been put into the writer's own words, without copying the sentence structure or the vocabulary of the original?
2. Which paraphrase uses synonyms for key words, while keeping a sentence structure similar to the original?

Paraphrase 1

Scientists are not sure if cell phones cause tumors, but they are looking at two types: an acoustic neuroma and a glioma. The first tumor doesn't cause cancer, but it can cause hearing problems. The second, a glioma, grows in the brain or central nervous system.

Paraphrase 2

Researchers are investigating a potential connection between cell phone usage and different kinds of tumors. One kind is named an acoustic neuroma. This kind of tumor is on the nerve between the ear and the brain. It's not the cause of cancer, but it may be responsible for other health issues, like deafness. Another kind researchers are investigating is a glioma. This is in the brain or central nervous system of the human body.

In the second case, the writer has supplied synonyms for key words, but the sentence structure is the same. It is too similar to the original and is therefore not acceptable.

Part III. Find a paragraph on a topic you are interested in and paraphrase it. Use at least one noun clause in your writing.

A helpful strategy for paraphrasing is to read a passage several times and take notes. Then try not to look at your notes when you write so that you can express the information in your own words. When you are finished, compare your paraphrase with your notes to make sure you have covered everything.

Part IV. Edit your writing. Check for the following:

1. ☐ all sentences contain a subject and a verb
2. ☐ use of one or more noun clauses in your paragraph
3. ☐ use of a singular subject when the noun clause begins the sentence
4. ☐ correct word order in noun clauses (statement word order)
5. ☐ correct spelling (use a dictionary or spell-check)

▨▨■■■ Go to the Essential Online Resources for Self-Study: Gerunds and Infinitives 12

13

Adjective Clauses

PRETEST: What do I already know?

Write "C" if a sentence has the correct sentence structure and "I" for incorrect. Check your answers below. After you complete each chart listed, make any necessary corrections.

1. _____ I enjoyed listening to the tour guide that took us around the city. (13-1)

2. _____ The gift is for you that is on the coffee table. (13-1)

3. _____ A movie a friend recommended it turned out to be very entertaining. (13-2)

4. _____ There is the professor from whom I received the award. (13-3)

5. _____ I spoke with a couple who his son created a popular social media app. (13-4)

6. _____ Each hotel room has a safe which you can keep your valuables. (13-5)

7. _____ I'll never forget the moment when I first met your dad. (13-6)

8. _____ Anyone wants to volunteer is welcome to come. (13-7)

9. _____ Is everything your lawyer says true? (13-7)

10. _____ Indonesia, that consists of thousands of islands, is the fourth most populated country in the world. (13-8)

11. _____ In my chemistry study group, there are eight students, two of whom are repeating the class. (13-9)

12. _____ The apartment building has ten floors and no elevator, which it will be a challenge for me. (13-10)

Incorrect sentences: 2, 3, 5, 6, 8, 10, 12

EXERCISE 1 ▶ Warm-up. (Chart 13-1)

The sentences are all correct. The words in blue are all pronouns. What nouns do they refer to? How does the noun affect the choice of the pronoun?

1. a. A ring floated past a diver. She was exploring some undersea rocks.
   b. A ring floated past a diver who was exploring some undersea rocks.
   c. A ring floated past a diver that was exploring some undersea rocks.

2. a. The diver saw a ring. It was sinking to the bottom of the sea.
   b. The diver saw a ring that was sinking to the bottom of the sea.
   c. The diver saw a ring which was sinking to the bottom of the sea.

13-1 Adjective Clause Pronouns Used as the Subject

I thanked the woman. **She** helped me. ↓ (a) I thanked the woman *who helped me*. (b) I thanked the woman *that helped me*.	In (a): *I thanked the woman* = a main clause *who helped me* = an adjective clause* An adjective clause modifies a noun. In (a): the adjective clause modifies **woman**.
The book is mine. **It** is on the table. ↓ (c) The book *that* *is on the table* is mine. (d) The book *which* *is on the table* is mine.	In (a): **who** is the subject of the adjective clause. In (b): **that** is the subject of the adjective clause. Examples (a) and (b) have the same meaning. In speaking, **who** and **that** are both commonly used as subject pronouns to describe people. **Who** is more common in writing. Examples (c) and (d) have the same meaning. In contemporary American English, **that** is preferred to **which**.** In British English, **that** and **which** are used interchangeably.
	SUMMARY: **who** = used for people **that** = used for both people and things **which** = used for things
(e) *CORRECT:* The book *that is on the table* is mine. (f) *INCORRECT:* The book is mine ~~that is on the table~~.	An adjective clause closely follows the noun it modifies.

*See Chapter 12 for information about clauses.
Which must be used in nonrestrictive clauses in both American and British English. See Chart 13-8.

EXERCISE 2 ▸ Looking at grammar. (Chart 13-1)
Choose <u>all</u> the possible completions for each sentence. Do not add commas or capital letters.

Identity Theft

1. I read a scary article _____ detailed how easy it is for someone to steal your ID.
   a. who   (b.) that   c. it   d. Ø

2. People _____ own a smartphone have a higher rate of identify theft.
   a. who   b. that   c. which   d. Ø

3. The article mentioned one thief _____ enjoys the challenge of hacking. He does it for fun.
   a. who   b. that   c. he   d. Ø

4. A fact _____ surprised me is that online thieves are rarely caught.
   a. who   b. that   c. it   d. Ø

EXERCISE 3 ▸ Looking at grammar. (Chart 13-1)
Combine the two sentences with **who** or **that**. Use the second sentence as an adjective clause.

On a Subway

1. I know the girl. She is sleeping. → *I know the girl* {*who* / *that*} *is sleeping.*

2. The guy is in my math class. He is talking loudly on his phone.

3. The passenger is from Argentina. He is sitting next to me.

4. The students are from Turkey. They are standing behind us.

5. We are going on a route. It is very crowded in the mornings.

6. We are on the train. It often breaks down.

EXERCISE 4 ▸ Let's talk. (Chart 13-1)
Make true sentences by using a word or phrase from each column. Use *who* or *that*.

		work hard.
		like a lot of rules.
		exercise every day.
		are smarter than me.
	friends	tell lies.
I like to spend time with	classmates	are quiet.
I don't like to spend time with	co-workers	talk a lot.
	adults	talk about themselves a lot.
	people	like to relax.
		are serious.
		tell a lot of jokes.

EXERCISE 5 ▸ Listening. (Chart 13-1)
Part I. When *who* is contracted with an auxiliary verb, the contraction is often hard to hear. Listen to the following sentences. What is the full, uncontracted form of the *italicized* verb?

1. He has a friend *who'll* help him.
   (*full form = who will*)
2. He has a friend *who's* helping him.
3. He has a friend *who's* helped him.
4. He has friends *who're* helping him.

5. He has friends *who've* helped him.
6. He has a friend *who'd* helped him.
7. He has a friend *who'd* like to help him.
8. He has a friend *who's* been helping him.

Part II. Complete the sentences with the verbs you hear, but write the full, uncontracted form of each verb.

Example: You will hear: I work with a man who's lived in 20 different countries.

   You will write: I work with a man who _____*has lived*_____ in 20 different countries.

1. We know a person who _____ great for the job.

2. We know a person who _____ to apply for the job.

3. That's the man who _____ to our department.

4. I know of three people who _____ to transfer to another location.

5. I'd like to talk to the people who _____ to move.

6. There are two people at this company who _____ here all their adult lives.

7. The manager who _____ from the company quit.

EXERCISE 6 ▸ Game. (Chart 13-1)

Work in teams. Make sentences using **who** or **that**. One team member can write them down. The team that finishes first with the most correct answers wins.

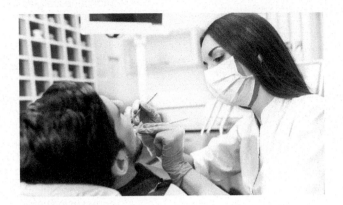

At the Dentist

Example: 1. A dentist is a person who/that treats problems with teeth.

1. A dentist is a person ___e___ .
2. A dental hygienist is a person _____ .
3. A cavity is a part of the tooth _____ .
4. A filling is a material _____ .
5. Novocain is a drug _____ .
6. A crown is an artificial covering _____ .
7. Braces are a device _____ .
8. Orthodontists are dentists _____ .
9. Pediatric dentists are dentists _____ .

a. is decayed
b. straightens teeth
c. is put into a cavity
d. treat children
✓ e. treats problems with teeth
f. put braces on teeth
g. cleans teeth
h. is put around a tooth
i. numbs the tooth area so the patient doesn't feel pain

EXERCISE 7 ▸ Warm-up. (Chart 13-2)

Work with a partner. Read the passage and complete the sentences using the correct verb forms.

William has been a stay-at-home dad for the last seven years, but now both children are in school, and he's going back to work. He's looking for a job that will still allow him to spend time with his children. What kind of job do you think he is looking for?

He is looking for a job that … OR *He is not looking for a job that …*

1. leave him free on weekends
2. require him to work on weekends
3. include a lot of long-distance travel
4. have a long commute
5. be close to home
6. have flexible hours

13-2 Adjective Clause Pronouns Used as the Object of a Verb

	The man was Mr. Jones.			Notice in the examples: The adjective clause pronouns are placed at the beginning of the clause.
	I saw *him*.			
	↓			
(a) The man	*who(m)*	*I saw*	was Mr. Jones.	In (a): *who* is usually used instead of *whom*, especially in speaking. *Whom* is generally used only in very formal English.
(b) The man	*that*	*I saw*	was Mr. Jones.	
(c) The man	Ø	*I saw*	was Mr. Jones.	

The movie wasn't very good.
We saw *it* last night.
↓

(d) The movie	*that*	*we saw last night*	wasn't very good.	In (c) and (e): An object pronoun is often omitted (Ø) from an adjective clause. (A subject pronoun, however, may not be omitted.)
(e) The movie	Ø	*we saw last night*	wasn't very good.	
(f) The movie	*which*	*we saw last night*	wasn't very good.	As an object pronoun for people, *that* is more common than *who*, but Ø is the most common in speaking and writing.

To describe things, *that* and Ø are the most common in speaking. In writing, *that* is the most common, and Ø is rare.

SUMMARY:

    who(m) = used for people
    that = used for both people and things
    which = used for things (common in British English but not in contemporary American English)

(g) *INCORRECT:* The man who(m) I saw ~~him~~ was Mr. Jones. The man that I saw ~~him~~ was Mr. Jones. The man I saw ~~him~~ was Mr. Jones.	In (g): The pronoun *him* must be removed. It is unnecessary because *who(m)*, *that*, or Ø functions as the object of the verb *saw*.

EXERCISE 8 ▸ Looking at grammar. (Chart 13-2)

Decide if the word in blue is a subject or object pronoun.

Online Reviews

1. Did you read the online reviews that were written by fake customers?   S   O
2. Every review that I read gave the product five stars.   S   O
3. All the writers that posted this week were paid to write a positive review.   S   O
4. The reviewers that gave five stars used similar vocabulary and sentence structure.   S   O
5. I've decided not to buy products that this particular company makes.   S   O

EXERCISE 9 ▸ Looking at grammar. (Chart 13-2)

Choose all the possible completions for each sentence. Do not add commas or capital letters.

Your Trip

1. Tell me about the people ＿＿＿ you met when you were in Norway.
    (a.) who   (b.) that   c. they   (d.) whom   (e.) Ø

2. Was the hotel ＿＿＿ you found on the Internet a nice play to stay?
    a. who   b. that   c. it   d. whom   e. Ø

3. Did you see your Norwegian friend _____ you met in college?
   a. who   b. that   c. he   d. whom   e. Ø

4. Tell me about the other cities _____ you went to.
   a. who   b. that   c. they   d. whom   e. Ø

5. Have you downloaded all the pictures _____ you took yet?
   a. who   b. that   c. they   d. whom   e. Ø

6. Did you find the Norwegian phrases _____ you had learned before you left helpful?
   a. who   b. that   c. they   d. whom   e. Ø

7. I'd like to know more about your cousins _____ you visited in the fishing village.
   a. who   b. that   c. they   d. whom   e. Ø

EXERCISE 10 ▸ Looking at grammar. (Chart 13-2)

Combine the two sentences. Use the second sentence as an adjective clause. Give <u>all</u> the possible patterns, orally or in writing. Use **who, that,** or **Ø**.

Recommendations

1. The book was good. You suggested I read it.
   → *The book that / Ø you suggested I read was good.*
2. I bought the TV. A consumer guide rated it highly.
3. The doctor was very helpful. You advised me to see him.
4. The tour guide recommended a restaurant. His cousin owns it.
5. I didn't like the plumber. My friend told me to call him.

EXERCISE 11 ▸ Warm-up. (Chart 13-3)

Compare the <u>underlined</u> adjective clause in sentence a. with the one in sentence b. What differences do you notice? NOTE: Both sentences are correct.

1. a. I think Lee is a person <u>who you can have fun with</u>.
   b. Do you think Lee is a person <u>with whom you can have fun</u>?

2. a. The art school <u>which Lori applied to</u> is very demanding.
   b. Do you know the name of the art school <u>to which Lori applied</u>?

13-3 Adjective Clause Pronouns Used as the Object of a Preposition

	She is the woman. I told you **about her**. ↓		In very formal English, the preposition comes at the beginning of the adjective clause, as in (a) and (e). Usually, however, in everyday usage, the preposition comes after the subject and verb of the adjective clause, as in the other examples.
(a) She is the woman	*about whom*	*I told you.*	
(b) She is the woman	*who*(m)	*I told you about.*	
(c) She is the woman	*that*	*I told you about.*	NOTE: If the preposition comes at the beginning of the adjective clause, only **whom** or **which** may be used. A preposition is never immediately followed by **that** or **who**.
(d) She is the woman	Ø	*I told you about.*	

	The music was good. We listened **to it** last night. ↓				INCORRECT: She is the woman ~~about who~~ I told you.
(e) The music	*to which*	*we listened*	*last night*	was good.	INCORRECT: The music ~~to that~~ we listened last night was good.
(f) The music	*that*	*we listened to*	*last night*	was good.	
(g) The music	Ø	*we listened to*	*last night*	was good.	
(h) The music	*which*	*we listened to*	*last night*	was good.	

EXERCISE 12 ▸ Looking at grammar. (Chart 13-3)
Choose all the possible completions for each sentence. Which one seems the most formal?

1. The scholarship _____ requires an essay.
   a. that they are applying for
   b. they are applying for
   c. they are applying
   d. they are applying for it
   e. for which they are applying

2. The counselor _____ had sample essays.
   a. who they spoke to
   b. that they spoke to
   c. who they spoke to her
   d. to whom they spoke
   e. to who they spoke
   f. they spoke to

EXERCISE 13 ▸ Looking at grammar. (Chart 13-3)
Combine the two sentences. Use the second sentence as an adjective clause. Give all the possible patterns, orally or in writing.

1. The man is standing over there. I was telling you about him.
2. I must thank the people. I got a present from them.
3. The meeting was interesting. Omar went to it.

EXERCISE 14 ▸ Looking at grammar. (Charts 13-1 → 13-3)
Give all the possible completions for each sentence. Use **who, that,** or **Ø**.

A Party

1. a. Did I tell you about the party _____*that / Ø*_____ I went to last night?

   b. Did I tell you about the party _____*that**_____ lasted until early morning?

2. a. I want to tell you about a woman _____ I met at the party.

   b. I want to tell you about the woman _____ hosted the party.

---

*Ø cannot be used for the subject position.

3. a. She works for a company _____ is hiring. She told me to apply.

   b. She said the company _____ she works for is excellent.

4. a. A man _____ I was dancing with stepped on my toes.

   b. The man _____ stepped on my toes also tripped and fell down.

5. a. My boyfriend wasn't at the party. He attended an event _____ was

   raising money for an animal shelter.

   b. We should donate to the animal shelter _____ he is supporting.

EXERCISE 15 ▶ Check your knowledge. (Charts 13-1 → 13-3)
Correct the errors in the adjective clauses.

1. In our village, there were many people didn't have much money.

2. I enjoyed the book that you told me to read it.

3. I still remember the man who he taught me to play the guitar when I was a boy.

4. I showed my father a picture of the car I am going to buy it as soon as I save enough money.

5. The man about who I was talking about walked into the room. I hope he didn't hear me.

6. The people appear in the play are amateur actors.

7. I don't like to spend time with people which loses their temper easily.

8. In one corner of the marketplace, an elderly man who was playing a violin.

9. People who works in the hunger program they estimate that 45,000 people worldwide die from starvation and malnutrition-related diseases every single day of the year.

EXERCISE 16 ▶ Let's talk: pairwork. (Charts 13-1 → 13-3)
Work with a partner. Take turns making statements that end in adjective clauses. Use words from each column and *who, that,* or Ø. Try to make the sentences true for you.

On Airplanes

Example: I enjoy people who like to have fun.

		are scary.
		have subtitles.
		have had interesting experiences.
	flights	are short.
I enjoy	people	are long.
I dislike	friends	are long-winded.★
I like to sit next to	passengers	make me think.
I like to talk to	pilots	like to have fun.
I don't like to talk to	movies	are sleeping.
	books	want to know more about me.
		are talkative.
		are busy doing other things.

★*long-winded* = boring because they talk too much

EXERCISE 17 ▶ Warm-up. (Chart 13-4)
Check (✓) the sentences that are grammatically correct.

1. _____ I have a friend. His purpose in life is to help others.

2. _____ I have a friend whose purpose in life is to help others.

3. _____ I have a friend who his purpose in life is to help others.

4. _____ I have a friend that his purpose in life is to help others.

13-4 Using *Whose*

I know the man. **His bike** was stolen. ↓ (a) I know the man *whose bike was stolen*.	**Whose** is used to show possession. It carries the same meaning as other possessive pronouns used as adjectives: *his, her, its,* and *their*. Like *his, her, its,* and *their*, **whose** is connected to a noun. *his bike → whose bike* *her composition → whose composition*
The student writes well. I read **her composition**. ↓ (b) The student *whose composition I read* writes well.	Both **whose** and the noun it is connected to are placed at the beginning of the adjective clause. **Whose** cannot be omitted.
(c) I worked at a **company** *whose employees* wanted to form a union.	**Whose** usually modifies people, but it may also be used to modify things, as in (c).
(d) That's the boy *whose parents* you met. (e) That's the boy *who's* in my math class. (f) That's the boy *who's been living* with our neighbors since his mother became ill.*	**Whose** and **who's** have the same pronunciation. **Who's** can mean **who is**, as in (e), or **who has**, as in (f).

*When **has** is a helping verb in the present perfect, it is usually contracted with **who** in speaking and sometimes in informal writing, as in (f).

When **has** is a main verb, it is NOT contracted with **who**: *I know a man **who has** a cook.*

EXERCISE 18 ▶ Looking at grammar. (Chart 13-4)
Change the words in blue to a clause with **whose**.

1.   A co-worker drives an old taxi to work.

         Her parents own a taxi company.
       ↓

A co-worker _____ own a taxi company drives an old taxi to work.

2.   The workers got a bonus.

         Their department had the most sales.
       ↓

The workers _____ had the most sales got a bonus.

3.   The hospital is temporarily closed.

         Its health-care workers are on strike.
       ↓

The hospital _____ is temporarily closed.

EXERCISE 19 ▸ Looking at grammar. (Chart 13-4)
Complete the sentences with *who* or *whose*.

Acquaintances

1. a. I know a doctor _____ last name is Doctor.

   b. I know a doctor _____ lives on a sailboat.

2. a. The professor _____ teaches art history is excellent.

   b. The professor _____ course I almost dropped is excellent.

3. a. I apologized to the man _____ coffee I spilled.

   b. I made friends with that man _____ is now in my math class.

EXERCISE 20 ▸ Let's talk: pairwork. (Chart 13-4)
Work with a partner. Imagine you are in a room full of people. You and your partner are speaking. Together, take turns identifying various people in the room. Begin with *There is*.

1. That man's wife is your teacher. → PARTNER A: *There is the man whose wife is my teacher.*
2. That woman's husband is a football player. → PARTNER B: *There is the woman whose husband is a football player.*
3. That girl's mother is a surgeon.
4. That person's picture was in the newspaper.
5. That woman's car was stolen.
6. You found that woman's keys.
7. You are in that teacher's class.
8. You read that author's book.

EXERCISE 21 ▸ Looking at grammar. (Chart 13-4)
Combine the two sentences. Use the second sentence as an adjective clause with *whose* or *who*.

College Orientation Day

1. We were taken on a tour by a student. Her major is popular culture.
   → *We were taken on a tour by a student whose major is popular culture.*
2. I have been assigned a roommate. His parents teach at this school.
3. The people seem nice. They live on my dorm floor.
4. I have a professor. She won a prestigious award.
5. I met the man. His wife is the president of the college.

EXERCISE 22 ▸ Listening. (Chart 13-4)
Choose the words you hear: *who's* or *whose*.

Example: You will hear: The man who's standing over there is Mr. Smith.
          You will choose: (who's)   whose

1. who's	whose	5. who's	whose
2. who's	whose	6. who's	whose
3. who's	whose	7. who's	whose
4. who's	whose	8. who's	whose

EXERCISE 23 ▶ Listening. (Chart 13-4)
Listen to the sentences in normal, contracted speech. You will hear: ***whose*** or ***who's*** (meaning ***who is*** or ***who has***). Choose the correct meaning.

Example: You will hear: I know a woman who's a taxi driver.
            You will choose: whose   (who is)   who has

1. whose	who is	who has		5. whose	who is	who has
2. whose	who is	who has		6. whose	who is	who has
3. whose	who is	who has		7. whose	who is	who has
4. whose	who is	who has		8. whose	who is	who has

EXERCISE 24 ▶ Warm-up. (Chart 13-5)
All of these sentences have the same meaning, and all of them are grammatically correct. The adjective clauses are in blue. What differences do you notice?

1. The **town** where I grew up is very small.
2. The **town** in which I grew up is very small.
3. The **town** which I grew up in is very small.
4. The **town** that I grew up in is very small.
5. The **town** I grew up in is very small.

13-5 Using *Where* in Adjective Clauses

	The building is very old. He lives **there** (**in that building**).			***Where*** is used in an adjective clause to modify a place (*city, country, room, house, etc.*).
(a)	The building	*where*	*he lives*	is very old.
				If ***where*** is used, as in (a), a preposition is NOT included in the adjective clause.
(b)	The building	*in which*	*he lives*	is very old.
	The building	*which*	*he lives in*	is very old.
	The building	*that*	*he lives in*	is very old.
	The building	Ø	*he lives in*	is very old.

If ***where*** is not used, the preposition must be included, as in (b). ***In which*** is more common in academic writing.

EXERCISE 25 ▶ Looking at grammar. (Chart 13-5)
Combine the two sentences. Use the second sentence as an adjective clause.

Hiding Places

1. That is the special book. My daughter puts her money there (in that book).

   → *That is the special book where my daughter puts her money.*
   → *That is the special book in which my daughter puts her money.*
   → *That is the special book which/that/Ø my daughter puts her money in.*

2. This is the mattress. My grandmother hid some money there (under the mattress).

3. That is the drawer. Johnny keeps a supply of candy there (in the drawer).

4. Here is the safe. My mom locks up her jewelry there (in that safe).

EXERCISE 26 ▸ Looking at grammar. (Chart 13-5)
Study the examples. Note how the sentences are combined with the words in blue. Then complete the sentences with *where, which,* or *in which*.

Examples: The city is beautiful. I was born there.

The city _____*where*_____ I was born is beautiful.

The city _____*in which*_____ I was born is beautiful.

The city is beautiful. It is next to my hometown.

The city _____*which*_____ is next to my hometown is beautiful.

1. The house is very old. We want to buy it.

   a. The house _____ we want to buy is very old.

   The house is very old. We lived there.

   b. The house _____ we lived is very old.

   c. The house _____ we lived is very old.

2. The town is a nice place to visit. I grew up there.

   a. The town _____ I grew up is a nice place to visit.

   b. The town _____ I grew up is a nice place to visit.

   The town is a nice place to visit. It is near us.

   c. The town _____ is near us is a nice place to visit.

3. The room is empty. It is in the basement.

   a. The room _____ is in the basement is empty.

   The room is unheated. I sleep there.

   b. The room _____ I sleep is unheated.

   c. The room _____ I sleep is unheated.

4. The park is next to the shopping center. It has a nice soccer field.

   a. The park _____ has a nice soccer field is next to the shopping center.

   The park is now a shopping center. I met your dad there.

   b. The park _____ I met your dad is now a shopping center.

   c. The park _____ I met your dad is now a shopping center.

EXERCISE 27 ▸ Looking at grammar. (Charts 13-1 → 13-5)

Complete the sentences with *who, that,* or *where.*

Euphemisms

1. A euphemism ("you-fuh-mism") is a word or phrase _____ makes something sound more pleasant.

2. For example, a "used" car is a car _____ has been "pre-owned." "Used" doesn't sound appealing to buyers.

3. A "landfill" is a place _____ people take their garbage. It used to be called a "dump."

4. A person _____ picks up your garbage is a "sanitation engineer."

5. "Pass away" is a phrase _____ sounds more gentle and indirect than "die."

6. People _____ are sick are "under the weather."

7. A guard _____ works at a jail is known as a "corrections officer."

8. The place _____ prisoners stay is a "correctional facility."

9. An employee _____ is fired is "let go."

EXERCISE 28 ▸ Warm-up. (Chart 13-6)

All of these sentences have the same meaning, and all of them are grammatically correct. The adjective clauses are in blue. What differences do you notice?

1. I clearly remember the **day** when I rode a bike for the first time.
2. I clearly remember the **day** on which I rode a bike for the first time.
3. I clearly remember the **day** that I rode a bike for the first time.
4. I clearly remember the **day** I rode a bike for the first time.

13-6 Using *When* in Adjective Clauses

	I'll never forget the day. I met you **then** (**on that day**).	*When* is used in an adjective clause to modify a noun of time (*year, day, time, century, etc.*).
(a) I'll never forget the day	*when* *I met you.*	The use of a preposition in an adjective clause that modifies a noun of time is somewhat different from that in other adjective clauses: a preposition + *which* is used, as in (b). Otherwise, there is no preposition. The use of a preposition is very formal.
(b) I'll never forget the day	*on which* *I met you.*	
(c) I'll never forget the day	*that* *I met you.*	
(d) I'll never forget the day	*Ø* *I met you.*	

EXERCISE 29 ▸ Looking at grammar. (Chart 13-6)

My Kuwaiti Cousins

Part I. Complete the sentences with the correct preposition.

1. My cousins from Kuwait will come _____ Monday.

2. Their plane arrives _____ 7:05.

3. I last saw them _____ 2010.

4. They asked to visit _____ July.

Part II. Combine the two sentences using **when** and **which**.

1. Monday is the day. My cousins from Kuwait will come then.
   → *Monday is the day when my cousins from Kuwait will come.*
   → *Monday is the day on which my cousins from Kuwait will come.*
2. 7:05 is the time. Their plane arrives then.
3. 2010 is the year. I last saw them then.
4. July is the month. The weather is usually the hottest then.

EXERCISE 30 ▶ Looking at grammar. (Charts 13-5 and 13-6)

Combine the two sentences. Use **where** or **when** to introduce an adjective clause.

Town Memories

1. That is the building. The fire began there. → *That is the place **where** the fire began*
2. I remember the day. The fire began then. → *I remember the day **when** the fire began.*
3. This used to be a movie theater. I was young then.
4. We liked that restaurant. You could get a good meal for a great price.
5. The bakery is no longer there. They made the best chocolate cake.
6. There was a time. There were no stoplights then.
7. The house is now an office building. I was born there.

EXERCISE 31 ▶ Let's talk: interview. (Charts 13-1 → 13-6)

For each question, interview two classmates. Encourage them to use adjective clauses in their responses. Share a few of their answers with the class.

Example:

What kind of **food** don't you like? → *I don't like **food** that is too sugary.*

1. What kind of **people** do you like to spend time with?
2. What kind of **people** do you prefer to avoid?
3. What kind of **cities** do you like to visit?
4. What kind of **teachers** do you learn best from?
5. What kind of **place** would you like to live in?
6. What **time of day** do you feel most energetic?

EXERCISE 32 ▶ Listening. (Charts 13-1 → 13-6)

Listen to the sentences. Choose the correct meanings for each sentence.

Example: You will hear: The nurse who gave the medicine to the patients seemed confused.
  You will choose: a. The patients were confused.
    (b.) The patients received medicine from the nurse.
    (c.) The nurse was confused.

1. a. A man gave an interview.
   b. The man is the speaker's friend.
   c. The speaker gave an interview.

2. a. Two people were killed in an accident.
   b. Two people blocked all lanes of the highway for two hours.
   c. An accident blocked all lanes of the highway for two hours.

3. a. The speaker lives in a large city.
   b. The speaker was born in a small town.
   c. The speaker was born in a large city.

4. a. The music teacher gives music lessons.
   b. The music teacher is a rock star.
   c. The speaker took music lessons.

5. a. The speaker got a phone from his parents.
   b. The phone takes excellent pictures.
   c. The speaker wants to get a phone that takes excellent pictures.

6. a. The speaker often invites the neighbor to dinner.
   b. The neighbor often visits at dinnertime.
   c. The speaker visits the neighbor at dinnertime.

EXERCISE 33 ▸ Grammar and writing. (Charts 13-1 → 13-6)

On a separate piece of paper, combine the sentences into a paragraph using adjective clauses.

Robert Ballard is an oceanographer.
He made headlines in 1985.
Ballard led a team.
They discovered the remains of the *Titanic*.
The *Titanic* was an "unsinkable" passenger ship.
It has rested on the floor of the Atlantic Ocean since 1912.
It had struck an iceberg in 1912.
After Ballard finished his exploration of the ship, he left a memorial plaque.
It honored all those who died on that terrible night.

EXERCISE 34 ▸ Warm-up. (Chart 13-7)

Underline each adjective clause. Draw an arrow to the word it modifies.

1. A: Management needs someone at the top who understands our jobs.
   B: You can say that again!*

2. A: We're the ones who seem to know everything.
   B: I couldn't agree more!

3. A: Everything they want to do slows us down and costs more.
   B: You said it!

---

*All of the responses are ways to express strong agreement.

13-7 Using Adjective Clauses to Modify Pronouns

(a) There is *someone* I want you to meet.	Adjective clauses can modify indefinite pronouns (e.g., *someone, everybody*).
(b) *Everything* he said was pure nonsense.	Object pronouns (e.g., *who(m), that, which*) are usually omitted in the adjective clause, as in (a) and (b).
(c) *Anybody* who wants to come is welcome.	
(d) Paula was *the only one* I knew at the party.	Adjective clauses can modify **the one(s)** and **those**.*
(e) Scholarships are available for *those* who need financial assistance.	
(f) *INCORRECT:* ~~I who am a student at this school~~ come from a country in Asia.	Adjective clauses are almost never used to modify personal pronouns. Native English speakers would not say or write the sentence in (f).
(g) It is *I* who am responsible.	Example (g) is possible, but very formal and uncommon.
(h) *He* who laughs last laughs best.	Example (h) is a well-known saying in which **he** is used as an indefinite pronoun (meaning "anyone" or "any person").

*An adjective clause with **which** can also be used to modify the demonstrative pronoun **that**:
  *We sometimes fear **that which** we do not understand.*
  *The bread my mother makes is much better than **that which** you can buy at a store.*

EXERCISE 35 ▶ Looking at grammar. (Chart 13-7) ⬅

Complete the sentences with adjective clauses.

Help

1. Ask your mom. She's the one ___who can help you.___
2. I have a problem. There is something ___I need your help with.___
3. This problem is harder than the ones ___we finished yesterday.___
4. Those ___who did not take the the exam.___ should stay after class.
5. I'm sorry, but I'm powerless to do anything. There's nothing more ___we can do.___
6. Could I talk to someone else? I've tried to explain my situation, but I don't think you heard anything _____
7. I did everything _____, but it didn't work.

   We need to find someone _____
8. You are the only one _____

EXERCISE 36 ▶ Let's talk. (Charts 13-1 → 13-7)

Work with a partner or in small groups. Complete this sentence: *The ideal ... is one ....* Use a word in the box and finish it with your own words. Use **who** or **that**.

Examples: The ideal friend is one who(m) you can always trust.
             The ideal job is one that has flexible hours.

friend	father	spouse	doctor
student	mother	job	city

Listen to your teacher read the sentences aloud. Both are correct. Notice the use of pauses. Then answer the questions for both sentences.

1. I just found out that Lara Johnson, who speaks Russian fluently, has applied for the job at the Russian embassy.
2. That's not the job for you. Only people who speak Russian fluently will be considered for the job at the Russian embassy.

- Which adjective clause can be omitted with no change in the meaning of the noun it modifies?
- What do you notice about the use of commas?

13-8 Punctuating Adjective Clauses

General guidelines for the punctuation of adjective clauses:
(1) **DO NOT USE COMMAS IF** the adjective clause is necessary to identify the noun it modifies.*
(2) **USE COMMAS IF** the adjective clause simply gives additional information and is not necessary to identify the noun it modifies.**

(a) *The professor* who teaches Chemistry 101 is an excellent lecturer.	In (a): No commas are used. The adjective clause is necessary to identify which professor is meant.
(b) *Professor Wilson,* who teaches Chemistry 101, is an excellent lecturer.	In (b): Commas are used. The adjective clause is not necessary to identify Professor Wilson. We already know who he is: he has a name. The adjective clause simply gives additional information.
(c) *Hawaii,* which consists of eight principal islands, is a favorite vacation spot.	GUIDELINE: Use commas, as in (b), (c), and (d), if an adjective clause modifies a proper noun. (A proper noun begins with a capital letter.)
(d) *Mrs. Smith,* who is a retired teacher, does volunteer work at the hospital.	NOTE: A comma reflects a pause in speech.
(e) *The man* { who(m) / that / Ø } *I met* teaches chemistry.	In (e): If no commas are used, any possible pronoun may be used in the adjective clause. Object pronouns may be omitted.
(f) *Mr. Lee,* whom I met yesterday, teaches chemistry.	In (f): When commas are necessary, the pronoun *that* may not be used (only *who, whom, which, whose, where,* and *when* may be used), and object pronouns cannot be omitted. *INCORRECT:* Mr. Lee, ~~that~~ I met yesterday, teaches chemistry.
COMPARE THE MEANING: (g) We took some children on a picnic. *The children, who wanted to play soccer,* ran to an open field as soon as we arrived at the park.	In (g): The use of commas means that *all* of the children wanted to play soccer and *all* of the children ran to an open field. The adjective clause is used only to give additional information about the children.
(h) We took some children on a picnic. *The children who wanted to play soccer* ran to an open field as soon as we arrived at the park. The others played a different game.	In (h): The lack of commas means that *only some* of the children wanted to play soccer. The adjective clause is used to identify which children ran to the open field.

*Adjective clauses that do not require commas are called *essential* or *restrictive* or *identifying*.
**Adjective clauses that require commas are called *nonessential* or *nonrestrictive* or *nonidentifying*.
NOTE: Nonessential adjective clauses are more common in writing than in speaking.

EXERCISE 38 ▶ Looking at grammar. (Chart 13-8)

Read each sentence, first with the adjective clause and then again without it. How does the meaning change? Does the adjective clause identify the noun? If it does not identify the noun, add commas.

1. Mercury which is the nearest planet to the sun is also the smallest planet in our solar system.
2. Research has shown that children who watch violent video games may become more aggressive.
3. People who live in glass houses shouldn't throw stones.
4. In a children's story, Little Red Riding Hood who went out one day to visit her grandmother found a wolf in her grandmother's bed.

EXERCISE 39 ▶ Grammar and listening. (Chart 13-8)

Work with a partner. Read the sentences aloud. Decide if the information in blue is necessary or simply provides additional information. If it is additional, add commas. Then listen to the sentences and correct your answers. Remember, pauses indicate commas.

1. a. Vegetables which are orange have a lot of vitamin A. (*necessary: no commas*)
   b. Vegetables, which come in many shapes and colors, have lots of vitamins.
      (*additional information: commas*)

2. a. Did you hear about the man who rowed a boat across the Atlantic Ocean?
   b. My uncle who loves boating rows his boat across the lake near his house nearly every day.

3. a. Rice which is grown in many countries is a staple food throughout much of the world.
   b. The rice which we had for dinner last night was very good.

4. a. The newspaper article was about a man who died two weeks ago of a rare tropical disease.
   b. The obituary said that Paul O'Grady who died two weeks ago of a sudden heart attack was a kind and loving man.

5. a. Tea which is a common drink throughout the world is made by pouring boiling water onto the dried leaves of certain plants.
   b. Tea which is made from herbs is called herbal tea.

6. a. Toys which contain lead paint are unsafe for children.
   b. Lead which can be found in paint and plastics is known to cause brain damage in children.

EXERCISE 40 ▶ Pronunciation and grammar. (Chart 13-8)

Work with a partner. Read the given sentence aloud. Choose the correct meaning.

1. The teacher thanked the students, who had given her some flowers.
   a. The teacher thanked *only some* of the students.
   (b.) The teacher thanked *all* of the students.

2. The teacher thanked the students who had given her some flowers.
   (a.) The teacher thanked *only some* of the students.
   b. The teacher thanked *all* of the students.

3. There was a terrible flood. The villagers who had received a warning of the flood escaped to safety.
   a. *Only some* of the villagers had been warned; only some escaped.
   b. *All* of the villagers had been warned; all escaped.

4. There was a terrible flood. The villagers, who had received a warning of the impending flood, escaped to safety.
   a. *Only some* of the villagers had been warned; only some escaped.
   b. *All* of the villagers had been warned; all escaped.

5. Natasha reached down and picked up the grammar book, which was lying upside down on the floor.
   a. There was *only one* grammar book near Natasha.
   b. There was *more than one* grammar book near Natasha.

6. Natasha reached down and picked up the grammar book which was lying upside down on the floor.
   a. There was *only one* grammar book near Natasha.
   b. There was *more than one* grammar book near Natasha.

EXERCISE 41 ▶ Looking at grammar. (Chart 13-8)

Add commas where necessary. Read the sentences aloud, paying attention to pauses.

1. a. We enjoyed the city where we spent our honeymoon.

   b. We enjoyed Mexico City where we spent our vacation.

2. a. One of the most useful materials in the world is glass which is made mainly from sand, soda, and lime.

   b. The glass which is used in windows is different from the glass which is used in eyeglasses.

3. a. You don't need to take heavy clothes when you go to Bangkok which has one of the highest average temperatures of any city in the world.

   b. Bangkok where my father was born is known as the Venice of the East.

4. a. Mr. Trang whose son won the spelling contest is very proud of his son's achievement.

   b. The man whose daughter won the science contest is also very pleased and proud.

5. a. I watched some beekeepers collect honey. They told me that beekeepers who wear protective clothing can avoid most bee stings.

   b. A person who doesn't wear protective clothing can get hundreds of bee stings within a minute.

EXERCISE 42 ▶ Listening. (Chart 13-8)

Listen to the sentences. Choose the correct meaning for each sentence.

1. a. She threw away all of the apples.
   b. She threw away only the rotten apples.

2. a. She threw away all of the apples.
   b. She threw away only the rotten apples.

3. a. Some of the students were excused from class early.
   b. All of the students were excused from class early.

4. a. Some of the students were excused from class early.
   b. All of the students were excused from class early.

EXERCISE 43 ▸ Reading and grammar. (Charts 13-1 → 13-8)

Part I. Answer these questions. Then read the web article. Note the adjective clauses in blue.

1. Do you have a computer?
2. Do you know the name of its operating system?

Do you know these words?
- computer programmer
- acquire the rights

DOS: The First Operating System

As you know, a computer needs to have an operating system in order to run programs. When most people think about the first operating systems that were developed for the personal computer, Microsoft or Bill Gates may come to mind. Actually, the truth is somewhat different.

In the late 1970s, there was a man in Seattle named Tim Paterson, who worked for a company that was called Seattle Computer. He was a computer programmer and needed an operating system for his computer. Paterson got tired of waiting for another company to create one and decided to develop his own program. He called it QDOS, which meant "quick and dirty operating system*." It took him about four months to develop it.

At the same time, Microsoft was quietly looking for an operating system to run a personal computer that IBM was developing. Microsoft saw the program that Paterson had written and in 1980, paid him $25,000 for a license for DOS. A year later they paid another $50,000 to acquire the rights. It became known as the Microsoft disk operating system (MS-DOS), and the rest is history. Microsoft and Bill Gates became very successful using Paterson's operating system.

quick and dirty = something that is done quickly or hastily

Part II. Complete the sentences with information from the article. Use adjective clauses in your completions.

1. Tim Paterson was the person who _____

2. Seattle Computer was the company that _____

3. The abbreviation for the program was QDOS, which _____

   _____

4. IBM was a company that _____

5. Microsoft, which _____

6. Microsoft acquired rights to a program that _____

   _____

EXERCISE 44 ▸ Warm-up. (Chart 13-9)
Choose the correct meaning (a. or b.) for each sentence.

1. The couple has 13 children, only a few of whom live at home.
   a. Ten children live at home.   b. A few of the couple's children live at home.
2. Victoria bought a dozen dresses, most of which she later returned to the store.
   a. Victoria returned a dozen dresses.   b. Victoria kept a few of the dresses.

13-9 Using Expressions of Quantity in Adjective Clauses

In my class there are 20 students. *Most of **them*** are from Asia.	An adjective clause may contain an expression of quantity with **of**: *some of, many of, most of, none of, two of, half of, both of,* etc.
(a) In my class there are 20 students, *most of **whom*** are from Asia.	
(b) He gave several reasons, *only a few of **which*** were valid.	The expression of quantity precedes the pronoun. Only **whom**, **which**, and **whose** are used in this pattern. This pattern is more common in writing than speaking. Commas are used.
(c) The teachers discussed Jim, *one of **whose problems*** was poor study habits.	

EXERCISE 45 ▸ Looking at grammar. (Chart 13-9)
Combine the two sentences in each item. Use the second sentence as an adjective clause.

At the Mall

1. The mall has 200 stores. Many of them are having sales this weekend.
   → *The mall has 200 stores, many of which are having sales this weekend.*
2. I went to a few sales. Only one of them had good discounts.
3. There are many clothing stores. The majority of them are for women and teenage girls.
4. I tried on five dresses. I liked two of them.
5. The movie theater is showing four movies. None sound good.
6. There are several ethnic restaurants in the food court. All of them have reasonable prices.
7. There are two cafés side by side. Both of them serve excellent coffee.

EXERCISE 46 ▸ Grammar and writing. (Chart 13-9)
Complete the sentences with your own words. Use adjective clauses.

About Me

1. I have several friends, two of _____*whom grew up with me.*_____
2. I own three _____, one of _____
3. I have many _____, all of _____
4. I bought two _____, neither of _____
5. I am taking _____ courses, one of _____
6. This term I had to buy _____ books, most of _____
7. For this class I need _____, some of _____

EXERCISE 47 ▸ Warm-up. (Chart 13-10)
What does *which* refer to in each sentence?

1. The soccer team worked very hard to win, **which** made their coach very proud.
2. Some of the athletes attended practice during vacation, **which** pleased their coach.

13-10 Using *Which* to Modify a Whole Sentence

(a) Tom was late. **That** surprised me.	The pronouns *that* and *this* can refer to the idea of a whole sentence which comes before.
(b) Tom was late, *which surprised me.*	In (a): The word *that* refers to the whole sentence *Tom was late*.
(c) The elevator is out of order. **This** is too bad.	Similarly, an adjective clause with *which* may modify the idea of a whole sentence.
(d) The elevator is out of order, *which is too bad.*	In (b): The word *which* refers to the whole sentence *Tom was late*.
	Using *which* to modify a whole sentence is informal and occurs most frequently in spoken English. This structure is generally not appropriate in formal writing. Whenever it is written, however, it is preceded by a comma to reflect a pause in speech.

EXERCISE 48 ▸ Looking at grammar. (Chart 13-10)
Combine the two sentences. Use the second sentence as an adjective clause.

Sonya's Challenges

1. Sonya lost her job. That wasn't surprising.
   → *Sonya lost her job, which wasn't surprising.*
2. She usually came to work late. That upset her boss.
3. So her boss fired her. That made her angry.
4. She hadn't saved any money. That was unfortunate.
5. So she had to borrow some money from me. I didn't like that.
6. She has found a new job. That is lucky.
7. So she has repaid the money she borrowed from me. I appreciate that.
8. She has promised herself to be on time to work every day. That is a good idea.

EXERCISE 49 ▸ Looking at grammar. (Charts 13-1 → 13-10)
Combine sentences a. and b. Use b. as an adjective clause. Use formal written English. Punctuate carefully.

1. a. An antecedent is a word.
   b. A pronoun refers to this word.
   → *An antecedent is a word to which a pronoun refers.*

2. a. The blue whale is considered the largest animal that has ever lived.
   b. It can grow to 100 feet and 150 tons.

3. a. The plane was met by a crowd of 300 people.
   b. Some of them had been waiting for more than four hours.

4. a. In this paper, I will describe the basic process.
   b. Raw cotton becomes cotton thread by this process.

5. a. The researchers are doing case studies of people to determine the importance of heredity in health and longevity.
   b. These people's families have a history of high blood pressure and heart disease.

6. a. At the end of this month, scientists at the institute will conclude their AIDS research.
   b. The results of this research will be published within six months.

7. a. According to many education officials, "math phobia" (that is, a fear of mathematics) is a widespread problem.
   b. A solution to this problem can and must be found.

8. a. The art museum hopes to hire a new administrator.
   b. Under this person's direction, it will be able to purchase significant pieces of art.

9. a. The giant anteater licks up ants for its dinner.
   b. Its tongue is longer than 30 centimeters (12 inches).

10. a. The anteater's tongue is sticky.
    b. It can go in and out of its mouth 160 times a minute.

EXERCISE 50 ▸ Reading and grammar. (Charts 13-1 → 13-10)

Read about Ellen and her commute to work. <u>Underline</u> what the words in blue refer to.

Ellen's Commute

Ellen <u>commutes to work by ferry</u>, which (1) means she takes a boat from the island where she lives to the city where (2) she works. She leaves her house at 6:00, which (3) is earlier than she'd like but necessary because the ferry ride takes 30 minutes. Ellen needs 20 minutes to drive to the parking lot where (4) she leaves her car and boards the ferry. Once she's on the other side, she catches a bus that (5) takes her to her office. Traffic is usually heavy at that hour, so she's on the bus for another 30 minutes. On the bus, she usually reads reports that (6) she was too tired to finish the night before. The bus drops her off a few blocks from her office. Sometimes she stops at an espresso stand and picks up coffee for her co-workers, for which (7) they reimburse her later. By the time she gets to her office, she has been commuting for an hour and a half, which (8) she wishes she didn't have to do but isn't going to change because she enjoys her life on the island so much.

EXERCISE 51 ▸ Warm-up. (Chart 13-11)
Look at the words in blue. What differences do you notice between each pair of sentences?
NOTE: Sentences a. and b. have the same meaning.

1. a. I talked to the people who were sitting beside me at the ball game.
   b. I talked to the people sitting beside me at the ball game.

2. a. The notebooks that are on my desk are mine.
   b. The notebooks on my desk are mine.

3. a. I read an article about Gregor Mendel, who is known as the father of genetics.
   b. I read an article about Gregor Mendel, known as the father of genetics.

13-11 Reducing Adjective Clauses to Adjective Phrases

CLAUSE: *A clause* is a group of related words that contains a subject and a verb.	
PHRASE: *A phrase* is a group of related words that does not contain a subject and a verb.	

(a) CLAUSE:	The girl *who is sitting next to me* is Mai.	An adjective phrase is a reduction of an adjective clause. It modifies a noun. It does not contain a subject and verb.
(b) PHRASE:	The girl *sitting next to me* is Mai.	Examples (a) and (b) have the same meaning.
(c) CLAUSE:	The girl *(whom) I saw* was Mai.	
(d) PHRASE:	*(none)*	Only adjective clauses that have a subject pronoun — *who, that,* or *which* — can be reduced to modifying adjective phrases. The adjective clause in (c) cannot be reduced to an adjective phrase.
(e) CLAUSE:	The man *who is talking* to John is from Korea.	There are two ways in which an adjective clause is changed to an adjective phrase.
PHRASE:	The man Ø Ø *talking* to John is from Korea.	**1.** if the adjective clause contains the *be* form of a verb, omit the subject pronoun and the *be* form, as in (e), (f), and (g).*
(f) CLAUSE:	The ideas *that are presented* in this book are good.	
PHRASE:	The ideas Ø Ø *presented* in this book are good.	
(g) CLAUSE:	Ann is the woman *that is responsible* for the error.	
PHRASE:	Ann is the woman Ø Ø *responsible* for the error.	
(h) CLAUSE:	English has an alphabet *that consists* of 26 letters.	**2.** If there is no *be* form of a verb in the adjective clause, it is sometimes possible to omit the subject pronoun and change the verb to its *-ing* form, as in (h) and (i).
PHRASE:	English has an alphabet Ø *consisting* of 26 letters.	
(i) CLAUSE:	Anyone *who wants* to come with us is welcome.	
PHRASE:	Anyone Ø *wanting* to come with us is welcome.	
(j) **Paris,** *which is the capital of France,* is an exciting city.		If the adjective clause requires commas, as in (j), the adjective phrase also requires commas, as in (k). An adjective phrase in which a noun follows another noun, as in (k), is called an *appositive*.
(k) **Paris,** *the capital of France,* is an exciting city.		

*If an adjective clause that contains *be* + *a single adjective* is changed, the adjective is moved to its normal position in front of the noun it modifies.

    CLAUSE: ***Fruit that is fresh*** *tastes better than old, soft, mushy fruit.*
    CORRECT PHRASE: ***Fresh fruit*** *tastes better than old, soft, mushy fruit.*
    INCORRECT PHRASE: *Fruit fresh tastes better than old, soft, mushy fruit.*

nge the adjective clauses to adjective phrases.

Early Failures of Famous People

Many famous people did not enjoy immediate success in their early lives:

1. Abraham Lincoln, ~~who was~~ one of the truly great presidents of the United States, ran for public office 26 times and lost 23 of the elections.
2. Walt Disney, who was the creator of Mickey Mouse and the founder of his own movie production company, once was fired by a newspaper editor because he had no good ideas.
3. Thomas Edison, who was the inventor of the light bulb and the phonograph, was believed by his teachers to be too stupid to learn.
4. Albert Einstein, who was one of the greatest scientists of all time, performed badly in almost all of his high school courses and failed his first college entrance exam.

EXERCISE 53 ▶ Looking at grammar. (Chart 13-11)
Change the adjective phrases to adjective clauses.

A Class Trip

1. Our biology class is going to Montreal to see the Biodome, a dome-like structure housing five ecosystems.
   → *Our class is going to Montreal to see the Biodome, which is a dome-like structure that/which houses five ecosystems.*
2. Ecosystems are biological communities containing living and non-living things found in one particular environment.
3. The ecosystems being studied in our class include a tropical rain forest and Antarctic islands.
4. An optional trip to the Montreal Insectarium, considered North America's leading museum of insects, is also being offered.
5. Students not wanting to see insects can spend more time at the Biodome.

tropical rain forest

EXERCISE 54 ▶ Listening. (Chart 13-11)
Listen to the sentences. Choose the correct meaning (a. or b.) for each sentence. In some cases, both are correct.

Example: You will hear: The experiment conducted by the students was successful.
    You will choose: (a.) The students conducted an experiment.
        (b.) The experiment was successful.

1. a. There is a fence around our house.
   b. Our house is made of wood.

2. a. All schoolchildren receive a good education.
   b. That school provides a good education.

3. a. The university president will give a speech.
   b. Dr. Stanton will give a speech.

4. a. There is a galaxy called the Milky Way.
   b. Our solar system is called the Milky Way.

the Milky Way

EXERCISE 55 ▸ Game. (Chart 13-11)
Work in teams. Complete the sentences by turning the information in the box into adjective phrases. Use commas as necessary. The team that finishes first with the most correct answers wins.

> a. It is the lowest place on the earth's surface.
> ✓ b. It is the highest mountain in the world.
> c. It is the capital of Iraq.
> d. It is the capital of Argentina.
> e. It is the largest city in the Western Hemisphere.
> f. It is the largest city in the United States.
> g. It is the most populous country in Africa.
> h. It is the northernmost country in Latin America.
> i. They are sensitive instruments that measure the shaking of the ground.
> j. They are devices that produce a powerful beam of light.

1. Mount Everest _____, *the highest mountain in the world,*_____ is in the Himalayas.

2. One of the largest cities in the Middle East is Baghdad _____

3. Earthquakes are recorded on seismographs _____
   _____

4. The Dead Sea _____
   is located in the Middle East between Jordan and Israel.

5. The newspaper reported an earthquake in Buenos Aires _____

6. Industry and medicine are continually finding new uses for lasers _____
   _____

7. Mexico _____ lies just south of
   the United States.

8. The nation Nigeria _____ consists of
   over 250 different cultural groups even though English is the official language.

9. Both Mexico City _____
   and New York City _____ face challenging futures.

EXERCISE 56 ▶ Reading and grammar. (Charts 13-2 and 13-11)
Read the passage. Find the 7 adjective clauses where *who, that,* or *which* have been omitted. Rewrite them using *who, that,* or *which.*

Do you know these words?
- genius
- unconscious
- sought
- altered
- trauma

An Accidental
Genius

Jason Padgett was not much of a student. A college dropout, he worked for his father at a furniture store in Tacoma, Washington. He thought of himself as a playboy and didn't think that school was important.

In 2002, at the age of 31, Jason's life changed forever. He left a karaoke bar one night, and while he was walking home, two men attacked him. They knocked him to the ground unconscious. After treatment at a hospital, he went home. The next morning he woke up and noticed that his vision was different. He saw geometric designs in the objects he looked at. Water pouring from a faucet had crystal structures. These were details he had never seen before. He began to draw complex patterns, some taking him weeks to finish. Before his injury, Padgett had never studied beyond pre-algebra. Now he saw mathematical structures everywhere.

He sought the help of a doctor, who told Padgett that he had become a math genius because of the injury. Eventually he went to Finland to meet Dr. Berit Brogaard, a specialist in brain injuries. Dr. Brogaard used a special MRI machine* to study Padgett's brain and discovered that the part of the brain used for math was more active. The injury had altered his brain to make it very specialized in math.

Padgett went back to school to study advanced math. Sometimes he knew more than his teachers. He also wrote a book, *Struck by Genius,* in which he described the trauma he went through. He said it has changed his life for the better, and he has no regrets.

*MRI = magnetic resonance imaging; a machine that uses radio waves to take pictures of organs in the body

1. _____
2. _____
3. _____
4. _____
5. _____
6. _____
7. _____

EXERCISE 57 ▶ Looking at grammar. (Chart 13-11)
Change the adjective clauses to adjective phrases. Change the adjective phrases to adjective clauses.

The Diamond Head Hike

1. Diamond Head, a mountain near Waikiki, was formed by a volcano 300,000 years ago.
2. Scientists who study Diamond Head say it is no longer an active volcano.

3. Visitors can hike the Diamond Head Trail, which is located inside the volcano's crater.

Diamond Head Crater

4. The trail leading hikers to a 360-degree view at the top is 2.25 kilometers (1.4 miles) long.
5. Tourists who are planning to hike to the top should bring sunscreen and water because there is no shade on the trail.
6. The path, which ends with 250 steps, is very steep.
7. At the top is an observation point, which overlooks Honolulu and the ocean.
8. Signs posted on the trail warn hikers not to leave the trail.
9. The trails can become very crowded. Some people are asking for changes that allow more access for tourists.
10. Many people wanting to preserve the natural habitats oppose this change.

EXERCISE 58 ▶ Looking at grammar. (Chapter 13 Review)

Combine each group of short, choppy sentences into one sentence. Use the first sentence as the independent clause and build your sentence around it. Use adjective clauses and adjective phrases where possible.

1. Chihuahua is divided into two regions.
   It is the largest Mexican state.
   One region is a mountainous area in the west.
   The other region is a desert basin in the north and east.

   Chihuahua, the largest Mexican state, is divided into two regions, a mountainous area in the west and a desert basin in the north and east.

2. Disney World covers a large area of land.
   It is an amusement park.
   It is located in Orlando, Florida.
   The land includes lakes, golf courses, campsites, hotels, and a wildlife preserve.

   _____

   _____

   _____

3. The Republic of Yemen is an ancient land.
   It is located at the southwestern tip of the Arabian Peninsula.
   This land has been host to many prosperous civilizations.
   These civilizations include the Kingdom of Sheba and various Islamic empires.

   _____

   _____

   _____

EXERCISE 59 ▶ Check your knowledge. (Chapter 13 Review)
Correct the errors.

1. Baseball is the only sport in which I am interested in it.

2. My favorite teacher, Mr. Chu, he was always willing to help me after class.

3. It is important to be polite to people who lives in the same building.

4. My sister has two children, who their names are Ali and Talal.

5. Paulo comes from Venezuela that is a Spanish-speaking country.

6. There are some people in the government who is trying to improve the lives of the poor.

7. A myth is a story expresses traditional beliefs.

8. There is an old legend telling among people in my country about a man lived in the seventeenth century and saved a village from destruction.

9. An old man was fishing next to me on the pier was mumbling to himself.

10. The road that we took it through the forest it was narrow and steep.

11. There are ten universities in Thailand, seven of them are located in Bangkok is the capital city.

12. At the national park, there is a path leads to a spectacular waterfall.

13. At the airport, I was waiting for some relatives which I had never met them before.

14. It is almost impossible to find two persons who their opinions are the same.

15. On the wall, there is a colorful poster which it consists of a group of young people who dancing.

16. The sixth member of our household is Pietro that is my sister's son.

17. Before I came here, I didn't have the opportunity to speak with people who English is their native tongue.

EXERCISE 60 ▸ Grammar and writing. (Chapter 13)

Part I. Some writing assignments require extended definition. This type of writing asks you to explain or describe something, for example, a process, a disease, a device, or perhaps something historical. Read the following example. Underline the adjective clauses and phrases.

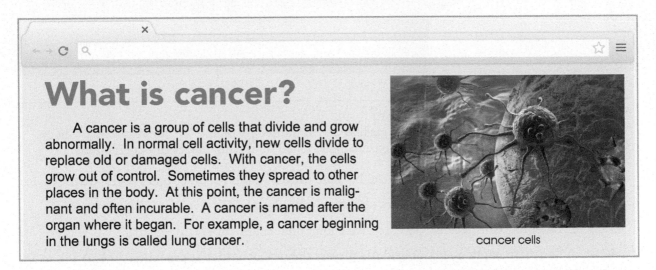

What is cancer?

A cancer is a group of cells that divide and grow abnormally. In normal cell activity, new cells divide to replace old or damaged cells. With cancer, the cells grow out of control. Sometimes they spread to other places in the body. At this point, the cancer is malignant and often incurable. A cancer is named after the organ where it began. For example, a cancer beginning in the lungs is called lung cancer.

cancer cells

Part II. Depending on your topic, it is helpful to address one or more of the following questions when you write an extended definition. Which question(s) does the paragraph above answer?

- What are the different parts? (e.g., the human heart)
- How does it work? (e.g., a seismograph — a machine to measure earthquakes)
- What happens? (e.g., a process like cell division)
- What does it look like? (e.g., an amoeba)
- What is its purpose? (e.g., a political movement)
- Is it similar to or different from anything? (e.g., a historical event)

Part III. Choose something you want to explain or describe. Write an extended definition.

WRITING TIP

Adjective clauses and phrases are useful because they can add interesting and relevant information to your writing in an efficient way. However, you want to be sure that the information is necessary or adds related information. Because adjective clauses can sound "academic" or very impressive, it may be tempting to use them too often. In the second sentence of the example paragraph, if the writer had written *In cell activity which is normal ...* , the adjective clause is forced. A simple adjective is all that is needed there.

Part IV. Edit your writing. Check for the following:

1. ☐ correct pronoun in adjective clauses (***who, which, that,*** *etc.*)
2. ☐ correct use of commas in adjective clauses
3. ☐ if reducing adjective clauses with ***be,*** delete ***be*** form and the pronoun
4. ☐ if reducing an adjective clause without ***be,*** change verb to ***-ing*** and omit the pronoun
5. ☐ correct spelling (use a dictionary or spell-check)

CHAPTER 1

Gerunds and Infinitives, Part 1

PRETEST: What do I already know?

Write "C" if a sentence has the correct gerund and infinitive form and "I" for incorrect. Check your answers below. After you complete each chart listed, make any necessary corrections.

1. _____ Shopping during the holidays can be more expensive than at other times of the year. (14-1)

2. _____ I appreciated to hear the news about your family. (14-2)

3. _____ The professor decided don't to give a long final exam. (14-3)

4. _____ The team captain encouraged the players they work harder at practices. (14-4)

5. _____ My boyfriend loves holding snakes, but I can't stand to even look at them. (14-5)

6. _____ Who is responsible for to clearing ice from the walkways? (14-6)

7. _____ I'd like to go hiking in the mountains, but I don't have the time right now. (14-7)

8. _____ The security guard caught the thief shoplifting a cell phone from the store. (14-8)

9. _____ It can be deadly driving a car and text at the same time. (14-9)

10. _____ How did you manage to learn four languages fluently? (14-10)

11. _____ Rey mentioned having some difficulty with his boss at work. (14-11)

12. _____ Instead of have a quiet night at home, why don't we invite a few friends over? (14-12)

Incorrect sentences: 2, 3, 4, 6, 9, 12

EXERCISE 1 ▶ Warm-up. (Chart 14-1)

Complete the sentences with the words in the box. Give your own opinion.

| baseball | golf | badminton |
| basketball | soccer | tennis |

1. My friends and I like to play

   _____.

2. I don't know much about playing

   _____.

3. Playing _____

   takes a lot of skill.

14-1 Gerunds and Infinitives: Introduction

(a) $\overset{S}{Playing}$ tennis $\overset{V}{is}$ fun.	A *gerund* is the *-ing* form of a verb used as a noun. A gerund is used in the same ways as a noun, i.e., as a subject or as an object.
(b) $\overset{S}{We}$ $\overset{V}{enjoy}$ $\overset{O}{playing}$ tennis.	In (a): *playing* is a gerund. It is used as the subject of the sentence. *Playing tennis* is a *gerund phrase*.
(c) He's excited $\overset{PREP}{about}$ $\overset{O}{playing}$ tennis.	In (b): *playing* is a gerund used as the object of the verb **enjoy**.
	In (c): *playing* is a gerund used as the object of the preposition **about**.
(d) $\overset{S}{To\ play}$ tennis well $\overset{V}{takes}$ a lot of practice.	An *infinitive* = **to** + *the simple form of a verb (to see, to be, to go, etc.)*.
(e) $\overset{S}{He}$ $\overset{V}{likes}$ $\overset{O}{to\ play}$ tennis.	Like gerunds, infinitives can also be used as the subject of a sentence, as in (d), or as the object, as in (e), but it is more common for the infinitive to be used as the object.

EXERCISE 2 ▶ Looking at grammar. (Chart 14-1)
Work with a partner. Compare the uses of the *-ing* form of verbs in the examples. Then check (✓) the sentences that have gerunds.

Examples:
Walking is good exercise.   (*walking* = a gerund used as the subject of the sentence)
Bob and Ann are playing tennis.   (*playing* = a present participle used as part of the present
                                              progressive tense)
That was a surprising win.   (*surprising* = a present participle used as an adjective)

Running

1. a. _____ Running uphill is hard work.

   b. _____ Martin isn't running in the race today.

   c. _____ I need new running shoes.

2. a. _____ I'm scheduling our team practices for the mornings.

   b. _____ Scheduling practices for the afternoons doesn't work.

   c. _____ Would you consider scheduling a practice in the evening?

3. a. _____ Drinking something with electrolytes is important after a race.

   b. _____ Is there any drinking water nearby?

EXERCISE 3 ▶ Looking at grammar. (Chart 14-1)
Work with a partner. Compare the uses of *to* in the examples. Then check (✓) the sentences on page 304 that have infinitives.

Examples:
Marta needs to leave early.   (*to leave* = an infinitive as the object)
To work without breaks is not permitted. (*to work* = an infinitive as the subject)
Is Elias committed to his job?   (*to* = a preposition)

Co-Workers

1. _____ Franco is engaged to Liz.
2. _____ Danielle is related to the CEO's wife.
3. _____ To become a CEO is Danielle's goal.
4. _____ Viktor has volunteered to mentor new interns.
5. _____ Rachel hasn't been feeling well, but she can't afford to take any sick days right now.
6. _____ Pedro will talk to new employees about texting during meetings.
7. _____ Karl's goal is to speak without any nervousness.

EXERCISE 4 ▶ Warm-up. (Chart 14-2)

Complete the sentences with phrases in the box that are true for you. What do you notice about the form of the verbs in these phrases?

buying things online	talking about politics
posting on social media	watching commercials on TV
surfing the Internet	watching TV news

1. I enjoy _____

2. I don't enjoy _____

3. I avoid _____

14-2 Common Verbs Followed by Gerunds

(a) I *enjoy* *playing* tennis. (verb + gerund)	Gerunds can be used as the objects of certain verbs. In (a): *enjoy* is followed by a gerund (*playing*). *Enjoy* is not followed by an infinitive. INCORRECT: *I enjoy to play tennis.* Common verbs that are followed by gerunds are listed below.
(b) Joe *quit smoking*. (c) Joe *gave up smoking*.	Some phrasal verbs are followed by gerunds. A *phrasal verb* consists of a verb and a particle (a small word such as a preposition) that together have a special meaning. For example in (c), *give up* means "quit." (Phrasal verbs are in parentheses below.)

Verb + gerund

enjoy	quit (give up)	avoid	consider
appreciate	finish (get through)	postpone (put off)	discuss
mind	stop*	delay	mention
		keep (keep on)	suggest**

*__Stop__ can also be followed by an infinitive of purpose. *He **stopped** at the station (**in order**) to get some gas.* See Charts 14-5 and 15-1, p. 335.

**__Suggest__ can also be used with a subjunctive noun clause. See Chart 12-9. p. 267.

EXERCISE 5 ▸ Looking at grammar. (Chart 14-2)
Complete the sentences with gerunds. Use the verbs in the box or any appropriate verbs.

be	drop	go	have	make	pay	read

College Plans

A: Aunt Kim, when you're done in the office, would you mind ____*reading*____ my college
    1
   application essay and checking for mistakes?

B: Sure. I just need to get through _____ the bills.
                                        2
   Where are you considering _____ to college?
                               3
A: I'm still not sure. I've put off _____ where to go.
                                     4
B: Don't you need to decide before you do your essay?

A: No, this is part of the general application. I have to do it for any college I'm interested in.

B: It doesn't seem like you can postpone _____ that decision much longer.
                                            5
A: Here's the problem. I want to study at a big school, but my mom and dad have suggested

   _____ to a smaller one. They said that's what they'll pay for.
       6
B: I went to a college with only about 4,000 students. I appreciated _____ small
                                                                        7
   classes. That's how I met your uncle.

A: You were a tutor, right? He mentioned _____ your student.
                                            8
B: Yes, for math. He was considering _____ the class, but I convinced him to
                                        9
   stay. It all worked out!

EXERCISE 6 ▸ Looking at grammar. (Chart 14-2)
Complete the sentences with any appropriate gerunds.

Roommates

1. Would you mind ___*opening / closing*___ the door? Thanks.

2. I want to order pizza. Sierra has suggested _____ burgers.

3. What are you considering _____ for dinner?

4. I'm not the best roommate. Sometimes I put off _____ the apartment
   when it's my turn. I know I shouldn't. Actually, when I think about it, all of us avoid

   _____ at some point. None of us enjoy _____ .

5. Tony mentioned _____ to a movie later tonight.

6. I have a lot of homework, but I'd still like to go out with you later on. I'll let you know when I
   get through _____ it.

7. No one will be here later. I appreciate _____ able to study in peace and quiet.

EXERCISE 7 ▸ Let's talk. (Chart 14-2)

Work with a partner. Take turns making sentences with the given words. Use any tense and subject.

1. mind \ turn off your phone
2. finish \ eat dinner
3. get through \ eat dinner
4. stop \ rain
5. keep \ work
6. keep on \ work

7. postpone \ do my work
8. put off \ do my work
9. delay \ leave on vacation
10. consider \ get a job
11. talk about \ go to a movie
12. mention \ go out of town

EXERCISE 8 ▸ Listening. (Chart 14-2)

Listen to the conversations. Complete the sentence summaries with appropriate verbs.

1. The speakers enjoy _____*watching*_____ movies on weekends.

2. The speakers have given up _____ for better weather.

3. The speakers are going to keep on _____.

4. The speakers are discussing _____ to a concert in the city.

5. The speakers have put off _____ their homework.

6. The speakers are going to delay _____ the office.

EXERCISE 9 ▸ Warm-up. (Chart 14-3)

Check (✓) the correct sentences.

1. a. _____ We hope winning the game.

   b. _____ We hope to win the game.

   c. _____ We hope win the game.

2. a. _____ The player promised not to react to the referee's decision.

   b. _____ The player promised not getting upset with the referee.

   c. _____ The player promised not yell at the referee.

14-3 Common Verbs Followed by Infinitives

(a) I *hope to see* you again soon.	Some verbs are followed immediately by an infinitive, as in (a) and (b).
(b) He *promised to be* here by ten.	
(c) He *promised not to be* late.	Negative form: ***not*** precedes the infinitive, as in (c).

Common verbs followed by infinitives

hope to (do something)	promise to	seem to	expect to
plan to	agree to	appear to	would like to
intend to*	offer to	pretend to	want to
decide to	refuse to	ask to	need to

*****Intend** is usually followed by an infinitive (*I **intend to go** to the meeting.*) but sometimes may be followed by a gerund (*I **intend going** to the meeting.*) with no change in meaning.

EXERCISE 10 ▶ Let's talk: interview. (Chart 14-3)

Work with a partner. Take turns asking and answering questions. Share your answers with the class.

1. what \ you \ need \ do \ today?
2. what \ you \ would like \ do \ this weekend?
3. what \ you \ plan \ do \ with English?
4. what \ should people \ refuse \ do?
5. what \ shouldn't people \ pretend \ do?
6. what \ should students \ expect \ do?

EXERCISE 11 ▶ Looking at grammar. (Chart 14-3)

Complete the sentences with your own words. In small groups or with a partner, compare your sentences.

In My Opinion

1. A hard-working employee expects _____
2. A nice teacher sometimes agrees _____
3. A serious student refuses _____
4. An honest police officer promises not _____
5. A lazy employee needs _____
6. A caring doctor offers _____
7. A good actor can appear _____

EXERCISE 12 ▶ Looking at grammar. (Charts 14-2 and 14-3)

Complete each sentence with a gerund or an infinitive.

Small Talk

1. *stop / talk / tell / text / turn off*

   A: How was the movie?

   B: The movie was good, but the guy in back of us

   kept _____*talking*_____ and _____ .

   A: Did you ask him _____?

   B: Yes, but it didn't help.

   A: At our theater, the audience is required _____ their electronic devices.

   B: I expected the usher _____ him to stop, but it didn't happen.

2. *have / help / join / lend / pay / see / talk*

   A: We're going out for dinner. Would you like _____ us?

   B: Would you mind _____ me some money?

   A: I thought you just got paid.

   B: I did, but Jens told me he was broke, so I offered _____ him out. I expected

   him _____ me back, but now I'm not sure he's going to. I think he's avoiding

   _____ to me. I saw him at the mall, and he pretended not _____ me.

   A: Good luck! You seem _____ a big problem on your hands.

3. *be / get / hear / take / wait*

A: Joan and David were considering _____ married in June, but they finally

decided _____ until August.

B: They're kind of an odd couple, aren't they? One minute they appear _____

happy, and the next minute they're fighting.

A: Their parents suggested _____ a break from each other, but they didn't

appreciate _____ that!

EXERCISE 13 ▸ Warm-up. (Chart 14-4)
Each sentence in blue is missing a person. Add *you* where appropriate.

1. Why didn't you call us?

   We told to call us.

2. Did Sami invite to the party?

   He said he was going to.

3. I'm not surprised you had a fender bender.

   I warned to drive more slowly.

a fender bender

14-4 Infinitives with Objects

Verb + Object + Infinitive

(a) Mr. Lee *told me to be* here at ten o'clock.	Some verbs are followed by a pronoun or noun object and then an infinitive, as in (a) and (b).
(b) The police *ordered the driver to stop*.	
(c) I *was told to be* here at ten o'clock.	These verbs are followed immediately by an infinitive when they are used in the passive, as in (c) and (d).
(d) The driver *was ordered* to stop.	

Common verbs followed by noun or pronoun + infinitive

tell someone to	invite someone to	require someone to	expect someone to
advise someone to*	permit someone to	order someone to	would like someone to
encourage someone to	allow someone to	force someone to	want someone to
remind someone to	warn someone to	ask someone to	need someone to

Verb + Infinitive / Verb + Object + Infinitive

(e) I *expect to pass* the test.	Some verbs have two patterns:
(f) I *expect Mary to pass* the test.	• *verb + infinitive*, as in (e)
	• *verb + object + infinitive*, as in (f)
	COMPARE:
	In (e): I think I will pass the test.
	In (f): I think Mary will pass the test.

Common verbs followed by infinitives or by objects and then infinitives

ask to OR ask someone to	want to OR want someone to
expect to OR expect someone to	would like to OR would like someone to
need to OR need someone to	

*A gerund is used after *advise* (active) if there is no noun or pronoun object.
COMPARE: (1) *He advised buying a Fiat.* (2) *He advised me to buy a Fiat. I was advised to buy a Fiat.*

EXERCISE 14 ▸ Looking at grammar. (Chart 14-4)

Complete the sentences with *to leave* or *me to leave*. In some cases, both are possible.

1. He told _____ *me to leave* _____ .

2. He decided _____ *to leave* _____ .

3. He asked _____ *to leave / me to leave* _____ .

4. He offered _____ .

5. She wanted _____ .

6. He agreed _____ .

7. She would like _____ .

8. He warned _____ .

9. She refused _____ .

10. He promised _____ .

11. She hoped _____ .

12. He permitted _____ .

13. She expected _____ .

14. He forced _____ .

15. She allowed _____ .

16. He reminded _____ .

17. She planned _____ .

18. He pretended _____ .

EXERCISE 15 ▸ Looking at grammar. (Chart 14-4)

Complete each sentence with the correct verb.

Advice and Obligations

1. *advised / was advised*

   a. Jack _____ me to get a new apartment.

   b. I _____ to get a new apartment.

2. *forced / was forced*

   a. The driver _____ to stop on the highway.

   b. The police _____ the driver to stop.

3. *encouraged / was encouraged*

   a. I _____ to go to college.

   b. My parents _____ me to go to college.

4. *do not allow / are not allowed*

   a. Residents _____ to have pets.

   b. The building rules _____ pets.

5. *warned / was warned*

   a. Mrs. Jackson _____ her son not
   to touch the hot stove.

   b. He _____ not to touch the
   hot stove.

EXERCISE 16 ▸ Looking at grammar. (Chart 14-4)

Summarize each statement by using the verbs in the box to introduce an infinitive phrase. In some cases, more than one verb is appropriate.

allow	expect	permit	require
ask	order	remind	tell

1. The professor said to Alan, "You may leave early."
   → *The professor allowed Alan to leave early.* OR
   → *Alan was allowed to leave early.*
2. Roberto said to me, "Don't forget to take your book back to the library."
3. I am very relieved because the Dean of Admissions said to me, "You may register for school late."
4. The law says, "Every driver must have a valid driver's license."
5. My boss said to me, "Come to the meeting ten minutes early."

EXERCISE 17 ▸ Let's talk: interview. (Chart 14-4)

Interview your classmates. Share some of their answers with the class.

1. What have you been told to do recently?
2. What are you often reminded to do?
3. What have you been asked to do recently?
4. What are you encouraged to do if you want to improve your English?
5. What is something children are warned not to do by their parents?
6. What is something teenagers are expected to do?
7. What is something parents are advised to do?
8. What are citizens in your country required to do?
9. What are citizens in your country not permitted to do?

EXERCISE 18 ▸ Warm-up. (Chart 14-5)

Which pairs have basically the same meaning? Which pairs have different meanings?

1. a. It began to snow.
   b. It began snowing.

2. a. I remembered to wear a warm jacket.
   b. I remembered wearing a warm jacket.

3. a. I forgot to bring gloves.
   b. I forgot bringing gloves.

4. a. We love to walk in the snow.
   b. We love walking in the snow.

5. a. We stopped to throw snowballs.
   b. We stopped throwing snowballs.

14-5 Common Verbs Followed by Either Infinitives or Gerunds

Some verbs can be followed by either an infinitive or a gerund, sometimes with no difference in meaning, as in Group A below, and sometimes with a difference in meaning, as in Group B below.

Group A: Verb + Infinitive or Gerund, with No Difference in Meaning

begin	like	hate	The verbs in Group A may be followed by either an infinitive or a gerund with little or no difference in meaning.
start	love	can't stand	
continue	prefer	can't bear	

(a) It *began to rain*. / It *began raining*. (b) I *started to work*. / I *started working*.	In (a): There is no difference between ***began to rain*** and ***began raining***.
(c) It *was beginning to rain*.	If the main verb is progressive, an infinitive (not a gerund) is usually used, as in (c).

Group B: Verb + Infinitive or Gerund, with a Difference in Meaning

remember	regret	stop	The verbs in Group B may be followed by either an infinitive or a gerund, but the meaning is different.
forget	try		

(d) Judy always *remembers to lock* the door.	***remember*** + *infinitive* = remember to perform responsibility, duty, or task, as in (d)
(e) Sam often *forgets to lock* the door.	***forget*** + *infinitive* = forget to perform a responsibility, duty, or task, as in (e)
(f) I *remember seeing* the Alps for the first time. The sight was impressive.	***remember*** + *gerund* = remember (recall) something that happened in the past, as in (f)
(g) I'll never *forget seeing* the Alps for the first time.	***forget*** + *gerund* = forget something that happened in the past, as in (g)*
(h) I *regret to tell* you that you failed the test.	***regret*** + *infinitive* = regret to say, to tell someone, to inform someone of some bad news, as in (h)
(i) I *regret lending* him some money. He never paid me back.	***regret*** + *gerund* = regret something that happened in the past, as in (i)
(j) I'm *trying to learn* English.	***try*** + *infinitive* = make an effort, as in (j)
(k) The room was hot. I *tried opening* the window, but that didn't help. So I *tried turning* on the fan, but I was still hot. Finally, I turned on the air conditioner.	***try*** + *gerund* = experiment with a new or different approach to see if it works, as in (k)
(l) The students *stopped talking* when the professor entered the room. The room became quiet.	***stop*** + *gerund* = stop an activity
(m) When Ann saw her professor in the hallway, she *stopped (in order) to talk* to him.	Notice that ***stop*** can also be followed immediately by an infinitive of purpose, as in (m): Ann stopped walking in order to talk to her professor. (See Chart 15-1, p. 335.)

*****Forget** followed by a gerund usually occurs in a negative sentence or in a question: e.g., *I'll never forget, I can't forget, Have you ever forgotten*, and *Can you ever forget* are often followed by a gerund phrase.

EXERCISE 19 ▶ Looking at grammar. (Charts 14-3 → 14-5)

Complete each sentence with the correct form of the verb in parentheses.

1. a. Maria loves (*swim*) _____*swimming / to swim*_____ in the ocean.

   b. Her husband likes (*swim*) _____ in freshwater lakes.

2. a. I hate (*see*) _____ any living being suffer.

   b. I can't bear (*watch*) _____ news reports of children who are homeless.

   c. I can't stand (*read*) _____ about animals that have been hurt by people.

3. a. I'm afraid of flying. When a plane begins (*move*) _____ down the runway, my heart starts (*race*) _____ .

   b. Uh-oh! The plane is beginning (*move**) _____ , and my heart is starting (*race*) _____ .

4. a. After a brief interruption, the professor continued (*lecture*) _____ .

   b. Even though the bell rang, the professor kept on (*talk*) _____ .

5. a. When I travel, I prefer** (*drive*) _____ to (*take*) _____ a plane.

   b. I prefer (*drive*) _____ rather than (*take*) _____ a plane.

6. a. I'm so sorry. I regret (*inform*) _____ you that your loan application has not been approved.

   b. I didn't listen to my father. I regret (*follow, not*) _____ his advice. He was right.

7. a. When my four-year-old asks the same question over and over, I try (*remain*) _____ patient as I give the exact same answer each time.

   b. The father tried everything, but his baby still wouldn't stop (*cry*) _____ . He decided to experiment. He tried (*hold*) _____ him, but that didn't help. He tried (*feed*) _____ him, but he refused the food and continued to cry. He tried (*burp*) _____ him. He tried (*change*) _____ his diaper. Nothing worked. His baby wouldn't stop crying.

---

*If possible, native speakers usually prefer to use an infinitive following a progressive verb instead of using two **-ing** verbs in a row.
    Usual: *The baby is starting **to walk**.* (instead of *walking*)
 If the main verb is not progressive, either form is used:
    *Babies **start to walk** around age one.* OR *Babies **start walking** around age one.*
Notice the patterns with **prefer:
    Prefer + *gerund: **I prefer staying** home **to going** to the concert.*
    Prefer + *infinitive: **I'd prefer to stay** home rather **than (to) go** to the concert.*

EXERCISE 20 ▶ Looking at grammar. (Chart 14-5)

Match the sentence in the left column with the meaning in the right.

1. _____ I remembered to turn off the lights.

2. _____ I remember playing with dolls when I was a child.

3. _____ What do you remember doing as a teenager?

4. _____ What did you remember to do before you left home?

5. _____ I forgot to pick up my sister.

6. _____ I forgot getting the mail.

7. _____ Stop driving so fast.

8. _____ I stopped to get gas.

9. _____ I stopped driving to work because of the high cost of gas.

a. I stopped one activity to do another.

b. What is your memory of that time?

c. I did something, but I forgot that I did it.

d. I quit the activity. I don't do it anymore.

e. I didn't remember to do something.

f. I have a memory of the event.

g. What didn't you forget?

h. Don't continue.

i. I didn't forget.

EXERCISE 21 ▶ Listening. (Chart 14-5)

Listen to each sentence and choose the sentence with the same meaning.

1. a. Joan thought about her phone call with her husband.
   b. Joan didn't forget to call her husband.

2. a. Rita was thinking about the times she went to the farmers' market with her grandmother.
   b. Rita didn't forget to go to the farmers' market with her grandmother.

3. a. Roger got a cigarette and began to smoke.
   b. Roger quit smoking.

4. a. Mr. and Mrs. Olson finished eating.
   b. Mr. and Mrs. Olson got something to eat before the movie.

5. a. The speaker is sorry about something he did.
   b. The speaker is delivering some bad news.

EXERCISE 22 ▶ Looking at grammar. (Chart 14-5)

Complete each sentence with the correct form of the verb in parentheses.

1. a. I remember (*visit*) _____visiting_____ my great-grandparents when I was very young.

   b. What do you remember (*do*) _____ before you leave for class every day?

   c. We almost had a fire. Eric didn't remember (*turn*) _____ off the oven before he went to bed.

   d. What do you remember (*do*) _____ when you were a child?

   e. Did you remember (*lock*) _____ the front door when you left?

   f. Uh-oh. I don't remember (*lock*) _____ it. I'd better go back and check.

2. a. Don't forget (*do*) _____ your homework tonight.

   b. What did Evan forget (*do*) _____ before he went to bed?

   c. I won't ever forget (*watch*) _____ our team score the winning goal in the last seconds of the championship game.

3. a. I want to tell Jeanne to stop (*talk*) _____ so much.

   b. I stopped on the way home (*get*) _____ some groceries.

   c. I stopped (*drink*) _____ coffee at night because it was keeping me awake.

EXERCISE 23 ▸ Let's talk. (Charts 14-1 → 14-5)

Thomas wanted to build a birdhouse for his wife, Eleni. After several hours, she found him like this. Make sentences about the situation. Use the verbs in the box. Work in pairs or small groups.

A Birdhouse Failure

advise	finish	keep on	put off	remind
consider	forgot	look forward to	regret	stop
encourage	intend	offer	remember	suggest

EXERCISE 24 ▸ Looking at grammar. (Charts 14-1 → 14-5)

Complete each sentence by restating the given idea.

1. Don't be late for the meeting.

   a. Nadia reminded ____*me not to be late for the meeting*_____ .

   b. Nadia told _____ .

   c. Nadia warned _____ .

2. Do you need help? I can carry the suitcases.

   a. I volunteered _____ .

   b. I offered _____ .

3. I have an idea. Let's quit our jobs and open our own business.

   a. We discussed _____.

   b. I suggested _____.

4. I wanted to pay with a check, but the taxi driver only took cash.

   a. The taxi driver refused _____.

   b. The taxi driver told _____.

5. The teacher asked a question. I didn't want to answer, so I didn't look at her.

   a. I avoided _____.

   b. I decided _____.

6. At my last doctor's appointment, the doctor said, "Don't smoke. It causes cancer."

   a. The doctor advised _____.

   b. The doctor reminded _____.

   c. The doctor warned _____.

7. I worked all day on my paper.

   a. I spent the day _____.

   b. I spent most of my time _____.

   c. I spent several hours _____.

8. Sam likes to talk to his friends in class. The teacher asks him to stop, but he doesn't.

   a. He keeps _____.

   b. He keeps on _____.

   c. He continues _____.

9. Roberto bought his wife an anniversary present. He didn't forget this time.

   a. He remembered _____.

   b. He didn't forget _____.

EXERCISE 25 ▸ Warm-up. (Chart 14-6)

Each phrase in blue contains a preposition. What do you notice about the form of the verb that follows each preposition?

1. Sonya is excited about moving to a new city.
2. You'd better have a good excuse for being late.
3. I'm looking forward to going on vacation soon.

14-6 Using Gerunds as the Objects of Prepositions

(a) We talked *about going* to Iceland for our vacation. (b) Sue is in charge *of organizing* the meeting. (c) I'm interested *in learning* more about your work.	A gerund is frequently used as the object of a preposition.
(d) I'm *used to sleeping* with the window open. (e) I'm *accustomed to sleeping** with the window open. (f) I *look forward to going* home next month.	In (d) through (f): *to* is a preposition, not part of an infinitive form, so a gerund follows.
(g) We *talked about not going* to the meeting, but finally decided we should go.	NEGATIVE FORM: *not* precedes a gerund.

Common preposition combinations followed by gerunds

be excited**
 be worried } *about doing it*

complain <br> dream <br> talk <br> think <br> apologize } *about /of doing it*

blame someone <br> forgive someone <br> have an excuse <br> have a reason <br> be responsible <br> thank someone } *for doing it*

keep someone <br> prevent someone <br> prohibit someone <br> stop someone } *from doing it*

be interested <br> believe <br> participate <br> succeed } *in doing it*

approve <br> be accused <br> be afraid**
 be capable <br> be guilty <br> be proud**
 instead <br> take advantage <br> take care } *of doing it*

be tired } *of /from doing it*

count <br> insist } *on doing* it

be accustomed <br> in addition <br> be committed <br> be devoted <br> look forward <br> object <br> be opposed <br> be used } *to doing it*

*Possible in British English: *I'm accustomed to sleep with the window open.*

***Be afraid, be excited,* and *be proud* can also be used with an infinitive. See Chart 15-2, page 337.

EXERCISE 26 ▶ Looking at grammar. (Chart 14-6)

Complete each sentence with a preposition and a form of *go*.

A Canceled Trip

1. We thought _____*about going*_____ to the beach for vacation.

2. We talked _____ there.

3. We were interested _____ there.

4. The kids were excited _____ there.

5. They were looking forward _____ there.

6. Heavy rain prevented us _____ there.

7. A windstorm kept us _____ there.

8. So we dreamed _____ there next year.

EXERCISE 27 ▸ Looking at grammar. (Chart 14-6)

Complete each sentence with a preposition and a form of the verb in parentheses.

On an Airplane Flight

1. Two children are excited (*take*) _____*about taking*_____ their first flight.

2. They have been looking forward (*be*) _____ above the clouds.

3. A first-time flyer is worried (*fly*) _____ in stormy weather.

4. One passenger is blaming another passenger (*spill*) _____ his coffee.

5. A man is complaining (*have*) _____ an aisle seat rather than a window seat.

6. The pilot was late, but he had an excuse (*be*) _____ late.

7. The co-pilot will be responsible (*fly*) _____ the plane.

8. A flight attendant is prohibiting a man (*stand*) _____ near the cockpit door.

At a Police Station

9. A teenager has been accused (*steal*) _____ a purse.

10. An elderly woman said he was responsible (*take*) _____ it.

11. The police are blaming him (*do*) _____ it.

12. The teenager said he was trying to prevent someone else (*take*) _____ it.

13. He is upset. The police are listening to the woman instead (*listen*) _____ to his version of the story.

14. He has not yet succeeded (*convince*) _____ the police of his innocence.

EXERCISE 28 ▸ Let's talk. (Chart 14-6)

Work with a partner. Take turns answering the questions on page 318 in complete sentences. Use prepositions followed by gerunds in your answers.

Example:

PARTNER A: People in some countries have their biggest meal at lunch. Are you used to doing that?

PARTNER B: Yes, I'm used to having my biggest meal at lunch. OR No, I'm not used to having my biggest meal at lunch.

PARTNER A	PARTNER B
1. Your neighbor helped you carry heavy boxes. Did you thank him/her?	1. Someone broke the window. Do you know who was responsible?
2. You're going to visit friends in another town this weekend. Are you looking forward to that?	2. The weather is hot/cold. What does that prevent you from doing?
3. You didn't come to class on time yesterday. Did you have a good excuse?	3. The advanced students have a lot of homework. Do they complain?
4. You're living in a cold/warm climate. Are you accustomed to that?	4. Your wallet was missing after your friend visited. Do you blame him?
5. You didn't study grammar last night. What did you do instead?	5. A customer interrupted you while you were talking to the store manager. Did she apologize?
6. The students in the class did role-plays. Did all of them participate?	6. You studied last weekend. What did you do in addition?
7. You're going to a deserted island for vacation. Are you excited?	7. Your friend was rude. Did she apologize?

EXERCISE 29 ▸ Looking at grammar. (Chart 14-6)

Complete each sentence with an appropriate preposition and the **-ing** form of the given verb.

At Work

1. Alice is interested (*get*) _____*in getting*_____ a promotion.

2. You are capable (*do*) _____ better work.

3. I'm accustomed (*get*) _____ to work before everyone else.

4. Thank you (*give*) _____ me an office with windows.

5. Donna insists (*take*) _____ the stairs instead of the elevator to the top floor.

6. Our company believes (*be*) _____ honest at all times with customers.

7. You should take advantage (*work*) _____ with so many experts here.

8. Lexi had a good reason (*come, not*) _____ to work yesterday.

9. Everyone participated (*find*) _____ a new administrative assistant.

10. I apologized (*come*) _____ late to the meeting.

11. Larry isn't used (*wear*) _____ a suit and tie every day.

12. In addition (work) _____ full-time, Spiro is going to night school.

13. I stopped the printer (make) _____ so much noise.

14. Would you object _____ my (leave) _____ early today?

15. Who was opposed to (have) _____ employees move offices?

16. Are you committed (do) _____ whatever it takes to be successful at this company?

17. Who is responsible (run) _____ the office while you are away?

18. Employees are prohibited (use) _____ the company email system for personal use.

EXERCISE 30 ▶ Listening. (Chart 14-6)
Listen to each conversation. Summarize it by completing each sentence with a preposition and a gerund phrase.

1. The man apologized ____*for being late*_____.

2. The woman succeeded _____.

3. Both speakers are complaining _____.

4. The man thanked his friend _____.

5. The man didn't have an excuse _____.

6. The woman isn't used _____.

7. The flu kept the man _____.

EXERCISE 31 ▶ Let's talk. (Chart 14-6)
By + a gerund or gerund phrase expresses how something is done. Answer the questions with **by** + a gerund or *gerund phrase* to express how something is done. Work in pairs, in small groups, or as a class.

How ... ?

1. How do you turn off a cell phone?
   → *By pushing a button.*
2. How can students improve their listening comprehension?
3. How do people satisfy their hunger?
4. How do people quench their thirst?
5. How did you find out what *quench* means?
6. What are some ways employees get in trouble with their manager?
7. How do dogs show they are happy?
8. How do cats show they are happy?
9. In a restaurant, how do you catch the server's attention?
10. How do you greet a friend you haven't seen in a long time? A family member?
11. How do you remove a blue ink stain from a white shirt?

EXERCISE 32 ▸ Let's talk: interview. (Chart 14-6)

Interview your classmates about the different ways people express emotions. Answers can include descriptions of facial expressions, actions, what people say, etc. Try to use **by** + *gerund* in your answers. Share some of the most interesting answers with the class.

Example: excitement
SPEAKER A: How do people show excitement at a sports event?
SPEAKER B: People show excitement at a sports event by clapping their hands, jumping up and down, and yelling.

1. happiness
2. sadness
3. anger
4. frustration
5. confusion
6. disagreement
7. agreement
8. surprise

EXERCISE 33 ▸ Reading and speaking. (Chart 14-6)

Part I. Read the passage. What do you notice about the forms in **bold**?

Do you know these words?
- awkward
- loss for words
- souvenir
- knick-knack
- discomfort
- gracefully

The Awkward Gift

Have you ever received a gift that left you at a loss for words? Perhaps it was an item of clothing a distant aunt chose for you, a souvenir a traveler brought back, or some knick-knack that a friend thought was cute. Moments like these can be a little awkward. But with a few generic comments, you can skillfully cover your discomfort. Here are some responses that can be useful when you open your present:

- Wow, what an interesting design!
- Oh, I've never seen one of these before. Where did you find it?
- It's so colorful. The artist/designer/creator must have spent a lot of time on it.
- It looks so warm/soft/comfortable.

The giver might respond **by saying,** "I'm glad you like it." You can finish the exchange with:

- **Thank you for giving** me … .
- **Thank you for thinking** of me.
- **Thanks for remembering** it was my birthday (or other special day).
- **I appreciate your* thinking** of me.
- It was very **kind of you to think** of me.

Speak enthusiastically — with a smile — and you have gracefully accepted the gift.

*In formal English, the possessive form adjective *your* is necessary. *You* may be used in informal speech.

Part II. Work with a partner. Partner A will give a gift to Partner B. You can choose one of the items pictured as a gift, or something you have in your bag or backpack. Complete the conversation. Then practice it and perform it for the class. Remember, you can look at your notes before you speak. When you speak, look at your partner.

A: I have a gift for you. (Pretend to give a wrapped gift to your partner.)

B: Should I open it now?

A: Yes, please. I can't wait to see your reaction!

(*Partner B pretends to open it.*)

B: _____

A: _____

B: _____

A: _____

EXERCISE 34 ▶ Warm-up. (Chart 14-7)
Complete the sentences by circling all the activities that are true for you. All the choices end in **-ing**. What do you notice about the verbs in blue?

1. Last week I went *shopping   running   biking   dancing.*

2. I like to go *hiking   swimming   camping   sightseeing.*

3. I've never gone *fishing   bowling   skiing   skydiving.*

14-7 Go + Gerund

(a) Did you *go shopping*? (b) We *went fishing* yesterday.	**Go** is followed by a gerund in certain idiomatic expressions to express, for the most part, recreational activities.

Go + gerund

go biking	go dancing	go running	go skiing
go birdwatching	go fishing*	go sailing	go skydiving
go boating	go hiking	go shopping	go sledding
go bowling	go hunting	go sightseeing	go snorkeling
go camping	go jogging	go skating	go swimming
go canoeing / kayaking	go mountain climbing	go skateboarding	go window shopping

*Also, in British English: *go angling.*

EXERCISE 35 ▶ Let's talk. (Chart 14-7)

Answer the questions about the activities in Chart 14-7. Work in pairs, in small groups, or as a class.

1. Which activities have you done? When? Briefly describe your experiences.
2. Which activities do you like to do?
3. Which activities do you never want to do?
4. Which activities have you not done but would like to do?

EXERCISE 36 ▶ Reading. (Chart 14-7)

Read the description of Ron's day and complete the sentences with a form of **go** and a verb.

Ron's Busy Saturday

Ron is an active individual. On his days off, he likes to do several activities in one day. His friends can't keep up with him. Last Saturday, for example, he woke up early and went to the lake with his canoe. He finds early mornings on the lake very calm and relaxing. He brought a fishing rod with him so he could catch something for dinner. He saw some friends getting their sailboat ready and thought about joining them but decided instead to take a swim. By that time, it was only noon!

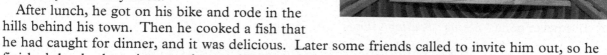

After lunch, he got on his bike and rode in the hills behind his town. Then he cooked a fish that he had caught for dinner, and it was delicious. Later some friends called to invite him out, so he finished the day by going to a dance with them.

1. Early Saturday morning, Ron ___went canoeing on the lake___ .

2. He brought a fishing rod so he could _____.

3. He saw some friends on a sailboat but didn't _____ with them.

4. He _____ instead.

5. After lunch, he _____ .

6. He finished the day by _____ with some of his friends.

EXERCISE 37 ▶ Let's talk. (Charts 14-2 and 14-7)

Work with a partner. Take turns giving your opinion about the following activities.

Example: I (enjoy, don't enjoy) \ go \ shop \ for clothes
PARTNER A: I don't enjoy going shopping for clothes. How about you?
PARTNER B: No, I don't enjoy it either. OR
Actually, I enjoy it.

1. I (go, never go) \ dance \ on weekends
2. I (like to go, don't like to go) \ bowl
3. Go \ hunt \ (sounds, doesn't sound) \ like fun to me

4. I (sometimes postpone, never postpone) \ do \ my homework

5. I (really appreciate, don't appreciate) \ get \ a lot of emails every day

6. I (am considering, am not considering) \ look \ for a new place to live

7. I (used to go, never went) \ fish \ as a child

8. I (go, never go) \ jog \ for exercise

9. I (enjoy, don't enjoy) \ play \ board games

EXERCISE 38 ▸ Warm-up. (Chart 14-8)

Agree or disagree with these statements. What do you notice about the verbs in blue?

1. It's easy to have fun shopping at a mall.   yes   no

2. I have a hard time spending my free time indoors.   yes   no

3. Teenagers spend a lot of time doing important things.   yes   no

4. People waste a lot of money buying unnecessary things.   yes   no

14-8 Special Expressions Followed by -ing

(a) We *had fun* We *had a good time* } *playing* volleyball.	*-ing* forms follow certain special expressions: **have fun / a good time + -ing** **have trouble / difficulty + -ing** **have a hard time / a difficult time + -ing**
(b) I *had trouble* I *had difficulty* I *had a hard time* I *had a difficult time* } *finding* his house.	
(c) Sam *spends most of his time studying.*	**spend** + *expression of time or money* + **-ing**
(d) I *waste a lot of time watching* TV.	**waste** + *expression of time or money* + **-ing**
(e) She *sat at her desk doing* homework.	**sit** + *expression of place* + **-ing**
(f) I *stood there wondering* what to do next.	**stand** + *expression of place* + **-ing**
(g) He *is lying in bed reading* a book.	**lie** + *expression of place* + **-ing**
(h) When I walked into my office, I *found George using* my telephone.	**find** + *(pro)noun* + **-ing**
(i) When I walked into my office, I *caught a thief looking* through my desk drawers.	**catch** + *(pro)noun* + **-ing** In (h) and (i): Both **find** and **catch** mean "discover." **Catch** often expresses anger or displeasure.

EXERCISE 39 ▸ Looking at grammar. (Charts 14-2, 14-3, 14-6, and 14-8)
Complete the sentences with the correct form of the verb in parentheses.

A Gem in the City

I had no idea Central Park was so big and had so much to offer! When I was in New York, I

spent a day (*explore*) _____ it, and I didn't even begin to see all of it. The weather
1

was quite hot, and I enjoyed (*walk*) _____ around the park in the shade. I
2

found a concert, and I sat on the grass (*listen*) _____ to the music for a
3

while. I noticed there were a lot of people lying on the ground (*relax*) _____,
4

(*read*) _____, or (*sleep*) _____. It was so peaceful
5   6

that I found myself (*get*) _____ sleepy too. I came across a lake for children to
7

fish in, and many parents stood nearby (*watch*) _____ their kids catch and
8

release fish. People told me about another lake that had rowboats for rent. I thought about

(*do*) _____ that, but I had difficulty (*find*) _____ the
9   10

boathouse. At the end of the day, I needed (*go*) _____ back to my hotel, but I had
11

a hard time (*leave*) _____. I definitely plan (*go*) _____ back.
12   13

EXERCISE 40 ▸ Grammar and speaking. (Chart 14-8)
Complete the sentences about yourself with appropriate **-ing** verbs. Compare your statements with
a classmate's.

About Me

1. Sometimes I have trouble _____

2. On weekends, I have fun _____

3. In the evenings, I spend my time _____

4. In the mornings, I stand in front of the mirror _____

5. At school, I sit in class _____

6. Sometimes in class I find myself _____

7. Sometimes in the middle of the night, I lie in bed _____

8. I am/am not a decisive person. I have a/an easy/hard time _____

9. You will never catch me _____

EXERCISE 41 ▶ Listening. (Chart 14-8)

Listen to the sentences. Complete the sentences, orally or in writing, using **-ing** verbs.

Example: You will hear:　　　　I play soccer every day. I love it!

You will write (or say): The speaker has fun ___*playing soccer*___ .

1. The speaker has trouble _____ .

2. The speaker caught his son _____ .

3. The speaker stands at the kitchen counter in the mornings _____ .

4. The speaker has a hard time _____ .

5. The speaker wasted two hours _____ .

6. The speaker had a good time _____ .

7. The speaker found Tom _____ .

8. The speaker spent an hour _____ .

EXERCISE 42 ▶ Warm-up. (Chart 14-9)

All of the sentences are grammatically correct. What differences do you notice in their structure? Do you agree or disagree with the statements? Why or why not?

1. Speaking a second language without an accent is nearly impossible for adult language learners.
2. To speak a second language without an accent is nearly impossible for adult language learners.
3. It is nearly impossible for adult language learners to speak a second language without an accent.

14-9 It + Infinitive; Gerunds and Infinitives as Subjects

(a) *It* is difficult *to learn* a second language.	Often an infinitive phrase is used with *it* as the subject of a sentence. The word *it* refers to and has the same meaning as the infinitive phrase at the end of the sentence. In (a): *It* means "to learn a second language."
(b) *Learning* a second language is difficult.	A gerund phrase is frequently used as the subject of a sentence, as in (b).
(c) *To learn* a second language is difficult.	An infinitive can also be used as the subject of a sentence, as in (c), but far more commonly an infinitive phrase is used with *it,* as in (a).
(d) It is easy *for young children* to learn a second language. *Learning* a second language **is** easy *for young children*. *To learn* a second language **is** easy *for young children*.	The phrase for (*someone*) may be used to specify exactly who the speaker is talking about, as in (d).

EXERCISE 43 ▶ Grammar and speaking. (Chart 14-9)

Work with a partner. Imagine a parent giving advice to a teenager. Make sentences beginning with *it*. Use a form of the given phrase followed by an infinitive phrase for each sentence.

Parent to Teenager

1. be dangerous
   → *It's dangerous to ride a skateboard without wearing a helmet.*
2. be important
3. not be easy
4. be silly
5. be smart
6. not cost much money
7. be necessary
8. take time

EXERCISE 44 ▶ Looking at grammar. (Chart 14-9)

Complete the sentences with the words in the box. Include a person and any other additional information. Make true statements.

be on time	learn English	take advanced math courses
have a visa	speak Spanish	use gerunds and infinitives correctly

1. It is/isn't possible for …
   → *It isn't possible for me to be on time for class when traffic is heavy.*
2. It is/isn't easy for …
3. It is/isn't important for …
4. It is/isn't essential for …
5. It's a good idea for …
6. It is/isn't difficult for …

EXERCISE 45 ▶ Let's talk: pairwork. (Chart 14-9)

Work with a partner. Partner A begins the sentence. Partner B completes it with an infinitive phrase. Partner A restates the sentence using a gerund phrase as the subject. Take turns.

Example:
PARTNER A: It's fun …
PARTNER B: … to ride a horse.
PARTNER A: Riding a horse is fun.

PARTNER A	PARTNER B
1. It's dangerous …	1. It's wrong …
2. It's easy …	2. It takes a lot of time …
3. It's a good idea …	3. It's impolite …
4. It's important …	4. Is it difficult … ?

14-10 Reference List of Verbs Followed by Infinitives

Verbs with a bullet (•) can also be followed by gerunds. See Chart 14-11.

Verbs Followed Immediately by an Infinitive

1. agree — They *agreed to help* us.
2. appear — She *appears to be* tired.
3. arrange — I'll *arrange to meet* you at the airport.
4. ask — He *asked to come* with us.
5. beg — He *begged to come* with us.
6. begin• — It *began to rain*.
7. can't afford — I *can't afford to buy* it.
8. can't bear• — I *can't bear to wait* in long lines.
9. can't stand• — I *can't stand to wait* in long lines.
10. can't wait — We *can't wait to see* you.
11. care — I *don't care to see* that show.
12. claim — She *claims to know* a famous movie star.
13. consent — She finally *consented to marry* him.
14. continue• — He *continued to speak*.
15. decide — I have *decided to leave* on Monday.
16. demand — I *demand to know* who is responsible.
17. deserve — She *deserves to win* the prize.
18. expect — I *expect to enter* graduate school in the fall.
19. fail — She *failed to return* the book to the library on time.
20. forget• — I *forgot to mail* the letter.
21. hate• — I *hate to make* silly mistakes.
22. hesitate — *Don't hesitate to ask* for my help.
23. hope — Jack *hopes to arrive* next week.
24. intend — He *intends to be* a firefighter.
25. learn — He *learned to play* the piano.
26. like• — I *like to go* to the movies.
27. love• — I *love to go* to operas.
28. manage — She *managed to finish* her work early.
29. mean — I *didn't mean to hurt* your feelings.
30. need — I *need to have* your opinion.
31. offer — They *offered to help* us.
32. plan — I'm *planning to have* a party.
33. prefer• — Ann *prefers to walk* to work.
34. prepare — We *prepared to welcome* them.
35. pretend — He *pretends not to understand*.
36. promise — I *promise not to be* late.
37. refuse — I *refuse to believe* his story.
38. regret• — I *regret to tell* you that you failed.
39. remember• — I *remembered to lock* the door.
40. seem — That cat *seems to be* friendly.
41. start• — It *started to rain*.
42. stop — Let's *stop to get* a snack.
43. struggle — I *struggled to stay* awake.
44. swear — She *swore to tell* the truth.
45. tend — He *tends to talk* too much.
46. threaten — She *threatened to tell* my parents.
47. try• — I'm *trying to learn* English.
48. volunteer — He *volunteered to help* us.
49. wait — I'll *wait to hear* from you.
50. want — I *want to tell* you something.
51. wish — She *wishes to come* with us.

Verbs Followed by a (Pro)noun + an Infinitive

1. advise• — She *advised me to wait* until tomorrow.
2. allow — She *allowed me to use* her car.
3. ask — I *asked John to help* us.
4. beg — They *begged us to come*.
5. cause — Her laziness *caused her to fail*.
6. challenge — She *challenged me to race* her to the corner.
7. convince — I couldn't *convince him to accept* our help.
8. dare — He *dared me to do* better than he had done.
9. encourage — He *encouraged me to try* again.
10. expect — I *expect you to be* on time.
11. forbid — I *forbid you to tell* him.
12. force — They *forced him to tell* the truth.
13. hire — She *hired a boy to mow* the lawn.
14. instruct — He *instructed them to be* careful.
15. invite — Harry *invited the Johnsons to come* to his party.
16. need — We *needed Chris to help* us figure out the solution.
17. order — The judge *ordered me to pay* a fine.
18. permit — He *permitted the children to stay* up late.
19. persuade — I *persuaded him to come* for a visit.
20. remind — She *reminded me to lock* the door.
21. require — Our teacher *requires us to be* on time.
22. teach — My brother *taught me to swim*.
23. tell — The doctor *told me to take* these pills.
24. urge — I *urged her to apply* for the job.
25. want — I *want you to be* happy.
26. warn — I *warned you not to drive* too fast.

14-11 Reference List of Verbs Followed by Gerunds

Verbs with a bullet (•) can also be followed by infinitives. See Chart 14-10.

1.	admit	He *admitted stealing* the money.
2.	advise•	She *advised waiting* until tomorrow.
3.	anticipate	I *anticipate having* a good time on vacation.
4.	appreciate	I *appreciated hearing* from them.
5.	avoid	He *avoided answering* my question.
6.	begin•	It *began raining*.
7.	can't bear•	I *can't bear waiting* in long lines.
8.	can't help	I *can't help worrying* about it.
9.	can't imagine	I can't *imagine having* no friends.
10.	can't stand•	I *can't stand waiting* in long lines.
11.	complete	I finally *completed writing* my term paper.
12.	consider	I *will consider going* with you.
13.	continue•	He *continued speaking*.
14.	delay	He *delayed leaving* for school.
15.	deny	She *denied committing* the crime.
16.	discuss	They *discussed opening* a new business.
17.	dislike	I *dislike driving* long distances.
18.	enjoy	We *enjoyed visiting* them.
19.	finish	She *finished studying* about ten.
20.	forget•	I'll never *forget visiting* Napoleon's tomb.
21.	hate•	I *hate making* silly mistakes.
22.	imagine	I *imagined* getting a scholarship, and I did.
23.	keep	I *keep hoping* he will come.
24.	like•	I *like going* to movies.
25.	love•	I *love going* to operas.
26.	mention	She *mentioned going* to a movie.
27.	mind	*Would* you *mind helping* me with this?
28.	miss	I *miss being* with my family.
29.	postpone	Let's *postpone leaving* until tomorrow.
30.	practice	The athlete *practiced throwing* the ball.
31.	prefer•	Ann *prefers walking* to driving to work.
32.	quit	He *quit trying* to solve the problem.
33.	recall	I *don't recall meeting* him before.
34.	recollect	I *don't recollect meeting* him before.
35.	recommend	She *recommended seeing* the show.
36.	regret•	I *regret telling* him my secret.
37.	remember•	I *can remember meeting* him when I was a child.
38.	resent	I *resent her interfering* in my business.
39.	resist	I *couldn't resist eating* the dessert.
40.	risk	She *risks losing* all of her money.
41.	start•	It *started raining*.
42.	stop	She *stopped going* to classes when she got sick.
43.	suggest	She *suggested going* to a movie.
44.	tolerate	She *won't tolerate cheating* during an examination.
45.	try•	I *tried changing* the light bulb, but the lamp still didn't work.
46.	understand	I *don't understand his leaving* school.
47.	urge	The official *urged using* caution.

14-12 Reference List of Preposition Combinations Followed by Gerunds

Preposition Combinations + Gerunds

1. apologize for	He *apologized for forgetting* his wife's birthday.	14. look forward to	I'm *looking forward to going* home.
2. approve of	The company manager *approved of hiring* me.	15. object to	The voters *objected to increasing* taxes.
3. blame someone for	She *blamed him for stealing* her phone.	16. participate in	The entire staff *participated in welcoming* students on the first day.
4. complain about / of	She *complained about working* too hard.	17. prevent someone from	Will the medicine *prevent me from getting* sick?
5. count on	I'm *counting on going* with you.	18. prohibit someone from	The police *prohibited them from leaving.*
6. dream about / of	He *dreamed about / of flying* an airplane	19. stop someone from	Security *stopped a passenger from getting* on the subway.
7. forgive someone for	She *forgave him for lying.*	20. succeed in	He *succeeded in getting* the job.
8. have a reason for	He *had a reason for being* absent.	21. take advantage of	I'm *taking advantage of having* a free day tomorrow.
9. have an excuse for	Did you *have an excuse for leaving* early?	22. take care of	She *took care of filling* out the paperwork.
10. in addition to	*In addition to studying,* I have to work this weekend.	23. talk about / of	He talked *about / of feeling* homesick.
11. insist on	I *insist on coming* with you.	24. thank someone for	They *thanked him for coming.*
12. instead of	*Instead of sitting* there, why don't you help us?	25. think about / of	She *thought about quitting* her job.
13. keep someone from	Can a special pillow *keep you from snoring*?		

Preposition Combinations with *Be* + Gerunds

1. be accused of	He *was accused of stealing.*	9. be interested in	I *am interested in learning* more about your country.
2. be accustomed to	She *is accustomed to working* hard.	10. be opposed to	He *is opposed to going* to war.
3. be afraid of	My kids *are afraid of being* alone.	11. be proud of	She *was proud of knowing* the answer.
4. be capable of	She *is capable of memorizing* long lists of words.	12. be responsible for	Who *is responsible for repairing* the roads?
5. be committed to	Dr. Pak *is committed to improving* medical care in rural areas.	13. be tired of / from	He *was tired of running.* He *was tired from running.**
6. be devoted to	*They are devoted to helping* the poor.	14. be used to	She *is used to working* weekends.
7. be excited about	She *is excited about starting* college.	15. be worried about	The driver *was worried about getting* a traffic ticket.
8. be guilty of	He *was guilty of lying* to the judge.		

*He was tired **of** running. = He doesn't want to run anymore.
He was tired **from** running. = He was tired because of running.

EXERCISE 46 ▸ Let's talk: pairwork. (Charts 14-10 → 14-12)
Work with a partner. Complete the sentences with ***doing it*** or ***to do it***. Partner A gives the prompt for the first group of ten. Then change roles where indicated. Check Charts 14-10 to 14-12 for the correct verb form if necessary.

Example: I promise
PARTNER A (*book open*):   I promise ...
PARTNER B (*book closed*):   ... to do it.

1. We plan ...
2. I can't afford ...
3. She didn't allow me ...
4. I don't care ...
5. Please remind me ...
6. I am considering ...
7. Our director postponed ...
8. He persuaded me ...
9. I don't mind ...
10. Everyone avoided ...

Change roles.

11. I refused ...
12. I hope ...
13. She convinced me ...
14. He mentioned ...
15. She complained about ...
16. I encouraged him ...
17. I warned him not ...
18. We prepared ...
19. I don't recall ...
20. Who is responsible for ... ?

Change roles.

21. He resented ...
22. When will you finish ... ?
23. Did you practice ... ?
24. She agreed ...
25. He was guilty of ...

26. Stop ...
27. I didn't force him ...
28. I couldn't resist ...
29. Somehow, the cat managed ...
30. Did the little boy admit ... ?

Change roles.

31. He denied ...
32. I didn't mean ...
33. She swore ...
34. I volunteered ...
35. He suggested ...
36. He advised me ...
37. He struggled ...
38. I don't want to risk ...
39. Do you recommend ... ?
40. I miss ...

Change roles.

41. I can't imagine ...
42. She threatened ...
43. He seems to dislike ...
44. The children begged ...
45. She challenged me ...
46. Did he deny ... ?
47. She taught me ...
48. Do you anticipate ... ?
49. They are opposed to ...
50. I'll arrange ...

EXERCISE 47 ▸ Game. (Charts 14-10 → 14-12)
Work in teams. Your teacher will begin a sentence by using any of the verbs in Charts 14-10 to 14-12. Complete the sentence with ***to do it*** or ***doing it***, or with your own words. Each correct answer gets one point.

Example:
TEACHER: I reminded Mario ...
STUDENT A: ... to do it. OR ... to be on time.
TEACHER: Yes. One point!

EXERCISE 48 ▶ Looking at grammar. (Chapter 14 Review)
Work in pairs. Choose all the correct sentences. Explain why each incorrect sentence is wrong.

1. a. Text while you are driving is dangerous.
   b. It is dangerous to text while you are driving.
   c. Texting while you are driving is dangerous.

2. a. We hope visiting them soon.
   b. We hope to visit them soon.
   c. We hope you to visit them soon.

3. a. Jay suggested going to the movies.
   b. Jay suggested that we go to the movies.
   c. Jay suggested me to go the movies.

4. a. Convincing me to take time off it is easy.
   b. It's easy to convince me to take time off.
   c. Convincing me to take time off is easy.

5. a. To run and playing on the beach are two things my kids love to do.
   b. Running and playing on the beach are two things my kids love to do.
   c. Run and play on the beach are two things my kids love to do.

6. a. My grandmother couldn't stand to touch cat fur.
   b. My grandmother couldn't stand to touching cat fur.
   c. My grandmother couldn't stand touching cat fur.

7. a. Roger spends two hours commuting to work.
   b. Roger spends two hours commute to work.
   c. Roger spends two hours for commuting to work.

EXERCISE 49 ▶ Check your knowledge. (Chapter 14 Review)
Correct the errors.

1. I don't mind to have a roommate.

2. Is hard for me understand people who speak very fast.

3. Learning about another country it is very interesting.

4. I tried very hard to don't make any mistakes.

5. Find an English tutor wasn't difficult.

6. All of us needed to went to the ticket office before the game yesterday.

7. I'm looking forward to go to swimming in the ocean.

8. Ski in the Alps it was a big thrill for me.

9. Don't keep to be asking me the same questions over and over.

10. During a fire drill, everyone is required leaving the building.

11. I don't enjoy to play card games. I prefer to spend my time for read or watch movies.

12. When I entered the room, I found my young son stand on the kitchen table.

13. Instead of work, Katie was lying on her bed think about her fiancé.

EXERCISE 50 ▸ Reading, grammar, and writing. (Chapter 14)

Part I. Read the thank-you note written after a job interview. Then read the tips that follow.

Dear Mr. Lopez,

Thank you for giving me the opportunity to interview with you. I enjoyed learning more about your business and having the chance to tell you about my skills and experience. Also, it was interesting to find out that you and my uncle went to school together.

As we discussed, I have an associate's degree in automotive technology and two years of on-the-job experience. Combined with my strong work ethic, I believe this background has prepared me well to be an entry-level mechanic with ABC Automotive.

I am excited to be considered for this position. If you have any further questions, please call or email me. I look forward to hearing from you.

Sincerely,

Gina DeVries

Gina DeVries

Although there are various ways to write a thank-you note after a job interview, notice the following important points:

- The writer begins by thanking the interviewer and telling him that she enjoyed the experience.
- In the second paragraph, she restates her skills and experience. She adds that she would be a good person for the specific job.
- In the final paragraph, she expresses enthusiasm for the position. She asks the interviewer to contact her if he has any further questions.
- A common way to end this type of letter is to write *I look forward to hearing from you.*
- *Sincerely, Best regards,* or *Kind regards* are polite ways to close.

You might be wondering if the letter should be sent by regular mail or if it can be emailed. It really depends on the culture of the company. For many companies, such as those with a tech or science focus, email is the norm. Also, if the decision is being made quickly, regular mail may be too slow. One rule of thumb is to communicate in the same way as you did previously. If everything has been online, for example, there's a good chance that an email will be preferred.

The thank-you letter is a nice touch. It shows that you are respectful and interested in the position. It may help the interviewer remember you better, especially if you can mention something specific that you talked about. Just be sure that you have someone check it for grammar and spelling! You want to make a good impression.

Part II. Write whether a gerund or infinitive follows each item in the sample letter.

1. Thank you for _____

2. enjoyed _____

3. am excited _____

4. look forward to _____

Part III. Choose one of the following options:

1. Write a thank-you letter to follow up on a job interview that you have had.
2. Write a thank-you letter for the following situation:

   Henry Sanson interviewed with Ms. Azizi for the position of hotel assistant manager.

   He has a recent degree in hotel management and one year's experience as a front desk clerk.

WRITING TIP

Thank-you notes, whether for business or otherwise, often have these key phrases:

- *thank you for* + gerund
- *be interested in* + gerund
- *enjoy* + gerund
- *look forward to* + gerund
- *appreciate your taking the time* + infinitive
- *have the opportunity/chance* + infinitive

When you use these words, be sure to check that you have the correct gerund or infinitive form after them.

Part IV. Edit your writing. Check for the following:

1. ☐ correct use of gerunds
2. ☐ correct use of infinitives
3. ☐ singular verb when a gerund is the subject
4. ☐ correct preposition if one is required
5. ☐ correct spelling (use a dictionary or spell-check)

CHAPTER 15

Gerunds and Infinitives, Part 2

PRETEST: What do I already know?

Write "C" if a sentence has the correct gerund and infinitive form and "I" for incorrect. Check your answers below. After you complete each chart listed, make any necessary corrections.

1. _____ Yasmin is returning home for to complete her medical studies. (15-1)

2. _____ I was sorry to hear that Mila and Pablo are moving away from here. (15-2)

3. _____ Your little puppy seems very eager to pleasing. (15-2)

4. _____ The baby isn't enough tired to sleep right now. (15-3)

5. _____ It's easy to be fool by Jordan's charm. (15-4)

6. _____ Marcus mentioned having lost a large sum of money. (15-5)

7. _____ I was happy to have been invited to the surprise party. (15-5)

8. _____ The car is really dirty. It needs to be wash. (15-6)

9. _____ The walls in our apartment are paper thin, and I could hear my roommate snoring loudly. (15-7)

10. _____ Could you help me to carry the groceries inside? There are several bags. (15-8)

11. _____ Rafael lets his young children to stay up past midnight on weekends. (15-8)

12. _____ Diana makes her kids clean their rooms once a week. (15-9)

13. _____ I appreciate your helping me with the plans for the party. (15-10)

Incorrect sentences: 1, 3, 4, 5, 8, 10, 11

EXERCISE 1 ▶ Warm-up. (Chart 15-1)

Which sentences answer the question "Why"?

1. The baby came to the hospital last week.
2. She has come to the hospital to get special treatment.
3. The doctor wore a clown nose to cheer up his patients.
4. The doctor will check the teddy bear first.
5. The doctor is going to check the teddy bear's heart to relax the baby.

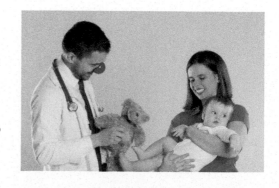

15-1 Infinitive of Purpose: *In Order To*

(a) He came here *in order to study* English. (b) He came here *to study* English.	*In order to* is used to express *purpose*. It answers the question "Why?" *In order* is often omitted, as in (b).
(c) *INCORRECT:* He came here ~~for studying~~ English. (d) *INCORRECT:* He came here ~~for to study~~ English. (e) *INCORRECT:* He came here ~~for study~~ English.	To express purpose, use (*in order*) *to*, not *for*, with a verb.*
(f) I went to the store *for* some bread. (g) I went to the store *to buy* some bread.	*For* can be used to express purpose, but it is a preposition and is followed by a noun object, as in (f).

*Exception: The phrase *be used for* expresses the typical or general purpose of a thing. In this case, the preposition *for* is followed by a gerund: *A saw **is used for cutting** wood.* Also possible: *A saw **is used to cut** wood.*

However, to talk about a particular thing and a particular situation, *be used* + *an infinitive* is generally used: *A chain saw **was used to cut** (NOT for cutting) down the old oak tree.*

EXERCISE 2 ▶ Looking at grammar. (Chart 15-1)
Complete the sentences with *to* or *for*.

Isabella spent a month in Miami. She went there ...

1. _____*to*_____ see her cousins.

2. _____*for*_____ a vacation.

3. _____ business.

4. _____ meet with company executives.

5. _____ discuss long-term plans for the company.

6. _____ spend time with her parents.

7. _____ a visit with childhood friends.

EXERCISE 3 ▶ Looking at grammar. (Chart 15-1)
Complete each sentence with an item from the right column.

Why?

1. Gina went to the grocery store for _____.
2. Gina went to the grocery store to _____.
3. My father swims every day to _____.
4. My mother runs every day for _____.
5. I went to the doctor for _____.
6. I made a doctor's appointment to _____.
7. I went to an ATM to _____.
8. I stopped at an ATM for _____.

    a. cash
    b. her health
    c. get a prescription
    d. food
    e. make a deposit
    f. pick up something for dinner
    g. stay in shape
    h. a prescription

EXERCISE 4 ▶ Looking at grammar. (Chart 15-1)
Add *in order* wherever possible. If nothing should be added, write Ø.

1. a. Lydia went to the dentist _____ to get some relief from her toothache.

   b. She doesn't go often _____ to get checkups.

   c. She's not enthusiastic about going _____ to the dentist.

   d. She's very sensitive _____ to pain, and she's allergic _____ to Novocain.

   e. She also works long hours _____ to support her family and doesn't have time for medical appointments.

2. a. Joe made cookies _____ to take a dessert to the party.

   b. He decorated them _____ to impress his girlfriend.

   c. He likes _____ to bake when he has free time.

   d. He cooks _____ to relax after a stressful day at work.

   e. His father was a pastry chef and taught him how _____ to bake.

EXERCISE 5 ▶ Let's talk: interview. (Chart 15-1)
Ask two classmates each question. Share some of their responses with the class.

What are two reasons why some people ...

1. go to Hawaii for vacation?
2. exercise?
3. cheat on exams?
4. meditate?
5. tell white lies?★
6. become actors?

EXERCISE 6 ▶ Warm-up. (Chart 15-2)
Look at the adjectives in blue. What do you notice about the words that come before and after them?

1. Eva *was* sorry *to hear* that the used car she liked had been sold.
2. She *is* certain *to find* another soon.
3. She *was* happy *to find* a helpful dealer.
4. Her friend Kevin had a different experience. He *was* upset *to learn* that the salesperson hadn't given him all the facts.
5. He *is* unlikely *to buy* a car from this dealer.

★*white lies* = lies that aren't considered serious, e.g., telling a friend her dress looks nice when you don't think it does

15-2 Adjectives Followed by Infinitives

(a) We *were **sorry to** hear* the bad news.	Certain adjectives can be immediately followed by infinitives, as in (a) and (b).
(b) I *was **surprised to** see* Ted at the meeting.	In general, these adjectives describe a person (or persons), not a thing. Many of these adjectives describe a person's feelings or attitudes.

Common adjectives followed by infinitives

glad to (do it)	sorry to*	ready to	careful to	surprised to*
happy to	sad to*	prepared to	hesitant to	amazed to*
pleased to*	upset to*	anxious to	reluctant to	astonished to*
delighted to	disappointed to*	eager to	afraid to	shocked to*
content to		willing to		stunned to*
relieved to	embarrassed to	motivated to	certain to	
lucky to	proud to	determined to	likely to	
fortunate to	ashamed to		unlikely to	
excited to				

*The expressions with asterisks are usually followed by infinitive phrases with verbs such as *see, learn, discover, find out, hear.*

EXERCISE 7 ▶ Let's talk. (Chart 15-2)

Work in small groups. Complete the sentences with adjectives from Chart 15-2 that make sense. Discuss your answers.

SITUATION 1: Mr. Wah was offered an excellent job in another country. He sees advantages and disadvantages to moving.

He is …

1. _____sad to / prepared to / reluctant to_____ leave his country.

2. _____ move away from his elderly parents.

3. _____ take his wife and children away from family and friends.

4. _____ try a new job.

5. _____ learn a new language.

SITUATION 2: There have been a lot of nighttime burglaries in the town of Viewmont.

The residents have been …

6. _____ leave their homes overnight.

7. _____ lock their doors and windows at night.

8. _____ watch for strangers on the streets.

9. _____ have weekly meetings with the police for updates on their progress.

10. _____ hear that the police suspect neighborhood residents.

EXERCISE 8 ▸ Writing or speaking. (Chart 15-2)

Complete the sentences using the expressions listed in Chart 15-2 and your own words. Use infinitive phrases in your completions.

1. Nicole always speeds on the expressway. She's ...
   → *She's certain to get stopped by the police.*
   → *She's likely to get a ticket.*
2. I've worked hard all day long. Enough! I'm ...
3. Next month, I'm going to a family reunion — the first one in 25 years. I'm very much looking forward to it. I'm ...
4. Some children grow up in unhappy homes. My family, however, has always been loving and supportive. I'm ...
5. Ivan's run out of money again, but he doesn't want anyone to know his situation. He needs money desperately, but he's ...
6. Rosalyn wants to become an astronaut. That has been her dream since she was a little girl. She has been working hard toward her goal and is ...
7. Our neighbors had extra tickets to the baseball game, so they invited us to go with them. Since both of us love baseball, we were ...
8. My sister-in-law recently told me what my brother is up to these days. I couldn't believe my ears! I was ...

EXERCISE 9 ▸ Let's talk: interview. (Chart 15-2)

Make questions using the words in parentheses. Ask two classmates each question. Share some of their answers with the class.

1. What are children sometimes (afraid \ do)?
2. When you're tired in the evening, what are you (content \ do)?
3. What should drivers be (careful \ do) in traffic?
4. If one of your friends has a problem, what are you (willing \ do)?
5. What are people who don't speak English well (reluctant \ do)?
6. What are you (determined \ do) before you are too old?
7. What are things some students are (motivated \ do)?
8. Can you tell me something you were (shocked \ find out)?
9. Can you tell me something you were (sad \ hear)?
10. What are you (eager \ do) in the near future?

EXERCISE 10 ▸ Warm-up. (Chart 15-3)

Complete the sentences with *too, to,* and *enough*.

MARIA: Will these chilies work for your recipe?
ALBERTO: They are too spicy. I don't want to cook with them.
RICARDO: They are spicy enough. I'll cook with them.

1. Alberto says they are _____ spicy

   _____ cook with.

2. Ricardo says they are spicy _____

   _____ cook with.

15-3 Using Infinitives with *Too* and *Enough*

COMPARE:	
(a) That box is *too heavy* for Bob to lift. (b) That box is *very heavy*, but Bob can lift it.	***Too*** can be followed by an infinitive, as in (a). In the speaker's mind, the use of ***too*** implies a negative result. In (a): ***too heavy*** = It is *impossible* for Bob to lift that box. In (b): ***very heavy*** = It is *possible but difficult* for Bob to lift that box.
(c) I am *strong enough to lift* that box. I can lift it. (d) I have *enough strength to lift* that box. (e) I have *strength enough to lift* that box.	***Enough*** can also be followed by an infinitive. Note the following: • ***Enough*** follows the adjective, as in (c). • Usually ***enough*** precedes a noun, as in (d). • In formal English, it may follow a noun, as in (e).

EXERCISE 11 ▸ Looking at grammar. (Chart 15-3)

Complete the sentences with ***too*** or ***enough***.

1. a. It's _____ stormy to go outside. I'll work inside today.

   b. The weather is severe _____ to keep emergency workers indoors.

2. a. Your room needs to be cleaned. You are old _____ to do it yourself.

   b. Please do it now. It's _____ messy to wait another day.

3. a. The conversation occurred _____ long ago to remember any specific details.

   b. It was long _____ ago to make the details seem unimportant.

4. a. It's _____ expensive to fly home on the weekend. We'll need to leave on a weekday.

   b. Jason has money _____ to fly anywhere in the world.

5. a. Rebecca's cold is really contagious. She has sense _____ to stay home.

   b. She has _____ sense to not expose others to her cold.

6. a. When I injure my back, it's often _____ painful to sleep at night.

   b. George's back injury was painful _____ to keep him in bed for a week.

EXERCISE 12 ▸ Let's talk. (Chart 15-3)

Answer the questions. Work in pairs, in small groups, or as a class.

Your Thoughts?

1. What is your backpack/bag big enough to hold? What is it too small to hold?
2. What do you have enough time to do after class today? Are you too busy to do something you'd like to do or should do?
3. Is there enough space in this classroom for 100 people? Or is it too small to hold that many people? How many people is this room big enough to hold comfortably?
4. Do you think it is very important to practice your English? Do you get enough practice? In your opinion, how much practice is enough?
5. Is it very difficult or too difficult to learn English articles (*a, an, the*)?
6. Think of a scientist you have learned about. What was he or she smart enough to do?

EXERCISE 13 ▸ Listening. (Chart 15-3)
Choose the sentence that has the same meaning as the sentence you hear.

Example: You will hear: I didn't fill your cup full enough.
            You will choose: (a.) You need more.
                         b. You have enough.

1. a. He's old enough to drive.
   b. He shouldn't drive.

2. a. She is too young to stay home alone.
   b. She stays home alone sometimes.

3. a. The test results are excellent.
   b. I'm not sure about the test results.

4. a. The room needs to be bigger.
   b. The room size is OK.

5. a. You will have enough time.
   b. You will need more time.

6. a. I want to eat them.
   b. I don't want to eat them.

EXERCISE 14 ▸ Warm-up. (Chart 15-4)
Choose the correct form of the passive verbs. Reminder: A passive verb has a form of **be** and a past participle, e.g., *the patient **was seen** by a specialist.*

1. The patient was hoping to be given / being given a good diagnosis.
2. He was worried about to be diagnosed / being diagnosed with cancer.
3. The patient appreciated to be seen / being seen by a specialist.
4. It was important for him to be seen / being seen by a specialist.

15-4	Passive Infinitives and Gerunds: Present
(a) I didn't *expect to be asked* to his party.	PASSIVE INFINITIVE: **to be** + *past participle* In (a): **to be asked** is a passive infinitive. The understood *by*-phrase is *by him: I didn't expect to be asked to his party (by him).*
(b) I *appreciated being asked* to his party.	PASSIVE GERUND: **being** + *past participle* In (b): **being asked** is a passive gerund. The understood *by*-phrase is *by him: I appreciated being asked to his party (by him).*

EXERCISE 15 ▸ Looking at grammar. (Chart 15-4)
Complete the sentences with the passive form of **invite**.

Ann's Party

1. Sam would like _____ *to be invited* _____ to Ann's party.

2. Mara also hopes _____ .

3. Maria has no doubts. She expects _____ to it.

4. Omar is looking forward to _____ too.

5. I would enjoy _____ to it, but I probably won't be.

6. Everyone I know wants _____ to Ann's party.

EXERCISE 16 ▶ Looking at grammar. (Chart 15-4)
Complete each sentence with the correct form of the verb in parentheses.

Complaints

1. I don't enjoy (*laugh*) _____*being laughed*_____ at by other people.

2. Ryan lied again. Unfortunately, it's easy (*fool*) _____*to be fooled*_____ by his lies.

3. It's not unusual for teenagers to complain about not (*understand*) _____
_____ by their parents.

4. Your compositions are not supposed (*handwrite*) _____ . They're
supposed to (*type*) _____ .

5. Dr. Davis is upset. She doesn't want (*call*) _____ at home unless there
is an emergency.

6. Please don't lie again. From now on, I insist on (*tell*) _____
_____ the truth.

7. Lars is hoping (*elect*) _____ to the city
council, but he's not qualified at all.

8. My sister is a helicopter parent.* Her kids need (*give*) _____
_____ more independence.

_____

a helicopter parent = an overprotective or overinvolved parent

EXERCISE 17 ▸ Reading and listening. (Chart 15-4)
First, read the paragraph and try to complete the sentences using the words in the box.
Then listen to the paragraph and check your answers.

to be understood	to solve	to read
able to read	using	being

An Issue in Health Care: Illiteracy

According to some estimates, well over half of the people in
the world are functionally illiterate. This means that they are
unable to perform everyday tasks because they can't read,
understand, and respond appropriately to information. One
of the problems this creates in health care is that millions of
people are not _____ directions on
1
medicine bottles or packages. Imagine _____ a parent with a sick child
2
and being unable _____ the directions on a medicine bottle. We all know
3
that it is important for medical directions _____ clearly. One solution
4
is pictures. Many medical professionals are working today _____ this
5
problem by _____ pictures to convey health-care information.
6

EXERCISE 18 ▸ Let's talk. (Chart 15-4)
Agree or disagree with the following statements and give reasons. Work in pairs, in small groups, or
as a class.

1. I appreciate *being given* advice by my family and friends.
2. I always expect *to be told* the absolute and complete truth by everyone at all times.
3. I would like *to be invited* to an event where there are a lot of famous people.

EXERCISE 19 ▸ Warm-up. (Chart 15-5)
Look at the sentences. All are correct. Which forms are you most familiar with? What differences
do you see between "b." and "c."?

1. a. Liam denied that he cheated on the test.
   b. Liam denied cheating on the test.
   c. Liam denied having cheated on the test.

2. a. He was surprised that he was caught by the teacher.
   b. He was surprised to be caught by the teacher.
   c. He was surprised to have been caught by the teacher.

15-5 Past Forms of Infinitives and Gerunds: Active and Passive

SIMPLE	PAST ACTIVE	PAST PASSIVE	Past infinitives and gerunds use a form of **have** + past participle.
to tell	*to have told*	*to have been told*	
telling	*having told*	*having been told*	

(a) Tim appeared *to have told* his wife about his job promotion.	PAST INFINITIVE: **to have** + *past participle* The event expressed in past phrases happened before the time of the main verb. The meaning in (a): It appeared that Tim had told his wife about his job promotion.
(b) Tim's wife was happy *to have been told* immediately about his job promotion.	PAST PASSIVE INFINITIVE: **to have been** + *past participle* The meaning in (b): Tim's wife was happy that she had been told immediately about his job promotion.
(c) He mentioned *having told* his wife immediately about his job promotion.	PAST GERUND: **having** + *past participle* The meaning in (c): He mentioned that he had told his wife immediately about his job promotion.
(d) She appreciated *having been told* immediately about his job promotion.	PAST PASSIVE GERUND: **having been** + *past participle* The meaning in (d): She appreciated that she had been told immediately about his job promotion.
(e) Tim mentioned *telling* his wife. Tim mentioned *having told* his wife. (f) She was happy *to be told*. She was happy *to have been told*.	Use of the past infinitive or gerund emphasizes that something occurred in the past, prior to another event. In practice, however, there is little difference in meaning between the simple and past forms, as in (e) and (f).

EXERCISE 20 ▸ Looking at grammar. (Chart 15-5)
Rewrite the sentences with the appropriate past infinitive or gerund phrase.

1. It seems that Thomas has received some upsetting news. → *Thomas seems to have received some upsetting news.*
2. The workers mentioned that they lost the contract. → *The workers mentioned having lost the contract.*
3. Mr. and Mrs. Sanchez regret that they missed your wedding.
4. It appears that Nicholas has gotten a new job.
5. The mechanic admitted that he had overcharged for repairs.
6. Mariah claims that she has met several celebrities.

EXERCISE 21 ▸ Looking at grammar. (Chart 15-5)
Complete the sentences with the correct form of the verb in parentheses.

1. I'm not sure I've ever met Billy Williams. (*meet*)

   a. I don't remember that I _____ *met* _____ him.

   b. I don't recall having _____ *met* _____ him.

   c. I don't recall _____ him.

   d. I don't remember _____ him.

   e. I don't remember having _____ him.

2. Ben was in the army during the war. He was caught by the enemy, but he was able to escape. (*survive*)

a. He was lucky to _____ _____ the war.

b. He was lucky to have _____ the war.

c. He was fortunate to _____ the war.

d. He told us about having _____ the war.

e. He told us about _____ the war.

f. It was fortunate that he _____ the war.

EXERCISE 22 ▸ Looking at grammar. (Charts 15-4 and 15-5)

Work with a partner. Choose the correct verbs. Several sentences have more than one correct answer. Discuss your answers.

1. Carlos looks great! He appears _____ some weight.
   a. losing
   b. to have lost
   c. to losing

2. I don't like _____ by friends.
   a. being lied to
   b. lying to
   c. to lie to

3. Mr. Gow mentioned _____ in an accident as a child.
   a. being injured
   b. having been injured
   c. injured

4. I was expecting _____ to the party, but I wasn't.
   a. being invited
   b. to be invited
   c. to have been invited

5. My husband talked of _____ by his parents.
   a. being misunderstood
   b. having been misunderstood
   c. misunderstood

6. The employees were happy _____ Mr. Larson as their next president.
   a. to choose
   b. to have chosen
   c. to have been chosen

7. Mr. Larson was happy _____ as the next company president.
   a. to choose
   b. to be chosen
   c. to have been chosen

EXERCISE 23 ▸ Warm-up. (Chart 15-6)

Make statements that are true for you. Use the same noun to complete each sentence. Do the sentences have the same or different meanings?

1. I need to clean my _____.

2. My _____ needs cleaning.

3. My _____ needs to be cleaned.

15-6 Using Gerunds or Passive Infinitives Following *Need*

(a) I *need to paint* my house. (b) John *needs to be told* the truth.	Usually an infinitive follows **need**, as in (a) and (b).
(c) My house *needs painting*. (d) My house *needs to be painted*.	In certain circumstances, a gerund may follow **need**, as in (c). In this case, the gerund carries a passive meaning. Usually the situations involve fixing or improving something. Examples (c) and (d) have the same meaning.

EXERCISE 24 ▶ Looking at grammar. (Chart 15-6)

Complete the sentences with the correct form of the verb in parentheses. Some verbs are active, and some are passive.

Farm Chores

1. The tractor is broken. I need (*fix*) _____*to fix*_____ it. The tractor needs

   (*fix*) _____*fixing / to be fixed*_____ .

2. The horses are hungry. They need (*feed*) _____ .

3. Their stalls are dirty. We need (*clean*) _____ them.

4. The hens have laid eggs. You need (*gather*) _____

   the eggs.

5. The dog's been digging in the mud. He needs (*wash*) _____ .

6. The vegetable garden is dry. It needs (*water*) _____ .

7. The apples on the tree are ripe. We need (*pick*) _____ them.

8. There is a hole in the fence. The fence needs (*repair*) _____ .

EXERCISE 25 ▶ Let's talk. (Chart 15-6)

Lawrence and Kara have been looking for a house. They've found one on a beautiful piece of land — shown in the photo — but it needs a lot of work. What needs doing or needs to be done? Make sentences using the words in the box or other appropriate vocabulary. Work in pairs or small groups.

A Fixer Upper

fix	paint	replace
foundation	porch	roof
front steps	rebuild	siding*
	repair	windows

Example: The windows need to be replaced. OR
The windows need replacing.

---

*siding = material, often wood, that goes around the outside of the house

Read the blog entry by author Stacy Hagen and answer the questions.

 BlueBookBlog **Multitasking**

Doing homework, checking text messages, group chatting — these are common activities, but are we capable of doing all of them at the same time and doing them well? According to research, it is impossible to multitask successfully. We either do the tasks more slowly, or we make mistakes. And with each additional task, the mistakes multiply. We make fewer mistakes with one task, more with two, and even more with three.

Our brain functions better when it stays focused on one task. This is why it is more efficient to do things in batches. We have a particular routine or mindset when we pay bills or answer emails, and these routines are different. So we want to pay all our bills or answer all our emails at one time before we move on to something else.

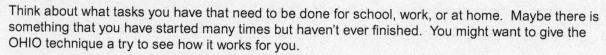

There is a related technique from organizational psychology that can help us stay on task. It is called "OHIO," which stands for "only handle it once." The idea is that once we start a single task like deleting photos from a phone, we should stay with it. We don't put some photos aside to make decisions about later. The result is that instead of looking at something multiple times, we deal with it only once.

Think about what tasks you have that need to be done for school, work, or at home. Maybe there is something that you have started many times but haven't ever finished. You might want to give the OHIO technique a try to see how it works for you.

1. What types of activities are you likely to multitask?
2. Is multitasking an effective approach for you?
3. Have you tried to do things in batches in order to be more efficient?
4. Do you have difficulty completing tasks you have started? Do you have any that still need to be finished?
5. Is OHIO a technique that could be helpful to you?

EXERCISE 27 ▸ Warm-up. (Chart 15-7)

See and *hear* are called "verbs of perception." In other words, they express things that we can perceive (become aware of) through our physical senses. What do you notice about the verb forms following *see* and *hear*?

1. a. CORRECT: I **saw** Mr. Reed give something to the boss.
   b. CORRECT: I **saw** Mr. Reed giving something to the boss.
   c. INCORRECT: I **saw** Mr. Reed ~~to~~ give something to the boss.

2. a. CORRECT: I **heard** Mr. Reed say something to the boss.
   b. CORRECT: I **heard** Mr. Reed saying something to the boss.
   c. INCORRECT: I **heard** Mr. Reed ~~to~~ say something to the boss.

15-7 Using Verbs of Perception

(a) I *saw* my friend *run* down the street.	Certain verbs of perception are followed by either *the simple form** or *the -ing form*** of a verb.
(b) I *saw* my friend *running* down the street.	
(c) I *heard* the rain *fall* on the roof.	Examples (a) and (b) have essentially the same meaning, except that the *-ing* form emphasizes the idea of "while." In (b): I saw my friend while she was running down the street.
(d) I *heard* the rain *falling* on the roof.	
(e) When I walked into the apartment, I *heard* my roommate *singing* in the shower.	Sometimes (not always) there is a clear difference between using the simple form or the *-ing* form.
(f) I *heard* a famous opera star *sing* at the concert last night.	The use of the *-ing* form gives the idea that an activity is already in progress when it is perceived, as in (e): The singing was in progress when I first heard it.
	In (f): I heard the singing from beginning to end. It was not in progress when I first heard it.

Verbs of perception followed by the simple form or the *-ing* form

see	look at	hear	feel	smell
notice	observe	listen to		
watch				

*The simple form of a verb = the infinitive form without *to*. INCORRECT: I saw my friend to run down the street.

The **-ing form is the present participle of the verb.

EXERCISE 28 ▸ Let's talk. (Chart 15-7)

Work in small groups. Describe what is going on.

1. Ask a classmate to stand up and sit back down. What did you just see him/her do?
2. Close your eyes. What do you hear happening right now?
3. Ask a classmate to go to the board and write something. As he/she does this, describe what you see and hear him/her doing.
4. If possible, find a hotel webcam on the Internet for a vacation spot. What do you see happening?

EXERCISE 29 ▸ Looking at grammar. (Chart 15-7)

Complete the sentences with any appropriate verbs. Both the simple form and the *-ing* form are possible with little or no difference in meaning.

An Earthquake

1. As I stood in the grocery store, I felt the ground _____shake / shaking_____.
2. I heard someone _____ "earthquake."
3. I saw cans of food _____ off shelves.
4. I watched customers in the store _____ outside.
5. I listened to people _____ the size of the earthquake.
6. I observed store staff _____ people outside.

EXERCISE 30 ▸ Looking at grammar. (Chart 15-7)

Read each situation. Complete the sentence below it with the verb form that seems better to you. Remember that the *-ing* form gives the idea that an activity is in progress when it is perceived.

SITUATION 1: I smell smoke. Something must be burning.

Do you smell something _____burning_____? I do.

SITUATION 2: The front door slammed. I got up to see if someone had come in.

When I heard the front door _____, I got up to see if someone had come in.

SITUATION 3: Uncle Ben is in the bedroom. He is snoring.

I know Uncle Ben is in the bedroom because I can hear him _____.

SITUATION 4: When I walked past the park, some children were playing softball.

When I walked past the park, I saw some children _____ softball.

SITUATION 5: It was graduation day in the auditorium. When the school principal called my name, I walked to the front of the room.

When I heard the school principal _____ my name, I walked to the front of the auditorium to receive my diploma.

SITUATION 6: I glanced out the window. Adam was walking toward the house. I was surprised.

I was surprised when I saw Adam _____ toward the house.

SITUATION 7: Someone is calling for help in the distance. I suddenly hear that.

Listen! Do you hear someone _____ for help? I do.

EXERCISE 31 ▸ Warm-up. (Chart 15-8)

Check (✓) the sentences that are grammatically correct.

1. _____ I'm not a morning person. My parents let me sleep late on weekends.
2. _____ My parents let me to sleep late on weekends.
3. _____ After I wake up, I help them do the chores.
4. _____ After I wake up, I help them to do the chores.

15-8	Using the Simple Form After *Let* and *Help*	
(a) My father *lets* me *drive* his car.	**Let** is followed by the simple form of a verb, not an infinitive.	
(b) I *let* my friend *borrow* my bike.	*INCORRECT:* My father lets me ~~to~~ drive his car.	
(c) *Let's go* to a movie.		
(d) My brother *helped* me *wash* my car.	**Help** is often followed by the simple form of a verb, as in (d).	
(e) My brother *helped* me *to wash* my car.	Although less common, an infinitive is also possible, as in (e). Both (d) and (e) are correct.	

EXERCISE 32 ▸ Looking at grammar. (Chart 15-8)

Complete the sentences with the verbs in parentheses.

At Breakfast

1. I forgot to tell you last night. My advisor is letting me (*challenge*) _____ a course. All I need to do is pass the test.
2. Could you help me (*figure*) _____ out my credit card statement before you go?
3. You really shouldn't let the dog (*sit*) _____ under the table.

4. How's our new neighbor, Mrs. Vitale? Did you help her (*move*) _____ her furniture?

5. Don't let me (*forget*) _____ to take my keys with me when I leave.

6. I need to go soon. Could you help me (*clear*) _____ the table?

7. You've been working so hard. Let me (*cook*) _____ dinner tonight.

EXERCISE 33 ▶ Warm-up. (Chart 15-9)
Match each of Andy's statements with the correct meaning.

a. "Weed the dandelions right now! I don't want you to leave until it's done."
b. "You did a good job with the dandelions. I'm glad I asked you to weed."
c. "I told my son I would double his allowance if he weeded the dandelions."

1. Andy got his son to weed the dandelions. _____

2. Andy made his son weed the dandelions. _____

3. Andy had his son weed the dandelions. _____

15-9 Using Causative Verbs: *Make, Have, Get*

(a) I *made* my brother *carry* my suitcase. (b) I *had* my brother *carry* my suitcase. (c) I *got* my brother *to carry* my suitcase.	*Make*, *have*, and *get* can be used to express the idea that "X" causes "Y" to do something. When they are used as causative verbs, their meanings are similar but not identical.
Simple form: X *makes* Y *do* something. Simple form: X *has* Y *do* something. Infinitive: X *gets* Y *to do* something.	In (a): My brother had no choice. I insisted that he carry my suitcase. In (b): My brother carried my suitcase because I asked him to. In (c): I managed to persuade my brother to carry my suitcase.

Causative *Make*

(d) Mrs. Lee *made* her son *clean* his room. (e) Sad movies *make* me *cry*.	Causative *make* is followed by the simple form of a verb, not an infinitive. *INCORRECT:* She made him ~~to~~ clean his room. ***Make*** gives the idea that "X" **gives** "Y" **no choice**. In (d): Mrs. Lee's son had no choice.

Causative *Have*

(f) I *had* the plumber *repair* the leak. (g) Jane *had* the waiter *bring* her some tea.	Causative *have* is followed by the simple form of a verb, not an infinitive. *INCORRECT:* I had him ~~to~~ repair the leak. ***Have*** gives the idea that "X" **requests** "Y" to do something. In (f): The plumber repaired the leak because I asked him to.

Causative *Get*

(h) The students *got* the teacher *to dismiss* class early. (i) Jack *got* his friends *to play* soccer with him after school.	Causative *get* is followed by an infinitive. ***Get*** gives the idea that "X" **persuades** "Y" to do something. In (h): The students managed to persuade the teacher to let them leave early.

Passive Causatives

(j) I *had* my watch *repaired* (by someone). (k) I *got* my watch *repaired* (by someone).	The past participle is used after *have* and *get* to give a passive meaning. In this case, there is usually little or no difference in meaning between *have* and *get*. In (j) and (k): I caused my watch to be repaired by someone.

EXERCISE 34 ▸ Looking at grammar. (Chart 15-9)
Match each conversation with the correct meaning.

a. ADAM: Mom, can I go out and play?
  MRS. LEE: No, Adam, you cannot go out and play until you clean up your room. I don't know how many times I have to say this. Go clean up your room, and I mean now!
  ADAM: OK, OK!

b. ADAM: Mom, can I go out and play?
  MRS. LEE: Well, let's make a deal. First you clean up your room. Then you can go out and play. How does that sound? It needs to be cleaned before Grandma comes for a visit this evening. And if you do it now, you can stay out and play until dark. You won't have to come home early to clean your room. OK?
  ADAM: OK.

c. ADAM: Mom, can I go out and play?
  MRS. LEE: Sure, but first you need to clean up your room. OK?
  ADAM: OK.

1. Mrs. Lee got Adam to clean up his room. _____
2. Mrs. Lee made Adam clean up his room. _____
3. Mrs. Lee had Adam clean up his room. _____

EXERCISE 35 ▸ Looking at grammar. (Chart 15-9)
Choose the meaning that is closest to the meaning of the verb in blue.

1. The teacher had her class write a composition.
  a. gave them no choice   b. persuaded them   c. requested them to do this

2. Mrs. Wilson made the children wash their hands before dinner.
  a. gave them no choice   b. persuaded them   c. requested them to do this

3. Kostas got some neighborhood kids to help him clean out his garage.
  a. gave them no choice   b. persuaded them   c. requested them to do this

4. My boss made me redo my report because he wasn't satisfied with it.
  a. gave me no choice   b. persuaded me   c. requested me to do this

5. I got Rosa to lend me some lunch money.
  a. gave her no choice   b. persuaded her   c. requested her to do this

6. The police officer had the driver get out of his car.
  a. gave him no choice   b. persuaded him   c. requested him to do this

EXERCISE 36 ▸ Looking at grammar. (Chart 15-9)
Complete the sentences with the correct form of the verbs in parentheses.

Tasks

1. Henry made his son (wash) _____ *wash* _____ the car before he could go outside to play.

2. Mrs. Crane had her house (paint) _____ *painted* _____.

3. I went to the bank to have a check (cash) _____.

4. Tom had a bad headache yesterday, so he got his roommate (cook) _____ dinner for him.

5. Scott needed a suit for work. The sleeves were too long, so he had them (*shorten*) _____ .

6. When my laptop stopped working, I took it to the computer store to have it (*fix*) _____ .

7. Benjamin was supposed to wash the windows, but he didn't want to. Somehow he got his little brother (*do*) _____ it for him.

8. We had our cousin (*take*) _____ pictures of everyone at the wedding. We had over 500 pictures (*take*) _____ .

EXERCISE 37 ▸ Let's talk. (Chart 15-9)

Think about the shopping area nearest your home. What can people do there? Make sentences with **can / can't + get**.

At the shopping area nearest my home, people can/can't get their …

1. car \ fix
2. hair \ cut
3. checks \ cash
4. laundry \ do
5. passport photo \ take
6. blood pressure \ check
7. shoes \ repair
8. clothes \ dry-clean
9. money \ exchange

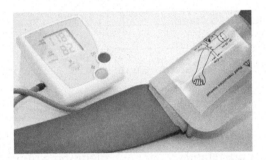

EXERCISE 38 ▸ Let's talk. (Chart 15-9)

Ask and answer the questions. Work in pairs, in small groups, or as a class.

1. What do children sometimes try to **get** their parents **to do** (perhaps at a toy store or grocery store)?
2. What do bosses sometimes **make** their employees **do**?
3. What does our teacher sometimes **have** us **do**?
4. Do teachers usually **let** their students **leave** the classroom whenever they want to? What kinds of things do teachers usually not **let** their students **do** inside a classroom?
5. What do your classmates (or friends) sometimes **help** you **do**?

(*Change roles if working in pairs.*)

6. What didn't your parents **let** you **do** when you were a child?
7. Will you **let** your children **do** those things? (Or, if you're a parent, do you **let** your children **do** those things?)
8. Did your parents **make** you **do** certain things when you were a child?
9. What do you sometimes **have** the server at a restaurant **do**?
10. What do you sometimes **get** your friends **to do**?

EXERCISE 39 ▸ Warm-up. (Chart 15-10)

Which sentence sounds more like everyday English to you? Which sounds more formal?

1. I appreciate your helping me.   2. I appreciate you helping me.

15-10 Using a Possessive to Modify a Gerund

— We came to class late. Mr. Lee complained about that fact. (a) FORMAL: Mr. Lee complained about *our coming* to class late. (b) INFORMAL: Mr. Lee complained about *us coming* to class late.	In formal English, a possessive adjective (e.g., **our**) is used to modify a gerund, as in (a). In informal English, the object form of a pronoun (e.g., **us**) is frequently used, as in (b).
(c) FORMAL: Mr. Lee complained about *Mary's coming* to class late. (d) INFORMAL: Mr. Lee complained about *Mary coming* to class late.	In formal English, a possessive noun (e.g., **Mary's**) is used to modify a gerund. As in (d), the possessive form is often not used in informal English.

EXERCISE 40 ▸ Looking at grammar. (Chart 15-10)

Complete the sentences with the correct form of the pronoun in parentheses.

Before the Wedding

1. (*I*)   a. FORMAL: My parents don't understand _____ wanting a small wedding.

        b. INFORMAL: My parents don't understand _____ wanting a small wedding.

2. (*she*) a. FORMAL: My mom has been too involved. We dislike _____ interfering in the wedding plans.

        b. INFORMAL: We dislike _____ interfering in the wedding plans.

3. (*we*)   a. FORMAL: Everyone else understands _____ planning a quiet celebration.

        b. INFORMAL: Everyone else understands _____ planning a quiet celebration.

4. (*they*) a. FORMAL: The Ricardos are coming from out of town. I look forward to _____ coming.

        b. INFORMAL: I look forward to _____ coming.

5. (*you*) a. FORMAL: We appreciate _____ helping us find a restaurant for the reception.

        b. INFORMAL: We appreciate _____ helping us find a restaurant for the reception.

6. (*he*)   a. FORMAL: Wait! Uncle Harry doesn't like Aunt Ethel. I insist on _____ being at a different table.

        b. INFORMAL: I insist on _____ being at a different table.

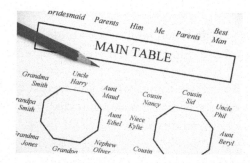

EXERCISE 41 ▸ Looking at grammar. (Chapters 14 and 15 Review)
Choose the correct completions.

1. My cousins helped me _____ into my new apartment.
     (a.) move   (b.) to move   c. moving   d. being moved

2. It was a hot day, and the work was hard. I could feel sweat _____ down my back.
     a. run   b. to run   c. running   d. ran

3. He's an amazing soccer player! Did you see him _____ that goal?
     a. make   b. to make   c. makes   d. made

4. We spent the entire class period _____ about the revolution.
     a. talk   b. to talk   c. talking   d. being talked

5. Fifty people applied for the sales job, so Maleek was fortunate _____ for an interview.
     a. chosen   b. being chosen   c. to choose   d. to be chosen

6. If you hear any news, I want _____ immediately.
     a. told   b. being told   c. to be told   d. telling

7. Victor stood in line _____ to buy a movie ticket.
     a. wait   b. waits   c. waiting   d. waited

8. _____ telling Roberto about the party was a mistake.
     a. We   b. My   c. I   d. Ø

9. I was getting sleepy, so I had my friend _____ the car.
     a. drive   b. being driven   c. to be driven   d. to drive

10. The witness to the murder wanted her name kept secret. She asked not _____ in the newspaper.
      a. identify   b. being identified   c. to be identified   d. to identify

EXERCISE 42 ▸ Looking at grammar. (Chapters 14 and 15 Review)
Complete each sentence with an appropriate form of the verb in parentheses.

1. My teenagers enjoy (*allow*) _____*being allowed*_____ to stay up later in the summer.

2. I couldn't get to sleep last night, so for a long time I just lay in bed (*think*) _____
   about my career and my future.

3. Jacob's at an awkward age. He's old enough (*have*) _____ adult problems but
   too young (*know*) _____ how (*handle*) _____ them.

4. I don't anticipate (*have*) _____ any difficulties (*adjust*) _____
   to a different culture when I go abroad.

5. I was tired, so I just watched my friends (*play*) _____ volleyball instead of (*join*)
   _____ them.

6. Emily stopped her car (*let*) _____ a cat (*run*) _____ across the street.

7. I'm tired. I wouldn't mind just (*stay*) _____ home tonight and (*get*) _____
   to bed early.

8. I don't like (*force*) _____ (*leave*) _____ the living room (*study*) _____ whenever my roommate decides (*have*) _____ a party.

9. Let's (*have*) _____ Ron and Maureen (*join*) _____ us for dinner tonight, OK?

10. Do you know that your co-workers complain about your (*come*) _____ late to work and (*leave*) _____ early?

11. Fish don't use their teeth for (*chew*) _____. They use them for (*grab*) _____, (*hold*) _____, or (*tear*) _____. Most fish (*swallow*) _____ their prey whole.

12. I can't seem (*get*) _____ rid of the cockroaches in my apartment. Every night I see them (*run*) _____ all over my kitchen counters. It drives me crazy. I'm considering (*have*) _____ the whole apartment (*spray*) _____ by a pest control expert.

EXERCISE 43 ▸ Looking at grammar. (Chapters 14 and 15 Review)
Complete each paragraph with the correct form of the given verbs.

1. *be / commute / do / move*

   Traffic has become too heavy for the Steinbergs _____ easily to their jobs in the city. They're considering _____ to an apartment in the city _____ closer to their work. They want to spend more time _____ things they really enjoy rather than being tied up on the highway during rush hour.

2. *ask / cough / feel / get / go / sneeze*

   Last week I was sick with the flu. It made me _____ awful. I didn't have enough energy _____ out of bed. I just lay there. When my father heard me _____ and _____, he opened my bedroom door to see if I needed anything. It was kind of him _____, but there wasn't anything he could do to make the flu _____ away.

EXERCISE 44 ▸ Check your knowledge. (Chapter 15 Review)
Correct the errors.

1. I went to the library ~~for~~ ^{to} study last night.

2. Barbara always makes me laughing. She has a great sense of humor.

3. The teacher opened the window for letting some fresh air into the room.

4. You shouldn't let children playing with matches.

5. I traveled to Osaka for to visit my sister.

6. My parents made me to promise contact them once a week.

7. I asked my roommate to let me borrowed his sleeping bag for my camping trip.

8. I heard a car door to open and closing.

9. I had my friend to lend me his car.

10. I've finally gathered enough information for beginning writing my research paper.

11. My parents want that I marry soon.

12. Lilly deserves to be tell the truth about what happened last night.

13. I went to the pharmacy for having my prescription to be filled.

14. Stop telling me what to do! Let me to make up my own mind.

15. Victoria didn't like her school photo, so she had it taking again.

16. Look at the kitchen windows. They really need to washing. Will you do it?

17. I saw Omar sitting on a park bench look at the ground. The blank expression on his face made me to worry about him.

EXERCISE 45 ▶ Reading and writing. (Chapter 15)

Part I. Read the passage. <u>Underline</u> the gerunds and infinitives. How many gerunds begin sentences? How many infinitives?

Do you know these words?
- *understatement*
- *remedies*
- *foolproof*

Why Do Onions Make Us Cry?

Cutting onions is no fun! Most people end up in tears, and the reason is quite simple. Onions contain a gas: sulfur. When an onion is cut, a very fine spray of sulfur is released into the air. It is an understatement to say that our eyes don't enjoy coming into contact with it. They immediately react by trying to wash the sulfur away with tears.

There are a few remedies that may be helpful to you, though not foolproof. Washing an onion with water can help to keep the sulfur away from your eyes. Refrigerating it weakens its strength. Some people find safety goggles effective. You might look foolish when you put them on, but there's a good chance they will keep you from crying. If you enjoy cooking, it's hard to avoid onions, but one of these simple solutions may be of help.

Part II. Think about an everyday problem that needs a remedy. Describe the problem and provide one or more solutions. Use one of the suggestions below or choose your own. Be sure to include some gerunds and infinitives.

- stopping the itch in a mosquito bite
- removing a stain from fabric
- removing something sticky from a surface
- soothing a sore throat
- soothing a sunburn

Using a gerund as the subject of a sentence rather than an infinitive is more common. In the passage about onions, *cutting onions* or *washing an onion* is preferable to the infinitive forms: *to cut* or *to wash.*

However, if you want to express the idea of *in order to,* use an infinitive: *To cut an onion, use a sharp knife*. The meaning is "In order to cut an onion, use a sharp knife."

Part III. Edit your writing. Check for the following:

1. ☐ correct use of gerunds with the required verbs
2. ☐ correct use of infinitives with the required verbs
3. ☐ correct use of infinitives with the required adjectives
4. ☐ correct use of a gerund if followed by a preposition
5. ☐ singular verb when a gerund is the subject
6. ☐ correct spelling (use a dictionary or spell-check)

Coordinating Conjunctions

PRETEST: What do I already know?

Write "C" if a sentence has the correct word choice and word forms, subject-verb agreement, and punctuation. Write "I" for incorrect. Check your answers below. After you complete each chart listed, make the necessary corrections.

1. _____ By obeying the speed limit, we can save energy, lives, and it costs us less. (16-1)

2. _____ My home offers me a feeling of security, warm, and love. (16-1)

3. _____ On my vacation, I lost a suitcase, broke my glasses, and I missed my flight home. (16-1)

4. _____ My sister brother-in-law, and I wanted to see a movie. The three of us went to the theater, but the line was too long. (16-2)

5. _____ I appreciate your help, I was feeling overwhelmed by all the work I had to do. (16-3)

6. _____ I refused Alicia's help, she became very angry and shouted at me. (16-3)

7. _____ Either the sales clerk or the manager have your refund. (16-4)

8. _____ Both the bride and the groom were late for their wedding. (16-4)

Incorrect sentences: 1, 2, 3, 4, 5, 6, 7

EXERCISE 1 ▸ Warm-up. (Chart 16-1)

Identify the parts of speech of the words in blue. Are they nouns, verbs, adjectives, or adverbs? What words connect them?

A Birthday Adventure

1. We hiked to a waterfall and a bridge.

2. The bridge was extremely high and scary.

3. I felt shaky but excited when I got on it.

4. The bridge rocked and swayed.

5. I tried not to hurry or to look down.

16-1 Parallel Structure

One use of a conjunction is to connect words or phrases that have the same grammatical function in a sentence. This use of conjunctions is called "parallel structure." The conjunctions used in this pattern are **and, but, or**, and **nor**. These words are called "coordinating conjunctions."

(a) *Steve* **and** his *friend* are coming to dinner.	In (a): *noun* + **and** + *noun*
(b) Susan *raised* her hand **and** *snapped* her fingers.	In (b): *verb* + **and** + *verb*
(c) He *is waving* his arms **and** *(is) shouting* at us.	In (c): *verb* + **and** + *verb* (The second auxiliary may be omitted if it is the same as the first auxiliary.)
(d) These shoes are *old* **but** *comfortable*.	In (d): *adjective* + **but** + *adjective*
(e) He wants *to watch* TV **or** *(to) listen* to some music.	In (e): *infinitive* + **or** + *infinitive* (The second *to* is usually omitted.)

EXERCISE 2 ▶ Looking at grammar. (Chart 16-1)
Choose <u>all</u> the words that are parallel with the given words.

1. *to watch*	hearing	to listen	saw	to decide	having thought
2. *beautiful*	friendly	nice	honest	happily	goodness
3. *texting*	contacted	to type	chatting	email	sending
4. *rapidly*	difficult	fast	good	slowly	wild

EXERCISE 3 ▶ Looking at grammar. (Chart 16-1)
Choose the correct completions.

My Roommate

1. My roommate, Kate, is friendly and _____.
   a. helpful b. kind c. kindness

2. Friendliness and _____ are admirable qualities in a roommate.
   a. kind b. kindness c. kindly

3. We are opposites. She likes to be busy and _____.
   a. actively b. activity c. active

4. I'm a quieter type. I prefer to stay home or _____ time with a few friends.
   a. spending b. spend c. to spending

5. Kate studies by listening to music and _____ at the same time.
   a. sing b. singing c. sings

6. I sit at the library and _____ in silence.
   a. work b. working c. worked

7. We get along well, though. We're both very neat and _____.
   a. tidy b. tidily c. have tidiness

8. We take turns cleaning our apartment and _____ the cooking.
   a. do b. to do c. doing

EXERCISE 4 ▸ Looking at grammar. (Chart 16-1)

Complete each sentence with <u>one</u> word that gives the same idea as the words in parentheses.

Road Rage

1. The driver ran a stop sign and _____*sped*_____ down the street.
   (*he was driving at a high speed*)

2. A pedestrian was shocked and _____ that she was almost hit in the crosswalk.
   (*her feelings were upset*)

3. A police officer stopped him, but the driver spoke impatiently and _____.
   (*his words were rude*)

4. He got out of his car and walked toward the officer. He was tall and _____.
   (*has a lot of strength*)

5. Another police officer arrived and _____ him into custody.
   (*she took*)

EXERCISE 5 ▸ Warm-up. (Chart 16-2)

Check (✓) the sentences that are correctly punctuated with commas.

1. _____ Oranges, and lemons are high in vitamin C. (*not correct*)

2. __✓__ Oranges and lemons are high in vitamin C.

3. _____ Oranges, lemons, and broccoli are high in vitamin C.

4. _____ Oranges, lemons and broccoli are high in vitamin C.

5. _____ Oranges lemons and broccoli are high in vitamin C.

6. _____ Oranges, lemons, and broccoli, are high in vitamin C.

16-2 Parallel Structure: Using Commas

(a) **Steve** and **Joe** are in class.	No commas are used when *and* connects **two** parts of a parallel structure, as in (a).
(b) *INCORRECT PUNCTUATION:* Steve, and Joe are in class.	
(c) **Steve, Joe** and **Rita** are in class. (d) **Steve, Joe,** and **Rita** are in class. (e) **Steve, Joe, Rita, Jan** and **Kim** are in class. (f) **Steve, Joe, Rita, Jan,** and **Kim** are in class.	When *and* connects **three or more** parts of a parallel structure, a comma is used between the first items in the series. A comma may also be used before *and,* as in (d) and (f). The use of this comma is optional (i.e., the writer can choose).* NOTE: A comma often represents a pause in speech.

*The purpose of punctuation is to make writing clear for readers. This chart and others in this chapter describe the usual use of commas in parallel structures. Sometimes commas are required according to convention (i.e., the expected use by educated language users). Sometimes use of commas is a stylistic choice made by the experienced writer.

EXERCISE 6 ▸ Looking at grammar. (Chart 16-2)
Add commas as necessary.

At a Hotel

1. The room includes a king-sized bed**,** a desk (*optional comma*)**,** and a balcony.
2. The price of the room includes Wi-Fi buffet breakfast and use of the exercise room.
3. The price of the room includes Wi-Fi and buffet breakfast.
4. We got an adjoining room for our son his wife and their daughter.
5. Our son's wife and daughter met us at the rooftop pool.
6. My wife called room service asked about vegetarian options and ordered a meal.
7. We searched for an on-demand movie with action adventure and suspense.
8. We enjoy action and adventure films.
9. The front-desk clerk the bellhop the concierge and the housekeeping staff were very attentive and courteous.

EXERCISE 7 ▸ Looking at grammar. (Charts 16-1 and 16-2)
Parallel structure makes repeating the same words unnecessary. Cross out the words that are unnecessary. Combine the given sentences into one concise sentence. Use parallel structure.

Molly's Party

1. Molly will open the door. ~~Molly will~~ greet her guests.
   → *Molly will open the door **and** greet her guests.*
2. She is opening the door. She is greeting her guests.
3. She is taking their coats. She is hanging them up in the closet.
4. Molly is kind. Molly is generous. Molly is trustworthy.
5. Since she is hard of hearing, please try to speak loudly. Please try to speak clearly.
6. Her boyfriend has come to the party. He has come with flowers. He has come with candy. He has come with a ring.
7. He has knelt down in front of her. He has taken her hand. He has asked her to marry him.
8. Molly is calm enough to listen. Molly is calm enough to say yes.
9. They talked about getting married in June. Or they could get married in August.
10. Molly had expected a surprise. She did not expect a ring.
    → *Molly had expected a surprise **but** not a ring*
11. Molly was surprised. She was not shocked.
12. They had discussed getting married at some point. They had not discussed getting married this year.

EXERCISE 8 ▶ Looking at grammar. (Charts 16-1 and 16-2)
First, complete the unfinished sentence in each group. Second, combine the sentences into one concise sentence that contains parallel structure.

1. The mountain road was curvy.
   The mountain road was steep.

   The mountain road was _____*narrow*_____.

   The mountain road was curvy, ___*steep, and narrow*___.

2. I dislike living in a city because of the air pollution.
   I dislike living in a city because of the crime.

   I dislike living in a city because of _____.

   I dislike living in a city because of the air pollution, _____

   _____.

3. Hawaii has a warm climate.
   Hawaii has beautiful beaches.
   Hawaii has many interesting tropical trees.

   Hawaii has many interesting tropical _____.

   Hawaii has a warm climate, beautiful beaches, _____

   _____.

4. Mary Hart would make a good president because she works effectively with others.
   Mary Hart would make a good president because she has a reputation for integrity.
   Mary Hart would make a good president because she has a reputation for independent thinking.

   Mary Hart would make a good president because she _____.

   Mary Hart would make a good president because she works effectively with others,

   _____.

EXERCISE 9 ▶ Let's talk. (Charts 16-1 and 16-2)
Work with a partner. Take turns completing each sentence. Share some of your partner's answers with the class.

1. A good friend needs to be _____ and _____.

2. English teachers should have these qualities: _____,

   _____, and _____.

3. _____, _____, and _____ are three

   easy ways for me to relax at the end of the day.

4. In my free time, I like to _____, _____, and

   _____.

5. Three activities I don't enjoy are _____, _____, and

   _____.

6. _____, _____, and _____ are difficult

   subjects for me.

EXERCISE 10 ▸ Warm-up. (Chart 16-3)
Check (✓) the three sentences with correct punctuation.

1. _____ Thunder clouds rolled by. Flashes of lightning lit the sky.
2. _____ Thunder clouds rolled by, flashes of lightning lit the sky.
3. _____ Thunder clouds rolled by, and flashes of lightning lit the sky.
4. _____ Thunder clouds rolled by. And flashes of lightning lit the sky.

16-3	Punctuation for Independent Clauses; Connecting Them with *And* and *But*	
(a) It was raining hard. There was a strong wind.	Example (a) contains two *independent clauses* (i.e., two complete sentences).	
(b) *INCORRECT PUNCTUATION:* It was raining hard, there was a strong wind.	PUNCTUATION: A period,* NOT A COMMA, is used to separate two independent clauses.	
(c) It was raining hard; there was a strong wind.	A semicolon may be used in place of a period. Semicolons are used between two *closely related* ideas.	
(d) It was raining hard, *and* there was a strong wind. (e) It was raining hard. *And* there was a strong wind. (f) It was raining hard *and* there was a strong wind. (g) It was late, *but* he didn't care. (h) It was late. *But* he didn't care.	*And* and *but* (coordinating conjunctions) are often used to connect two independent clauses. PUNCTUATION: Usually a comma immediately precedes the conjunction, as in (d) and (g). In informal writing, a writer might choose to begin a sentence with a conjunction, as in (e) and (h). In a very short sentence, a writer might choose to omit the comma in front of *and*, as in (f). (Omitting the comma in front of *but* is rare.)	

*In British English, a period is called a "full stop."

EXERCISE 11 ▸ Looking at grammar. (Chart 16-3)
Punctuate the sentences by adding commas and periods. Do not add any words. Capitalize as necessary.

Athletic Conditioning Class

1. Some members did push-ups some members lifted weights.
    → *Some members did push-ups. Some members lifted weights.*

2. Some members did push-ups and some members lifted weights.

3. The teacher demonstrated correct form a group of new members watched.

4. The teacher demonstrated correct form and a group of new members watched.

5. An assistant was available to help but only a few people needed him.

6. An assistant was available to help only a few people needed him.

EXERCISE 12 ▸ Looking at grammar. (Chart 16-3)
Check (✓) the correct sentences. Punctuate the incorrect ones. Do not add any words. Capitalize as necessary.

Email Excerpts

1. _____ I'd like to help, let me know what you need.
2. _____ I'll be happy to come. Thank you for inviting me.
3. _____ It's really hard to know what to do, we don't have much information yet.
4. _____ I'll pay you back. I get paid tomorrow.
5. _____ Let's wait to see what happens, we don't want to make a decision prematurely.

EXERCISE 13 ▸ Looking at grammar. (Chart 16-3)
Rewrite the email with correct punctuation. You may add *and* and *but*.

From: J.B. Leeds	
To: Majda	Today at 2:11 PM
Subject: Update/Thanks	

Dear Majda,

Thank you for offering to drive students to the track meet. We are still hoping we can get a bus, we will know later today. The first race starts at 4:00 the boys will be leaving school around 1:15 the girls can leave at 1:30 since their race is at 4:30. We always appreciate parent volunteers, thanks again for contacting me, I will be back in touch soon.

EXERCISE 14 ▸ Reading and grammar. (Charts 16-1 → 16-3)
Work with a partner. Find and correct the errors with parallel structure and punctuation.

Ziplining

Ziplining began as a way to get people across impassible places like canyons and crossing rivers. But in the 1980s, Costa Rica, with its emphasis on eco-tourism, turned it into a thrilling adventure. The opportunity to soar over spectacular scenery has made ziplining one of Costa Rica's top tourist attractions.

The concept is very simple, a cable is strung across a scenic area, for example, a lush forest or fast-moving river one end of the cable is higher than the other. A harness for the rider hangs from the cable, riders are strapped tightly into the harness. They climb to a platform, jump off, and flying through the air.

Ziplining's popularity has spread worldwide, the longest zipline is in Sun City, South Africa, where one cable is 1.2 miles (2 km) long. Average speeds are 75 miles (120 km) per hour! Not all zipline rides are as hair-raising, companies around the world strive to provide exciting and safety rides that will appeal to a variety of experience levels and age groups.

EXERCISE 15 ▸ Warm-up. (Chart 16-4)
What do you notice about the subject-verb agreement in each pair of sentences?

1. a. Either my brother or my sister is going to tutor me in science.
   b. Either my brother or my sisters are going to tutor me in science.

2. a. Neither my brother nor my sister is a teacher.
   b. Neither my brother nor my sisters are teachers.

3. a. Not only my brother but also my sister has a doctorate in science.
   b. Not only my brother but also my sisters have doctorates in science.

16-4 Paired Conjunctions: *Both ... And; Not Only ... But Also; Either ... Or; Neither ... Nor*

(a) *Both* my mother *and* my sister *are* here.	Two subjects connected by *both ... and* take a plural verb, as in (a).
(b) *Not only* my mother *but also* my sister *is* here. (c) *Not only* my sister *but also* my parents *are* here. (d) *Neither* my mother *nor* my sister *is* here. (e) *Neither* my sister *nor* my parents *are* here.	When two subjects are connected by *not only ... but also, either ... or,* or *neither ... nor*, the subject that is closer to the verb determines whether the verb is singular or plural. *Not only ... but also* is used for emphasis or to indicate surprise. It should be used sparingly.
(f) The research project will take *both* time *and* money. (g) Sue saw *not only* a fox in the woods *but also* a bear. (h) I'll take *either* chemistry *or* physics next quarter. (i) That book is *neither* interesting *nor* accurate.	Notice the parallel structure in the examples. The same grammatical form should follow each part of the paired conjunctions.* In (f): *both* + noun + *and* + noun In (g): *not only* + noun + *but also* + noun In (h): *either* + noun + *or* + noun In (i): *neither* + adjective + *nor* + adjective NOTE: Paired conjunctions are usually used for emphasis; they draw attention to both parts of the parallel structure.

*Paired conjunctions are also called "correlative conjunctions."

EXERCISE 16 ▸ Looking at grammar. (Chart 16-4)
Complete the sentences with *is/are*.

1. Both the teacher and the student _____*are*_____ here.

2. Neither the teacher nor the student _____ here.

3. Not only the teacher but also the student _____ here.

4. Not only the teacher but also the students _____ here.

5. Either the students or the teacher _____ planning to come.

6. Either the teacher or the students _____ planning to come.

7. Both the students and the teachers _____ planning to come.

8. Both the students and the teacher _____ planning to come.

EXERCISE 17 ▶ Looking at grammar. (Chart 16-4)

In the News

Part I. Answer the questions with *both ... and*.

1. The homeless received food. Did they receive clothing?
   → *Yes. The homeless received both food and clothing.*

2. Passengers were injured in the bus accident. Was the driver injured in the accident?

3. I know the government is increasing taxes. Is the government increasing spending too?

4. The city suffers from air pollution. Does it suffer from water pollution?

Part II. Answer the questions with *not only ... but also*.

5. I know crime is growing in the cities. Is crime growing in the suburbs?
   → *Yes. Crime is growing not only in the cities but also in the suburbs.*

6. I know our team lost its first game. Did it also lose its second game?

7. I know some tech companies need more workers. Do they need more office space too?

8. I know the city is building a new freeway. Is it also building a new subway too?

EXERCISE 18 ▶ Looking at grammar. (Chart 16-4)

At Our Apartment Building

Part I. Answer the questions with *either ... or*.

1. The manager has my package, or Mrs. Ramircz has my package. Is that right?
   → *Yes. Either the manager or Mrs. Ramirez has your package.*

2. Jonas is going to take care of the neighbor's cat, or William is going to take care of the neighbor's cat. Is that right?

3. Your sister is driving Ms. Androv to the airport, or your brother is driving her. Right?

4. We can use the front stairs, or we can use the back stairs. Is that right?

Part II. Answer the questions with *neither ... nor*.

5. The mail carrier isn't friendly. Is she unfriendly?
   → *No. She is neither friendly nor unfriendly.*

6. Her children don't speak English. Does her husband speak English?

7. They don't have an air conditioner in their apartment. Do they have a fan?

8. The window washers weren't fast. Were they slow?

EXERCISE 19 ▶ Listening. (Chart 16-4)

Choose the sentence (a. or b.) that has the same meaning as the sentence you hear.

Example: You will hear: Sarah is working on both a degree in biology and a degree in chemistry.
You will choose: a. Sarah is working on only one degree.
(b.) Sarah is working on two degrees.

1. a. Ben will call Mary and Bob.
   b. Ben will call one of them but not both.

2. a. My mother and my father talked to my teacher.
   b. Either my mother or my father talked to my teacher.

3. a. Simon saw both a whale and a dolphin.
   b. Simon didn't see a whale, but he did see a dolphin.

4. a. Our neighborhood had electricity but not water.
   b. Our neighborhood didn't have electricity or water.

5. a. We will have two teachers today.
   b. We will have one teacher today.

EXERCISE 20 ▸ Looking at grammar. (Chart 16-4)

Combine each pair of sentences into one new sentence with parallel structure. Use **both ... and;**
either ... or; neither ... nor.

At the Mall

1. I do not have my credit card. I do not have cash.
   → *I have neither my credit card nor cash.*

2. You can get some shoes now, or you can look online
   more.
   → *You can either get some shoes now or look online more.*

3. Rika enjoys shopping during sales. Bettina enjoys
   shopping during sales.

   _____

4. Matt is not joining us. Taka is not joining us.

   _____

5. Matt is sick. Taka is sick.

   _____

6. This store doesn't have the size I need. That store doesn't have the size I need.

   _____

7. We can eat lunch here, or we can look for other restaurants.

   _____

8. The manager was helpful. The assistant manager was helpful.

   _____

9. You need your receipt for a return, or you need your credit card.

   _____

10. The stores close at 10:00. The food court closes at 10:00.

    _____

11. We can take the bus home, or we can take the subway.

    _____

EXERCISE 21 ▸ Grammar and listening. (Chapter 16 Review)
Choose the correct completions. Then listen to the passage and check your answers.

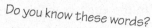
Do you know these words?
- *unreasoned*
- *tangle*
- *rabies*
- *pollinating*
- *overripe*
- *flourish*
- *train (a pet)*

Bats

What do people in your country think of bats? Are they mean and scary creatures, or are they symbols of both happiness and (luck)/ lucky?
1

In Western countries, many people have an unreasoned fear of bats. According to scientist Dr. Sharon Horowitz, bats are not only harm / harmless but also benefit / beneficial
2   3
mammals. "When I was a child, I believed that a bat would attack me and tangle / tangled itself in my hair. Now I know better,"
4
said Dr. Horowitz.

Contrary to popular Western myths, bats do not attack / attacking
5
humans. Although a few bats may have diseases, they are not major carriers of rabies or other frightening diseases. Bats help natural plant life by pollinating plants, spreading seeds, and to eat / eating insects. If you get rid of bats that eat overripe fruit, then
6
fruit flies can flourish and destroy / destruction the fruit industry.
7

According to Dr. Horowitz, bats are both gentle and train / trainable pets. Not many
8
people, however, own or train bats, and bats themselves prefer to avoid people.

EXERCISE 22 ▸ Reading, grammar, and speaking. (Chapter 16 Review)

Part I. Read the paragraph about Dr. Martin Luther King, Jr.

Martin Luther King, Jr., was the leader of the 1960s civil rights movement in the United States that sought to end segregation and racial discrimination against African-Americans. In 1964, Dr. King became the youngest person to receive the Nobel Peace Prize. He was assassinated in 1968, but his powerful and inspiring words live on.

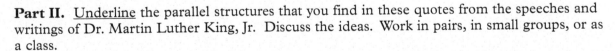

Part II. Underline the parallel structures that you find in these quotes from the speeches and writings of Dr. Martin Luther King, Jr. Discuss the ideas. Work in pairs, in small groups, or as a class.

1. "The hope of a secure and livable world lies with disciplined nonconformists who are dedicated to justice, peace, and brotherhood."

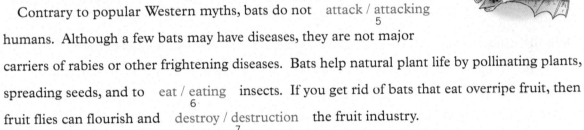

2. "The ultimate measure of a man is not where he stands in moments of comfort and convenience but where he stands at times of challenge and controversy."

3. "In the end, we will remember not the words of our enemies but the silence of our friends."

4. "Nonviolence is the answer to the crucial political and moral question of our time: the need for mankind to overcome oppression and violence without resorting to oppression and violence. Mankind must evolve for all human conflict a method which rejects revenge, aggression, and retaliation. The foundation of such a method is love."

EXERCISE 23 ▶ Check your knowledge. (Chapter 16 Review)
Correct the errors.

1. Slowly and being cautious, the firefighter climbed the burned staircase.

2. Janice entered the room and looked around she knew no one.

3. Derek made many promises but he had no intention of keeping any of them.

4. The pioneers hoped to clear away the forest and planting crops.

5. When Nadia moved, she had to rent an apartment, make new friends, and to find a job.

6. All plants need light, to have a suitable climate, and an ample supply of water and minerals from the soil.

7. Both the main earthquake and subsequent aftershocks was devastating to the town.

8. With their sharp eyesight, fine hearing, and they have a strong sense of smell, wolves hunt mainly at night.

9. Not only speed but also endurance determine a runner's success in a race.

10. The ancient Egyptians had good dentists archaeologists have found mummies that had gold fillings in their teeth.

EXERCISE 24 ▶ Writing. (Chapter 16)
Part I. Read the post from social media.

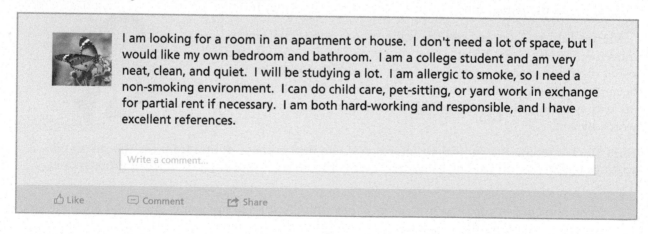

I am looking for a room in an apartment or house. I don't need a lot of space, but I would like my own bedroom and bathroom. I am a college student and am very neat, clean, and quiet. I will be studying a lot. I am allergic to smoke, so I need a non-smoking environment. I can do child care, pet-sitting, or yard work in exchange for partial rent if necessary. I am both hard-working and responsible, and I have excellent references.

Write a comment...

👍 Like   💬 Comment   ↪ Share

Part II. Following the example in Part I, write a social media post about something you are looking for: a place to rent, a car, a pet, etc.

Part III. Edit your writing. Check for the following:

1. □ clear, uncomplicated sentences
2. □ a period, not a comma, between two complete sentences
3. □ parallel structure
4. □ correct subject-verb agreement with paired conjunctions, e.g., ***both ... and***
5. □ correct spelling (use a dictionary or spell-check)

17

Adverb Clauses

PRETEST: What do I already know?

Write "C" if a sentence has the correct form, meaning, and punctuation and "I" for incorrect. Check your answers below. After you complete each chart listed, make any necessary corrections.

1. _____ The first time I met your parents at the party for Nicholas and his girlfriend. (17-1)

2. _____ After the movie ended. The audience stayed in their seats for a few minutes. (17-1)

3. _____ Whenever Josh died, his family was very sad. (17-2)

4. _____ Because Rosa inherited a large amount of money from her parents, she was an only child. (17-3)

5. _____ Now that I graduated, I need to look for a job. (17-3)

6. _____ Even though the movie is very popular, I don't think the theater will be crowded. (17-4)

7. _____ While some people enjoy being online a lot, others do. (17-5)

8. _____ If anyone needs me, I'll be in my office. (17-6)

9. _____ Are you coming with us? If so, could you hurry? (17-7)

10. _____ Even if he invites me to the party, I will go. (17-8)

11. _____ In case you've forgotten anything, I can always send it to you. (17-9)

12. _____ Unless you get below 70% on the next test, you'll pass the course. (17-10)

13. _____ Only if Abdul's foot is better he can play in the soccer match next month. (17-11)

Incorrect sentences: 1, 2, 3, 4, 5, 7, 10, 13

EXERCISE 1 ▶ Warm-up. (Chart 17-1)

The words in blue are adverb clauses. What do you notice about their placement in the sentence and punctuation?

1. The fireworks display began after it got dark.
2. Because it was New Year's Eve, thousands of people came to watch.
3. Although it was very crowded, everyone had good views.
4. There is a show every year even if the weather is bad.

17-1 Introduction

Adverb clauses are used to show relationships between ideas. They show relationships of *time, cause and effect, contrast,* and *condition.*

adverb clause main clause (a) *When the phone rang,* the baby woke up. (b) The baby woke up *when the phone rang.*	In (a) and (b): ***when the phone rang*** is an adverb clause of time. Examples (a) and (b) have the same meaning. PUNCTUATION: When an adverb clause precedes a main clause, as in (a), a comma is used to separate the clauses. When the adverb clause follows, as in (b), usually no comma is used.
(c) *Because he was sleepy,* he went to bed. (d) He went to bed *because he was sleepy.*	In (c) and (d), ***because*** introduces an adverb clause that shows a cause-and-effect relationship.

(e) *INCORRECT:*
   When we were in New York. We saw several plays.
 	
(f) *INCORRECT:*
   He went to bed. Because he was sleepy.
	Adverb clauses are dependent clauses. They cannot stand alone as a sentence in written English. They must be connected to a main (or independent) clause.*

Summary list of words used to introduce adverb clauses**

TIME		CAUSE AND EFFECT	CONTRAST	CONDITION
after	by the time (that)	because	even though	if
before	once	now that	although	unless
when	as/so long as	since	though	only if
while	whenever			whether or not
as	every time (that)		DIRECT CONTRAST	even if
as soon as	the first time (that)		while	in case
since	the last time (that)			
until	the next time (that)			

*See Chart 12-1, p. 248, for the definition of dependent and independent clauses.

**Words that introduce adverb clauses are called "subordinating conjunctions."

EXERCISE 2 ▶ Looking at grammar. (Chart 17-1)

Check (✓) the sentences that are grammatically complete and contain the correct punctuation.

Annoyances

1. a. __✓__ The door slammed.

    b. _____ When the door slammed.

    c. _____ I woke up. When the door slammed.

    d. _____ I woke up when the door slammed.

    e. _____ When the door slammed, I woke up.

    f. _____ The door slammed. I woke up.

2. a. _____ After I texted you, my phone died.

    b. _____ The last time I texted you, and you didn't answer.

    c. _____ Every time the phone rings, and no one is there.

    d. _____ Whenever the phone rings, no one is there.

    e. _____ As soon as we sit down to dinner, a telemarketer calls.

EXERCISE 3 ▶ Looking at grammar. (Chart 17-1)

<u>Underline</u> the adverb clauses. Add punctuation and capitalization as necessary. Do not add or delete any words.

A Snowstorm

1. *W*
   <u>when Adolfo came to Chicago</u>, he planned to stay with his cousins.

2. Adolfo planned to stay with his cousins when he came to Chicago.

3. As soon as the plane landed a blizzard began.

4. A blizzard began as soon as the plane landed.

5. Once the plane landed a blizzard began.

6. Adolfo didn't go outside the airport until it stopped.

7. When it stopped Adolfo went outside.

8. When he went outside there weren't any taxis.

9. He was stranded at the airport until the roads were cleared.

10. As soon as the roads were cleared he left the airport.

EXERCISE 4 ▶ Looking at grammar. (Chapter 16 and Chart 17-1)

Work with a partner. Add punctuation and capitalization as necessary. Do not add or delete any words.

1. Paulo is a member of a championship basketball team he is a wheelchair athlete Paulo's legs are paralyzed when he plays he moves around the basketball court in a wheelchair he has competed in many tournaments, and his team often wins.

2. Fritz is a golden retriever he appears to be a typical dog except he has an important job he is a service dog he has been trained to help a blind person whenever his owner needs to go downtown Fritz assists him Fritz can help him cross streets get on buses go down stairs and avoid obstacles.

3. Sometimes when people speak to someone who is hard of hearing they shout shouting is not necessary it is important to face the person and speak clearly people who are hard of hearing can often read lips my father is hard of hearing, but he can understand me when I look at him and say each word clearly.

EXERCISE 5 ▶ Warm-up. (Chart 17-2)

Add the word(s) in parentheses to the correct place in each sentence. Add commas and capitalization as necessary.

1. Oscar can't catch the meaning *when* people speak English too fast. (*when*)

2. The teacher speaks too fast Oscar is going to ask her to slow down. (*the next time*)

3. Oscar is listening to English he tries not to translate from his language. (*while*)

4. His teacher encourages students to figure out the meaning they check their dictionaries. (*before*)

5. Oscar began studying English he has wanted to speak fluently. (*ever since*)

17-2 Using Adverb Clauses to Show Time Relationships

after *	(a) **After** she graduates, she will get a job. (b) **After** she (had) graduated, she got a job.	A present tense, NOT a future tense, is used in an adverb clause of time, as in (a) and (c).
before *	(c) I will leave **before** he comes. (d) I (had) left **before** he came.	
when	(e) **When** I arrived, he *was talking* on the phone. (f) **When** I got there, he *had* already *left*. (g) **When** it began to rain, I *stood* under a tree. (h) **When** I was in Chicago, I *visited* the museums. (i) **When** I see him tomorrow, I *will ask* him.	**when** = *at that time* Notice the different time relationships expressed by the tenses.
while *as*	(j) **While** I was walking home, it began to rain. (k) **As** I was walking home, it began to rain.	**while, as** = *during that time*
by the time	(l) **By the time** he arrived, we *had* already *left*. (m) **By the time** he comes, we *will have* already *left*.	**by the time** = *one event is completed before another event* Notice the use of the past perfect and future perfect in the main clause.
since	(n) I *haven't seen* him **since** he left this morning. (o) I've *known* her **ever since** I was a child.	**since** = *from that time to the present* In (o): **ever** adds emphasis. NOTE: The present perfect is used in the main clause.
until *till*	(p) We stayed there *until* we finished our work. (q) We stayed there *till* we finished our work.	**until, till** = *to that time and then no longer* (**Till** is used more in speaking than in writing; it is generally not used in formal English.)
as soon as *once*	(r) **As soon as** it stops raining, we will leave. (s) **Once** it stops raining, we will leave.	**as soon as, once** = *when one event happens, another event happens soon afterward*
as long as *so long as*	(t) I will never speak to him again *as long as* I live. (u) I will never speak to him again *so long as* I live.	**as long as, so long as** = *during all that time, from beginning to end*
whenever *every time*	(v) **Whenever** I see her, I say hello. (w) **Every time** I see her, I say hello.	**whenever** = *every time*
the first time *the last time* *the next time*	(x) **The first time** (that) I went to New York, I went to a Broadway show. (y) I saw two plays **the last time** (that) I went to New York. (z) **The next time** (that) I go to New York, I'm going to see a ballet.	Adverb clauses can be introduced by: the { first / second / third, etc. / last / next / etc. } time (that)

After and *before* are commonly used in the following expressions:

shortly *after*   **shortly** *before*
a short time *after*   **a short time** *before*
a little while *after*   **a little while** *before*
not long *after*   **not long** *before*
soon *after*

EXERCISE 6 ▶ Looking at grammar. (Charts 17-1 and 17-2)
Complete the sentences with your own words. Add brackets around the adverb clause in each sentence.

1. *Don't worry.*

    a. I will call you [before I _____ *come over* _____.]

    b. I will go to bed after I _____ my homework.

    c. I did my chores before I _____ to my friend's house.

    d. By the time you get home, I _____ dinner for you.

2. *Dogs and spiders scare me.*

    a. Ever since I was a child, I _____ of dogs.

    b. One time a small dog bit me when I _____ it.

    c. Whenever I _____ spiders, I scream.

    d. A spider fell out of my shoe as I _____ this morning.

    e. By the time I stopped screaming, the spider _____.

3. *You need to protect your ID.*

    a. The last time I _____ overseas, I lost my passport. The next time I
       _____, I'm going to bring a photocopy of it.

    b. Whenever I _____ a password for a website, I make it very long.

    c. Ever since I _____ about identity theft, I have been very careful about sharing
       information online.

EXERCISE 7 ▶ Looking at grammar. (Charts 17-1 and 17-2)
Combine each pair of sentences with the words in parentheses. Add commas as necessary.

On a Flight

1. The baggage will be loaded soon. The plane will take off. (*as soon as*)
   → As soon as the baggage is loaded, the plane will take off.
2. The passengers got on the plane. The flight attendant closed the door. (*after*)
3. The passengers got on the plane. The flight attendant closed the door. (*before*)
4. Malea feels nervous. She flies. (*whenever*)
5. The plane was climbing. We hit turbulence. (*while*)
6. I was falling asleep. The pilot made an announcement. (*just as★*)
7. I fell asleep. He finished. (*as soon as*)
8. I stood up to walk to the restroom. The flight attendant told us to fasten our seat belts. (*just after*)
9. We had to stay in our seats. The pilot turned off the seat belt sign. (*until*)
10. We had lunch. The person next to me has been talking non-stop. (*since*)

★*Just* adds the idea of "immediately":
    just as = at that immediate or same moment
    just before = immediately before
    just after = immediately after

11. I fly. I will bring earplugs. (*the next time*)
12. I will text you. We land. (*as soon as*)
13. I get my bags. I will meet you in the passenger-loading zone. (*just as soon as*)
14. I flew this airline. My bags were lost. (*the first time*)
15. I will be happy to stretch my legs. We get off the plane. (*once*)
16. We land. We will have been on the plane for ten hours. (*by the time*)

EXERCISE 8 ▶ Looking at grammar. (Chart 17-2)
Choose the best completion for each sentence.

1. As soon as Martina saw the fire, she _____ the fire department.
   a. was telephoning   c. had telephoned
   b. telephoned   d. has telephoned

2. Before Jennifer won the lottery, she _____ any kind of contest.
   a. hasn't entered   c. wasn't entering
   b. doesn't enter   d. hadn't entered

3. Every time Prakash sees a movie made in India, he _____ homesick.
   a. will have felt   c. feels
   b. felt   d. is feeling

4. Since I left Venezuela six years ago, I _____ to visit friends and family several times.
   a. return   c. am returning
   b. will have returned   d. have returned

5. While he was washing his new car, Lawrence _____ some scratches on his front bumper.
   a. has discovered   c. is discovering
   b. was discovering   d. discovered

6. Yesterday while I was attending a sales meeting, Matthew _____ on the company's annual report.
   a. was working   c. has worked
   b. had been working   d. works

7. Tony _____ to have children until his little daughter was born. After she won his heart, he decided he wanted a big family.
   a. doesn't want   c. wasn't wanting
   b. hadn't wanted   d. hasn't wanted

8. After the horse threw her to the ground for the third time, Jennifer picked herself up and said, "I _____ on another horse as long as I live."
   a. never ride   c. will never ride
   b. have never ridden   d. do not ride

9. The next time Paul _____ to New York, he will visit the Metropolitan Museum of Art's famous collection of international musical instruments.
   a. will fly   c. has flown
   b. flies   d. will have flown

10. Ever since Maurice arrived, he _____ quietly in the corner. Is something wrong?
    a. sat   c. had been sitting
    b. has been sitting   d. will have sat

11. After Nela _____ for 20 minutes, she began to feel tired.
   a. jogging
   b. had been jogging
   c. has been jogging
   d. has jogged

12. Peter, _____ since you got home from football practice?
   a. have you eaten
   b. will you eat
   c. are you eating
   d. do you eat

13. The last time I _____ in Athens, the weather was hot and humid.
   a. had been
   b. was
   c. am
   d. will have been

14. By the time the young birds _____ the nest for good, they will have learned how to fly.
   a. will leave
   b. will have left
   c. are leaving
   d. leave

EXERCISE 9 ▶ Looking at grammar. (Charts 17-1 and 17-2)
Read the description of events. Make sentences using the words in the list.

Example: Just after
   → *Just after Judy parked her car, a thief broke into it.*

   4:00   Judy parked her car at the mall and went to buy some jeans.
   4:03   A thief broke into her car and stole her radio.
   4:30   Judy returned to her car.
   4:31   Judy called the police.
   4:35   The police arrived.
   4:35   Judy began crying in frustration.

   1. Just after   3. When   5. By the time
   2. Just as   4. While   6. As soon as

EXERCISE 10 ▶ Let's talk. (Charts 17-1 and 17-2)
Work in pairs or small groups. Complete the sentences. Each person should finish each sentence. Share a few things you learned about your classmates.

About Me

Example:
After I left class yesterday, ...
→ *After I left class yesterday, I met my cousin at a café.*

   1. After I leave class today, ...
   2. Before I go to bed tonight, ...
   3. As soon as I get up tomorrow, ...
   4. Whenever I feel nervous, ...
   5. The first time I came to this class, ...
   6. Ever since I was a child, ...
   7. As long as I live, ...
   8. Just as I was falling asleep last night, ...

EXERCISE 11 ▶ Reading, grammar, and writing. (Charts 17-1 and 17-2)

Part I. Read the passage and then complete the sentences.

Cultural Misunderstandings

Since Marco and Anya came to this country, they've had some memorable misunderstandings due to language and culture. The first time Marco met someone at a party, he was asked, "How's it going?" Marco thought that the person was asking him about leaving, and that seemed very strange.

   Once, Anya walked into class, and a native speaker said, "Hi. How are you?" When Anya started to give a long answer, the speaker looked at her rather oddly. This happened several times until Anya learned she was just supposed to say something like "OK" or "Fine, thanks. And you?"

   Another time, Marco was at a restaurant and wanted to get the server's attention. He snapped his fingers. The server was not pleased.

   Since coming here, Marco and Anya have learned that cultural misunderstandings are a normal part of learning another language. They can be valuable and even entertaining learning experiences. Marco and Anya just smile at these misunderstandings now.

1. The first time Marco was asked, "How's it going?" _____

_____

2. At first, every time someone asked Anya how she was, _____

_____

3. The next time Marco wants to get the server's attention at a restaurant, _____

_____

4. Since Marco and Anya have come to this country, _____

_____

5. Whenever they have a cultural misunderstanding, _____

_____

Part II. Write a paragraph about a cultural misunderstanding you have had or experienced.

EXERCISE 12 ▶ Warm-up. (Chart 17-3)
Which adverb clauses give the idea of "because"?

1. Now that I've finished art school, I can focus on finding work as an illustrator.
2. Since I was young, I have been artistic.
3. Since I've had formal training, maybe I can illustrate books.

17-3 Using Adverb Clauses to Show Cause and Effect

because	(a) **Because** he was sleepy, he went to bed. (b) He went to bed **because** he was sleepy.	An adverb clause may precede or follow the independent clause. Notice the punctuation in (a) and (b). Be sure to identify the correct cause and effect. *INCORRECT:* Because he went to bed, he was sleepy.
now that	(c) **Now that** I've finished the semester, I'm going to rest a few days and then take a trip. (d) Jack lost his job. **Now that** he's unemployed, he can't pay his bills.	**Now that** means "because now." In (c): **Now that I've finished the semester** means "because the semester is now over." *NOTE:* **Now that** is used with the present, present perfect, or future tenses.
since	(e) **Since** Monday is a holiday, we don't have to go to work. (f) **Since** you're a good cook and I'm not, you should cook the dinner.	When **since** is used to mean "because," it expresses a known cause; it means "because it is a fact that" or "given that it is true that." Cause-and-effect sentences with **since** say, "Given the fact that X is true, Y is the result." In (e): "Given the fact that Monday is a holiday, we don't have to go to work."
	(g) **Since** I came here, I have met many people.	*NOTE:* **Since** has two meanings. One is "because." It is also used in time clauses, as in (g). See Chart 17-2.

EXERCISE 13 ▶ Looking at grammar. (Chart 17-3)

Combine each pair of sentences with the words in parentheses. Add commas as necessary.

Travel

1. We have a lot of frequent-flier miles. We can visit several countries. (*now that*)
   → *Now that we have a lot of frequent-flier miles, we can visit several countries.*
2. We can compare hotel prices. They are posted online. (*since*)
3. We have read the online hotel reviews. We can choose our hotel. (*now that*)
4. There is little chance we will get lost. We have GPS on our phones. (*because*)
5. People post online reviews instantly. Customer service has improved. (*since*)
6. We won't get so homesick. We can video chat with our families. (*because*)

EXERCISE 14 ▶ Looking at grammar. (Chart 17-3)

Check (✓) the sentences that can be rewritten with **now that**, and then rewrite them.

My Grandmother

1. __✓__ Because my grandfather has died, my mom would like my grandmother to move in with us.
   Now that my grandfather has died, my mom would like my grandmother to move in with us.

2. _____ Because my grandmother lives alone, I visit her more often.

3. _____ Because my grandmother was a nurse, she took good care of her health.

4. _____ Because my grandparents saved for their retirement, she doesn't need to worry about finances.

5. _____ Because she is 90, I have asked her a few times if she should continue driving.

EXERCISE 15 ▸ Warm-up. (Chart 17-4)
Which sentence expresses an unexpected result?

1. Because I was very tired, I went to bed early.
2. Even though I was very tired, I stayed up late.

17-4	Expressing Contrast (Unexpected Result): Using *Even Though*	
(a)	*Because* the weather was cold, I *didn't go* swimming.	*Because* is used to express expected results.
(b)	*Even though* the weather was cold, I *went* swimming.	*Even though* is used to express unexpected results.*
(c)	*Because* I wasn't tired, I *didn't go* to bed.	NOTE: Like *because, even though* introduces an adverb clause.
(d)	*Even though* I wasn't tired, I *went* to bed.	

Although and *though* have basically the same meaning and use as *even though*. See Chart 19-7, p. 416, for information on the use of *although* and *though*.

EXERCISE 16 ▸ Looking at grammar. (Chart 17-4)
Choose the correct completion for each sentence.

1. Because it was a dark, cloudy day, _____.
   a. I didn't put on my sunglasses   b. I put on my sunglasses

2. Even though it was a dark, cloudy day, _____.
   a. I put on my sunglasses   b. I didn't put on my sunglasses

3. Even though Mira was cold, _____.
   a. she wore a heavy coat outside   b. she wore a light sweater outside

4. Because Mira enjoys the outdoors, _____.
   a. she goes for walks rain or shine   b. she doesn't go for walks in bad weather

EXERCISE 17 ▸ Looking at grammar. (Chart 17-4)
Complete the sentences with *even though* or *because*.

1. a. Tim's in good shape physically _____*even though*_____ he doesn't get much exercise.

   b. Barry's in good shape physically _____*because*_____ he gets a lot of exercise.

2. a. _____ Yoko has a job, she is able to pay her rent and feed her family.

   b. _____ Melissa has a job, she doesn't make enough money to support her four children.

3. a. Joe speaks Spanish well _____ he lived in Mexico for a year.

   b. Sherry didn't learn Spanish _____ she lived in Mexico for a year.

4. a. Jin jumped into the river to rescue a little girl who was drowning _____ he wasn't a good swimmer.

   b. _____ she was rescued right away, the girl survived.

5. a. _____ the flood washed away

   the bridge, the campers were able to cross the river

   _____ they had a boat.

   b. _____ the bridge was out

   of service for several months, people had to find

   alternate ways to get across the river.

EXERCISE 18 ▶ Let's talk. (Chart 17-4)

Work in pairs, in small groups, or as a class. Speaker A asks the question. Speaker B answers the
question beginning with **Yes/No** and followed by **Even though**.

Small Talk

Examples:
SPEAKER A: It was raining. Did you go to the zoo anyway?
SPEAKER B: Yes. Even though it was raining, I went to the zoo.

SPEAKER A: You studied hard. Did you pass the test?
SPEAKER B: No. Even though I studied hard, I didn't pass the test.

1. You stayed up all night. Did you go to work?
2. Your sister has a new baby. Have you met her yet?
3. The food was terrible. Did you eat it anyway?
4. You didn't study. Did you pass the test anyway?
5. The weather is terrible today. Did you stay home?
6. You fell down the stairs. Did you get hurt?
7. You sent in an excellent college application. Did you get accepted?
8. You rehearsed your speech several times. Were you nervous?

(Change roles if working in pairs.)

9. You told the truth, but did anyone believe you?
10. You bought a brand-new air conditioner. Does it work?
11. You changed your password. Did your account still get hacked?
12. You have a new cat and dog. Do you have enough pets?
13. Your grandfather is 100 years old. Is he still young at heart?
14. You didn't understand the joke. Did you laugh anyway?
15. Your friends gave you a surprise birthday party. Were you surprised?
16. You backed up your computer files. Could you find all your documents?

EXERCISE 19 ▶ Warm-up. (Chart 17-5)

Check (✓) the sentences that show contrast (i.e., show that "X" is the opposite of "Y").

1. _____ I am a vegetarian, while my husband is a meat-eater.
2. _____ While I was buying vegetables, I remembered that we had leftovers in the fridge.
3. _____ While many vegetarians eat eggs, I don't because they come from chickens.

17-5 Showing Direct Contrast: *While*

(a) Mary is rich, *while John is poor*. (b) John is poor, *while Mary is rich*. (c) *While John is poor*, Mary is rich. (d) *While Mary is rich*, John is poor.	*While* is used to show direct contrast: "this" is exactly the opposite of "that."* Examples (a), (b), (c), and (d) all have the same meaning. Note the use of the comma in (a) and (b): In using *while* for direct contrast, a comma is often used even if the *while*-clause comes second (unlike the punctuation of most other adverb clauses).
COMPARE: (e) The phone rang *while I was studying*.	REMINDER: *While* is also used in time clauses and means "during that time," as in (e). See Chart 17-2.

*****Whereas** can have the same meaning and use as *while*, but it occurs mostly in formal written English and occurs with considerably less frequency than *while*: *Mary is rich, **whereas** John is poor.*

EXERCISE 20 ▶ Looking at grammar. (Chart 17-5)
Choose the best completion for each sentence.

1. Some people are tall, while others are _____.
   a. intelligent
   b. thin
   c. short
   d. large

2. A box is square, while _____.
   a. a rectangle has four sides
   b. my village has a town square in the center
   c. we use envelopes for letters
   d. a circle is round

3. While some parts of the world get an abundance of rain, others _____.
   a. are warm and humid
   b. are cold and wet
   c. get little or none
   d. get a lot

4. In some nations the favorite beverage is coffee, while _____.
   a. I like tea
   b. it has caffeine
   c. in others it is tea
   d. they drink tea

5. Some people like cream and sugar in their coffee, while _____.
   a. others like it black
   b. others drink hot coffee
   c. milk is good in coffee too
   d. sugar can cause cavities

6. Steve is an interesting storyteller and conversationalist, while his brother _____.
   a. is a newspaper reporter
   b. bores other people by talking about himself all the time
   c. has four children
   d. knows a lot of stories too

EXERCISE 21 ▶ Let's talk. (Chart 17-5)
Work in pairs or small groups. Contrast each pair of words using *while*. You may need to research the words. Share some of your answers with the class.

Example: alligators/crocodiles
→ *Alligators are found in the U.S. and China, while crocodiles are found worldwide.*
→ *A crocodile has a V-shaped snout, while an alligator has a rounded snout.*
→ *Alligators can live in freshwater, while crocodiles prefer salt water.*

1. a college/a university
2. an island/a peninsula
3. tap water/filtered water
4. an immigrant/a refugee
5. the word *affect*/the word *effect*
6. a passport/a visa

EXERCISE 22 ▸ Warm-up. (Chart 17-6)

Check (✓) the sentence with *if* that is grammatically correct.

1. _____ If I will need help, I will ask you.

2. _____ If I need help, I will ask you.

3. _____ If I will need help, I ask you.

17-6	Expressing Conditions in Adverb Clauses: *If*-Clauses

(a) *If it rains tomorrow, I will take my umbrella.*	*If*-clauses (also called "adverb clauses of condition") present possible conditions. The main clause expresses RESULTS. In (a): POSSIBLE CONDITION = *it may rain tomorrow* RESULT = *I will take my umbrella* A present tense, not a future tense, is used in an *if*-clause even though the verb in the *if*-clause may refer to a future event or situation, as in (a).*

Words that introduce adverb clauses of condition (*if-clauses*)		
if	even if	unless
whether or not	in case	only if

*See Chapter 20 for uses of other verb forms in sentences with *if*-clauses.

EXERCISE 23 ▸ Looking at grammar. (Chart 17-6)

Make sentences with *if* using the given conditions.

Example: It may be cold tomorrow. → *If it's cold tomorrow, I'm going to stay home.*
→ *We can't go on a picnic if it's cold tomorrow.*

1. I will stay up all night.
2. I may be sick tomorrow.
3. Maybe I will wake up tomorrow and speak English fluently.
4. The power may be out for 24 hours.
5. The government might put a 20% tax on snack food.

EXERCISE 24 ▸ Reading and grammar. (Charts 17-1 → 17-6)

Underline the adverb clauses in the student handbook passage. Correct the errors in punctuation.

Forms of Address
Colleges and Universities

It's your first day of class, and you're not sure what to call your teacher. Is the first name acceptable or too informal? If you use a title, should it be *Dr.* or *Professor*?

At the college level, many teachers actually prefer to use first names, because it feels friendlier and less formal. They prefer not to have the psychological distance that a title creates.

While many teachers prefer first names some would rather use titles. *Dr.* is for someone with a Ph.D. degree. It is important to know that not all instructors have Ph.D.'s. In that case, *Professor* is more appropriate, as long as the teacher has the following job title: *Professor, Associate Professor,* or *Assistant Professor*. Note that the last name, not first name, is used with *Dr.* and *Professor*.

Even though many graduate students teach college courses. They are not professors. One option for addressing them is *Ms.* or *Mr.* + last name. But most prefer first names, since they are still technically students.

You can always ask your teacher: "What would you like to be called?" or "How would you like to be addressed?" Teachers like to have contact with students, and knowing your teacher's preference may make it easier for you to approach him or her.

EXERCISE 25 ▶ Warm-up. (Chart 17-7)

Check (✓) the sentences that logically follow the question and are grammatically correct.

Do you have your cell phone with you?

1. _____ If you do, could I use it?

2. _____ If so, could I use it?

3. _____ If not, I can use someone else's.

4. _____ If you don't, I can use someone else's.

5. _____ If you are, could I use it?

17-7 Shortened *If*-Clauses

(a) Are you a student? *If so / If you are,* the ticket is half-price. *If not / If you aren't,* the ticket is full price. (b) It's a popular concert. Do you have a ticket? *If so / If you do,* you're lucky. *If not / If you don't,* you're out of luck.	When an *if*-clause refers to the idea in the sentence immediately before it, it is sometimes shortened. In (a): **If so / If you are** = *If you are a student* **If not / If you aren't** = *If you aren't a student* In (b): **If so / If you do** = *If you have a ticket* **If not / If you don't** = *If you don't have a ticket*

EXERCISE 26 ▶ Looking at grammar. (Chart 17-7)

First, complete the sentences in two ways:

  a. Use *so* or *not*.

  b. Use a helping verb or main verb *be*.

Second, give the full meaning of the shortened *if*-clause.

1. Does Lisa want to go out to dinner with us?

  a. If _____*so*_____, tell her to meet us at 8:00.

  b. If she _____*does*_____, tell her to meet us at 8:00.

   → *Meaning: if Lisa wants to go out to dinner with us*

2. Are you free this weekend?

  a. If _____, do you want to go to a movie?

  b. If you _____, do you want to go to a movie?

3. Do you have a ride to the theater?

  a. If _____, would you like to ride with us?

  b. If you _____, would you like to ride with us?

4. Are you coming to the meeting?

  a. If _____, I'll see you there.

  b. If you _____, I'll see you there.

5. Did you use a spell-check on your email to me?

  a. If _____, it didn't catch all the spelling errors.

  b. If you _____, it didn't catch all the spelling errors.

6. We need some rice. Can you stop at the store on your way home today?

    a. If _____, I'll do it.

    b. If you _____, I'll do it.

EXERCISE 27 ▸ Warm-up. (Chart 17-8)
Check (✓) all the sentences that are true for David.

SITUATION: If David gets married, he will be happy. If he doesn't get married, he will be happy.

1. _____ David will be happy if he doesn't get married.
2. _____ If he gets married, David won't be happy.
3. _____ Even if David gets married, he won't be happy.
4. _____ Even if David doesn't get married, he will be happy.
5. _____ David will be happy whether or not he gets married.
6. _____ Whether or not David gets married, he will be happy.

17-8	Adverb Clauses of Condition: Using *Whether Or Not* and *Even If*

Whether or not

(a) I'm going to go swimming tomorrow *whether or not it is cold.* OR *whether it is cold or not.*	**Whether or not** expresses the idea that neither this condition nor that condition matters; the result will be the same. In (a): "If it is cold, I'm going swimming. If it is not cold, I'm going swimming. I don't care about the temperature. It doesn't matter."

Even if

(b) I have decided to go swimming tomorrow. *Even if the weather is cold,* I'm going to go swimming.	Sentences with **even if** are close in meaning to those with **whether or not**. **Even if** gives the idea that a particular condition does not matter. The result will not change.

EXERCISE 28 ▸ Looking at grammar. (Chart 17-8)
Choose the sentence (a. or b.) that has the same meaning as the given sentence.

1. Even if I get an invitation to the reception, I'm not going to go.
    a. I won't go to the reception without an invitation.
    b. I don't care if I get an invitation. I'm not going.

2. Even if the weather improves, I won't go to the beach.
    a. I'm going to the beach if the weather improves.
    b. I don't care if the weather improves. I'm not going to the beach.

3. Whether or not you want help, I plan to be at your house at 9:00.
    a. I'm going to help you because I think you need help.
    b. I'm going to help you because you want me to.

4. I won't tell even if someone pays me.

    a. I won't tell whether or not someone gives me money.

    b. If someone pays me enough money, I will tell.

5. I have to go to work tomorrow whether I feel better or not.

    a. Whether I go to work or not depends on how I feel.

    b. I'm going to work tomorrow no matter how I feel.

6. Even if John apologizes, I won't forgive him!

    a. John needs to apologize for me to forgive him.

    b. I don't care if John apologizes. It doesn't matter.

EXERCISE 29 ▸ Looking at grammar. (Chart 17-8)

Use the given information to complete sentences a. and b.

SITUATION 1: Usually people need to graduate from school to get a good job. But it's different for Ed. Maybe Ed will graduate from school, and maybe he won't. It doesn't matter because he has a good job waiting for him in his father's business.

    a. Ed will get a good job whether or not …

       → *Ed will get a good job whether or not he graduates.*

    b. Ed will get a good job even if …

       → *Ed will get a good job even if he doesn't graduate.*

SITUATION 2: Cindy's uncle tells a lot of jokes. Sometimes they're funny, and sometimes they're not. It doesn't matter.

    a. Cindy laughs at the jokes whether … or not.

    b. Cindy laughs at the jokes even if …

SITUATION 3: Maybe you are finished with the exam, and maybe you're not. It doesn't matter. The time is up.

    a. You have to hand in your examination paper whether … or not.

    b. You have to hand in your examination paper even if …

SITUATION 4: Max's family doesn't have enough money to send him to college. He would like to get a scholarship, but it doesn't matter because he's saved some money to go to school and has a part-time job.

    a. Max can go to school whether or not …

    b. Max can go to school even if …

SITUATION 5: Sometimes the weather is hot, and sometimes the weather is cold. It doesn't matter. My grandfather always wears his gray sweater.

    a. My grandfather wears his gray sweater whether or not …

    b. My grandfather always wears his gray sweater even if …

SITUATION 6: Your approval doesn't matter to me.

    a. I'm going to marry Harry whether … or not.

    b. I'm going to marry Harry even if …

SITUATION 7: It might snow, or it might not. We don't want to go camping in the snow, but it doesn't matter.

    a. We're going to go camping in the mountains whether … or not.

    b. We're going to go camping in the mountains even if …

EXERCISE 30 ▸ Warm-up. (Chart 17-9)

Choose the sentence (a. or b.) that has the same meaning as the given sentence.

If by chance you have a problem, you can reach me at this number.

    a. In case you have a problem, you can reach me at this number.
    b. When you have a problem, you can reach me at this number.

17-9	Adverb Clauses of Condition: Using *In Case*
(a) I'll be at my uncle's house *in case you (should)* need to reach me.	*In case* expresses the idea that something probably won't happen, but it might. *In case* means "if by chance this should happen." NOTE: Using ***should*** in an adverb clause emphasizes the speaker's uncertainty that something will happen.

EXERCISE 31 ▸ Looking at grammar. (Chart 17-9)

Combine each pair of sentences. Begin your new sentence with ***In case***.

I'm just letting you know …

1. You probably won't need to get in touch with me, but maybe you will. If so, I'll give you my cell number.
    → *In case you (should) need to get in touch with me, I'll give you my cell number.*
2. You probably won't need to see me, but maybe you will. If so, I'll be in my office tomorrow morning around ten.
3. I don't think you need any more information, but maybe you do. If so, you can call me.
4. You probably don't have any more questions, but maybe you do. If so, ask Dr. Smith.
5. The dentist probably won't call, but maybe she will. If so, come get me. I'll be outside.
6. I hope you're happy with your present, but maybe it won't work. If not, you can return it to the store and get something else.

EXERCISE 32 ▸ Looking at grammar. (Charts 17-7 → 17-9)

Complete the sentences with your own words. Work in pairs, in small groups, or as a class.

Bad Weather

1. Our boss doesn't accept bad weather as an excuse for missing work. We have to go to work even if …
2. The weather is getting worse. I may not be able to make it home tonight. If not, …
3. The trains might not be running. I'd better … in case …
4. I may stay in town tonight. If so, …
5. I packed a change of clothes today in case …

EXERCISE 33 ▸ Warm-up. (Chart 17-10)

Choose the logical completion for each sentence.

1. I'll be at the meeting on time if there   is / isn't   a lot of traffic.
2. I'll be at the meeting on time unless there   is / isn't   a lot of traffic.
3. My manager won't be coming unless she feels   better / worse.
4. My manager won't be coming if she feels   better / worse.

17-10 Adverb Clauses of Condition: Using *Unless*

(a) I'll go swimming tomorrow *unless* *it's cold*.	*unless* = *if* ... *not*
(b) I'll go swimming tomorrow *if* *it isn't cold*.	In (a): *unless it's cold* means "if it isn't cold."
	Examples (a) and (b) have the same meaning.

EXERCISE 34 ▸ Looking at grammar. (Chart 17-10)

Restate each sentence with **unless**.

FYI (For Your Information)

1. If you don't buy your ticket today, you won't get one.
    → *Unless you buy your ticket today, you won't get one.*
2. You can't travel to that country if you don't have a visa.
3. If you don't sign up for the test by Monday, you can't take it next month.
4. It's difficult to return a product to that store if you don't have a receipt.
5. You can't get a motorcycle license if you haven't passed a special training course.
6. The store won't accept your credit card if you don't have ID with you.
7. Traffic fines increase if you don't pay them right away.

EXERCISE 35 ▸ Looking at grammar. (Chart 17-10)

Complete the sentences with your own words. Work in pairs, in small groups, or as a class.

Sorry, but ...

1. You can't speak to the manager unless ...
    → *You can't speak to the manager unless you have an appointment.*
2. You can't pay with a check unless ...
3. Some students won't be able to pass unless ...
4. ... unless you save more money.
5. Unless you spend more time with your kids, ...
6. Some stores will close permanently unless ...
7. ... unless I get a raise in salary.
8. I'm going to ... unless ...
9. Unless you ...
10. Interest and penalties on your bill will continue to increase unless ...
11. Unless ... , I won't ...

EXERCISE 36 ▸ Warm-up. (Chart 17-11)

Answer the questions about Scott.

SITUATION: Scott closes his bedroom window at night only if it's raining hard.

1. Does Scott close his bedroom window if the temperature is below freezing?
2. Does Scott close his bedroom window if it's windy outside?
3. Does Scott close his bedroom window if there's a light rain?
4. Does Scott close his bedroom window if there is a heavy rain?

17-11 Adverb Clauses of Condition: Using *Only If*

(a) The picnic will be canceled *only if it rains*. 　　If it's windy, we'll go on the picnic. 　　If it's cold, we'll go on the picnic. 　　If it's damp and foggy, we'll go on the picnic. 　　If it's unbearably hot, we'll go on the picnic.	*Only if* expresses the idea that there is only one condition that will cause a particular result.
(b) *Only if* it rains **will** the picnic **be canceled**.	When *only if* begins a sentence, the subject and verb of the main clause are inverted, as in (b).* This is a less common usage. No commas are used.

*Other subordinating conjunctions and prepositional phrases preceded by *only* at the beginning of a sentence require subject-verb inversion in the main clause:

Only when the teacher dismisses us **can we stand** and **leave** the room.
Only after the phone rang **did I realize** that I had fallen asleep in my chair.
Only in my hometown **do I feel** at ease.

EXERCISE 37 ▶ Looking at grammar. (Chart 17-11)

Check (✓) the sentences that are true for the situation.

SITUATION: You can take Saturday off only if you work Thursday.

1. _____ You must work Thursday if you want Saturday off.
2. _____ You can take Saturday off if you work another day of your choice.
3. _____ If you work Thursday, you don't have to work Saturday.
4. _____ You can work Thursday, but it's not a requirement if you want Saturday off.

EXERCISE 38 ▶ Looking at grammar. (Chart 17-11)

Read the situations and complete the sentences. Work in pairs, in small groups, or as a class.

SITUATION 1: John must take an additional science class in order to graduate. That is the only condition under which he can graduate. If he doesn't take an additional science class, he can't graduate.

　　He can graduate only if ...
　　→ *He can graduate only if he takes an additional science class.*

SITUATION 2: You have to have an invitation in order to go to the party. That is the only condition under which you will be admitted. If you don't have an invitation, you can't go.

　　You can go to the party only if ...

SITUATION 3: You have to have a student visa in order to study here. Unless you have a student visa, you can't go to school here.

　　You can attend this school only if ...

SITUATION 4: Jimmy's mother doesn't want him to chew gum, but sometimes he chews it anyway.

　　Jimmy ... only if he's sure his mother won't find out.

SITUATION 5: If you want to go to the movie, we'll go. If you don't want to go, we won't go.

　　We ... only if you want to.

SITUATION 6: The temperature has to reach 32°F / 0°C before water will freeze.

　　Water will freeze only if ...

SITUATION 7: You must study hard. Then you will pass the exam.

　　Only if you study hard ...

SITUATION 8: You have to have a ticket. Then you can get into the soccer stadium.

Only if you have a ticket …

SITUATION 9: His parents make Joseph finish his homework before he can have screen time.

Only if Joseph finishes his homework …

SITUATION 10: I have to get a job. Then I will have enough money to go to school.

Only if I get a job …

EXERCISE 39 ▶ Looking at grammar. (Charts 17-10 and 17-11)

Make sentences with the same meaning as the given sentences. Use ***only if*** and ***unless***.

An Illness

1. If you don't stay in bed and rest, you won't recover quickly from the virus.
   → *You will recover quickly from the virus only if you stay in bed and rest.*
   → *You won't recover quickly from the virus unless you stay in bed and rest.*
2. If you don't see the doctor in person, she won't give you a prescription.
3. If you don't have a fever, you can go back to work.
4. If you don't need my help right now, I will leave for a few hours.
5. If you don't have a doctor's note, you can't take sick time.
6. If you don't call the pharmacy now, your prescription won't be ready on time.
7. If you don't take your medicine, you won't get well quickly.

EXERCISE 40 ▶ Looking at grammar. (Charts 17-6 → 17-11)

Combine these two sentences using the words in the list.

It may or may not rain. The party will be held indoors/outdoors.

Example: If
        → *If it rains, the party will be held indoors.*
        → *If it doesn't rain, the party will be held outdoors.*

1. Even if
2. Whether or not
3. In case
4. Unless
5. Only if

EXERCISE 41 ▶ Check your knowledge. (Chapter 17 Review)

Correct the errors.

1. Once we will pay our bills, we'll have little money left over for the holidays.
2. In the case there is an emergency, call the number on this paper.
3. While my parents live nearby, my siblings don't.
4. Unless you have a doctor's note, you can take sick time from work.
5. If tenants will have any questions about the apartment, they need to contact the manager.
6. Only if you help me I will clean the apartment.
7. When Yusef finished medical school at the age of 21.
8. The last time we were at the theater on a holiday weekend.
9. Even I get a promotion to manager, I won't relocate to another city.
10. I care about you if or not you believe me.

EXERCISE 42 ▶ Reading, grammar, and writing. (Chapter 17)

Part I. <u>Underline</u> the words that introduce adverb clauses. What tense is used in these clauses?

How Do People Learn Best?

How do people learn best? There is not one answer since much depends on individual learning styles and needs. Over 300 years ago, however, the noted inventor Benjamin Franklin made some observations regarding learning that still hold true for a great many learners today: "Tell me and I forget. Teach me and I remember. Involve me and I learn."

Imagine that you are learning how to fold a paper airplane. Before you ever pick up a piece of paper, the person says the following:

- Take a piece of paper.
- Fold it in half.
- Open the paper.
- Look at the crease in the middle.
- Now take one corner and fold it down along the crease.

All of the information is presented verbally. How well are you going to learn how to fold a paper airplane so long as the instructor continues in this manner?

Now imagine that your instructor is standing before you with paper and gives the directions while she folds the paper herself. Will this help you more?

Finally, imagine that both you and your instructor have paper. Every time she gives you instructions, both you and she fold your own papers.

Of the three methods, which one will be the most effective in helping you learn how to fold a paper airplane?

It's interesting to think about Benjamin Franklin's quote in relation to learning English. How do you learn English best? Is "being told" effective for you? What about "being taught"? How about "being involved"?

Part II. Think about your experiences learning English vocabulary and complete the sentences with your own words. Punctuate carefully.

1. I remember new words best when _____

2. I often forget the meanings of new words unless _____

3. Even if I _____
_____

4. I _____ only if _____

5. If students want to increase their vocabulary, _____
_____

6. If teachers want to help their class learn new vocabulary, they _____
_____

7. Although _____
_____

8. When I am involved in my learning, I feel _____
_____

Part III. Write one or more paragraphs about how you learn best. Use the questions in the reading and your statements in Part II to help you develop your ideas. You can also include what does not work for you. Organize the points you want to make and support them with examples.

> **WRITING TIP**
>
> Remember that adverb clauses do not always need to come at the beginning of a sentence. In fact, it can become boring if the writer always puts them in the same place. Try to vary your writing by changing the position of the adverb clauses, putting some at the beginning and some later in your sentences.

Part IV. Edit your writing. Check for the following:

1. ☐ a comma at the end of an adverb clause when it begins a sentence
2. ☐ a period, not a comma, between two complete sentences
3. ☐ correct meaning of adverb clauses
4. ☐ the use of *even though* or *even if* instead of *even*
5. ☐ when *only if* begins a sentence, inversion of the subject and verb in the main clause
6. ☐ placement of adverb clauses: not all at the beginning of sentences
7. ☐ correct spelling (use a dictionary or spell-check)

Reduction of Adverb Clauses to Modifying Adverbial Phrases

PRETEST: What do I already know?

Write "C" if a sentence has the correct sentence structure and "I" for incorrect. Check your answers below. After you complete each chart listed, make any necessary corrections.

1. _____ While checking text messages at the bus stop, Janice dropped her phone in a mud puddle. (18-1)

2. _____ Before accepting the job, the company offered Joseph additional vacation days. (18-1)

3. _____ After having completed two years of medical training, Marisa was ready to begin life as a paramedic. (18-2)

4. _____ Since came to this country, I have experienced some interesting cultural traditions. (18-2)

5. _____ Sitting outdoors in the sun, Jenn realized she had forgotten to put on sunscreen. (18-3)

6. _____ While hotel guests were checking in, they were told about holiday specials. (18-3)

7. _____ Not have spent much time with her grandparents when she was younger, Lauren was happy about their summer visit. (18-4)

8. _____ Needed the package by the weekend, Barry paid for express delivery. (18-4)

9. _____ Upon hearing about the promotion of her assistant, Nela sat down at her desk in surprise. (18-5)

10. _____ On learning about genetics and eye color, Sofia began looking more closely at the eye color of her friends and their parents. (18-5)

Incorrect sentences: 2, 4, 7, 8

EXERCISE 1 ▶ Warm-up. (Charts 18-1 and 18-2)
Check (✓) the sentences that are grammatically correct.

1. _____ While riding the elevator, Zac heard a strange noise.

2. _____ While Zac was riding the elevator, it suddenly stopped.

3. _____ While riding the elevator, it suddenly stopped.

4. _____ While ride the elevator, it suddenly stopped.

18-1 Introduction

(a) Adverb clause:	*While I was walking* to class, I ran into an old friend.	In Chapter 13, we discussed changing adjective clauses to modifying phrases. (See Chart 13-11, p. 295.) Some adverb clauses may also be changed to modifying phrases, and the ways in which the changes are made are the same:
(b) Modifying phrase:	*While walking* to class, I ran into an old friend.	
(c) Adverb clause:	*Before I left* for work, I ate breakfast.	• If there is a *be* form of the verb, omit the subject of the dependent clause and *be* verb, as in (b).
(d) Modifying phrase:	*Before leaving* for work, I ate breakfast.	OR • If there is no *be* form of a verb, omit the subject and change the verb to *-ing*, as in (d).
(e) Change possible:	*While I was sitting in class, I* fell asleep. *While sitting in class, I* fell asleep.	An adverb clause can be changed to a modifying phrase **only when the subject of the adverb clause and the subject of the main clause are the same.**
(f) Change possible:	*While Ann was sitting in class, she* fell asleep. (clause) *While sitting in class, Ann* fell asleep.	A *modifying adverbial phrase* that is the reduction of an adverb clause *modifies the subject* of the main clause.
(g) No change possible:	*While the teacher was lecturing to the class, I* fell asleep.*	No reduction (i.e., change) is possible if the subjects of the adverb clause and the main clause are different, as in (g).
(h) INCORRECT:	~~While watching TV last night,~~ the phone rang.	In (h): *While watching* is called a "dangling modifier" or a "dangling participle," i.e., a modifier that is incorrectly "hanging alone" without an appropriate noun or pronoun subject to modify.

While lecturing to the class, **I fell asleep means "While **I** was lecturing to the class, **I** fell asleep."*

EXERCISE 2 ▸ Looking at grammar. (Chart 18-1)

Choose the correct sentence in each pair.

1. a. While sitting at my computer, the fire alarm went off.
   b. While sitting at my computer, I heard the fire alarm go off.

2. a. While standing on the top floor of the building, the crowd below looked like ants.
   b. While standing on the top floor of the building and looking down, Patrick suddenly felt dizzy.

3. a. Before getting up, Mary likes to lie in her warm bed and plan her day.
   b. Before getting up, Mary's alarm clock went off three times by accident.

4. a. While working on his new novel, William found himself telling the story of his childhood.
   b. After finishing his novel, many of William's childhood friends contacted him.

5. a. After standing in line for hours to buy tickets, the manager told us the concert was sold out.
   b. After standing in line for hours to buy tickets, we were told the concert was sold out.

6. a. Before turning in your essay, it is important to check the grammar and spelling.
   b. Before you turn in your essay, it is important to check the grammar and spelling.

18-2 Changing Time Clauses to Modifying Adverbial Phrases

(a) Clause: *Since Maria came* to this country, she has made many friends.	Adverb clauses beginning with **after**, **before**, **when**,* **while**, and **since** can be changed to modifying adverbial phrases.
(b) Phrase: *Since coming* to this country, Maria has made many friends.	
(c) Clause: *When Tyrell cooks,* he uses a lot of spices.	
(d) Phrase: *When cooking,* Tyrell uses a lot of spices.	
(e) Clause: *After he (had) finished* his homework, Peter went to bed.	In (e): There is no difference in meaning between *After he finished* and *After he had finished*.
(f) Phrase: *After finishing* his homework, Peter went to bed.	In (f) and (g): There is no difference in meaning between *After finishing* and *After having finished*.
(g) Phrase: *After having finished* his homework, Peter went to bed.	
(h) Phrase: Peter went to bed *after finishing* his homework.	The modifying adverbial phrase may follow the main clause, as in (h).

*When can also mean "upon." If it has this meaning, it cannot be reduced to a phrase. See Chart 18-5.

EXERCISE 3 ▸ Looking at grammar. (Charts 18-1 and 18-2)

<u>Underline</u> the subject of the adverb clause and the subject of the main clause in each sentence. Change the adverb clauses to modifying adverbial phrases if possible.

1. a. While <u>Joe</u> was driving to school yesterday, <u>he</u> had an accident.
   → *While driving to school yesterday, Joe had an accident.*
   b. While <u>Joe</u> was talking to his insurance company, <u>the police arrived</u>. (*no change*)

2. a. Before I came to class, I stopped in a café for a cup of coffee.
   b. Before the students came to class, they met at a café for lunch.

3. a. Since Alberto moved here, he has been taking business classes.
   b. Since Alberto opened his new business, his family hasn't seen much of him.

4. a. Omar's wife drove Omar to his downtown office after he (had) finished breakfast.
   b. Omar walked up ten flights of stairs to his office after he (had) entered the building.

5. a. When the waiter took my order, I forgot to order a beverage.
   b. When I order coffee, I always ask for extra cream and sugar.

6. a. You should always read a contract carefully before you sign your name.
   b. Before I signed my name, I had a lawyer look over the contract.

7. a. After Karl had been climbing for several hours, his muscles began to ache.
   b. After Karl slipped and lost his footing, he held onto the ledge with all his strength.

EXERCISE 4 ▸ Let's talk: interview. (Chart 18-2)

Ask two classmates each question. Ask them to answer in complete sentences. Share some of their answers with the class.

What do you do …

1. before going to bed?
2. after waking up?
3. after arriving at school?
4. while sitting in class?
5. before leaving school for the day?
6. while preparing for a difficult exam?

EXERCISE 5 ▸ Warm-up. (Charts 18-3 and 18-4)

Read the sentences and answer the questions.

1. Hiking through the woods yesterday, Alan saw a bear.
   QUESTION: Who was hiking through the woods?

2. Walking through the woods, a bear spotted Alan.
   QUESTION: Who was walking through the woods?

18-3	**Expressing the Idea of "During the Same Time" in Modifying Adverbial Phrases**	
(a)	*While I was walking* down the street, *I* ran into an old friend.	Sometimes *while* is omitted, but the *-ing* phrase at the beginning of the sentence gives the same meaning (i.e., "during the same time").
(b)	*While walking* down the street, *I* ran into an old friend.	
(c)	*Walking* down the street, *I* ran into an old friend.	Examples (a), (b), and (c) have the same meaning.

18-4	**Expressing Cause and Effect in Modifying Adverbial Phrases**	
(a)	*Because she needed* some money to buy a book, *Sue* went to a cash machine.	Often an *-ing* phrase at the beginning of a sentence gives the meaning of "because."
(b)	*Needing* some money to buy a book, *Sue* went to a cash machine.	Examples (a) and (b) have the same meaning.
(c)	*Because he lacked* the necessary qualifications, *he* was not considered for the job.	*Because* is not included in a modifying phrase. It is omitted, but the resulting phrase expresses a cause-and-effect relationship, as in (b) and (d).
(d)	*Lacking* the necessary qualifications, *he* was not considered for the job.	
(e)	*Having seen* that movie before, *I don't want* to go again.	*Having* + *past participle* gives the meaning not only of "because" but also of "before."
(f)	*Having seen* that movie before, *I didn't want* to go again.	
(g)	*Because he is* a doctor, Oskar often gets calls in the middle of the night.	A form of *be* in the adverb clause may be changed to *being*. The use of *being* makes the cause-and-effect relationship clear.
(h)	*Being* a doctor, Oskar often gets calls in the middle of the night.	
(i)	*Because she was unable* to afford a car, *she* bought a bike.	Examples (i), (j), and (k) have the same meaning.
(j)	*Being unable* to afford a car, *she* bought a bike.	
(k)	*Unable* to afford a car, *she* bought a bike.	

EXERCISE 6 ▸ Looking at grammar. (Charts 18-3 and 18-4)

<u>Underline</u> the modifying adverbial phrases. Which ones have the meaning of "because"? Which ones have the meaning of "while"? Do some of the sentences give the idea of both?

1. a. <u>Driving to my grandparents' house last night,</u> I saw a young woman who was selling flowers. I stopped so that I could buy some for my grandmother. _____*while*_____

   b. Being a young widow with three children, my grandmother had no choice but to go to work. _____

2. a. Sitting on the airplane and watching the clouds pass beneath me, I let my thoughts wander to the new experiences that were in store for me during the next two years of living abroad. _____

   b. Tapping her fingers loudly on the tray table in front of her, the woman next to me talked about her fear of flying. _____

3. a. Having guessed at the answers for most of the test, I did not expect to get a high score. _____

   b. Realizing that I didn't know much, I began to panic. _____

4. a. Walking down the icy steps without using the handrail, Elena slipped and fell.

   _____

   b. Having broken her arm in the fall, Elena had to learn to write with her left hand.

   _____

EXERCISE 7 ▸ Looking at grammar. (Chart 18-4)

Change the adverb clauses to modifying adverbial phrases.

1. Because David didn't want to hurt her feelings, he ate his girlfriend's salty soup.
   → *Not wanting to hurt her feelings, David ate his girlfriend's salty soup.*

2. Because his girlfriend hadn't tasted the soup, she didn't realize how bad it was.

3. Because David thinks that honesty can be hurtful, he doesn't tell her how he really feels.

4. Because David is a better cook, he does most of the cooking for them.

EXERCISE 8 ▸ Looking at grammar. (Charts 18-2 → 18-4)

Choose <u>all</u> the possible answers for each sentence.

1. Before _____ to you, I had never understood that formula.
   a. talked   b. talking   c. I talked

2. After _____ the chapter four times, I finally understood the author's theory.
   a. I read   b. read   c. reading

3. Since _____ his bachelor's degree, he has had three jobs, each one better than the last.
   a. he completed   b. completing   c. completed

4. _____ across Canada, I could not help being impressed by the great differences in terrain.
   a. Traveling   b. While I was traveling   c. While traveling

5. _____ national fame, the union leader had been an electrician in a small town.
   a. Before gaining   b. He had gained   c. Before he gained

6. _____ in an airplane before, the little girl was surprised and a little frightened when her ears popped.
   a. Had never flown   b. Having never flown   c. Because she had never flown

7. Before _____ vice president of marketing and sales, Peter McKay worked as a sales representative.
   a. became   b. becoming   c. he became

8. _____ the cool evening breeze and listening to the sounds of nature, we lost track of time.
   a. Because enjoying   b. Enjoying   c. We were enjoying

9. _____ to spend any more money this month, Jim decided against going to a café for lunch. He took a sandwich to work instead.
   a. Not wanting   b. Because he didn't want   c. Because not wanting

EXERCISE 9 ▶ Looking at grammar. (Charts 18-3 and 18-4)

Where possible, combine each pair of sentences by making a modifying phrase out of the first sentence.

A Visit Home

1. a. I am a college student. My family doesn't see me so often now. (*no change*)
   b. I am a freshman in college. I spend most weekends in my dorm room doing homework.
      → *Being a freshman in college, I spend most weekends in my dorm room doing homework.*

2. a. My younger siblings had made a "Welcome Home" sign. They were excited to see me.
   b. The kids were excited. I offered to play with them right away.

3. a. My mom lives a long distance from her job. She has to leave early every morning.
   b. My mom spends four hours a day commuting. Her job needs to change.

4. a. I heard that my cousin was in the hospital. I called my aunt to find out how she was doing.
   b. We decided to visit my cousin. A nurse told us she was resting.

5. a. My brother was picking blackberries in the garden. A bee stung him.
   b. My brother didn't want to yell. He began taking deep breaths.

6. a. I recognized my neighbor, but I had forgotten his name. I just smiled and said, "Hi."
   b. He remembered my name as well as my girlfriend's. I felt pretty embarrassed.

7. a. My little sister was convinced she couldn't learn math. I helped her with some lessons.
   b. I was convinced that she had the ability. I encouraged her to keep trying and not give up.

EXERCISE 10 ▸ Game. (Charts 18-3 and 18-4)

Work in teams. Make sentences by combining the ideas in each column. Use the idea on the left as a modifying adverbial phrase. Show logical relationships. The first group to combine all the ideas correctly is the winner.

Example: 1. They give birth only every five years.
→ *Giving birth only every five years, female elephants do not have many offspring.*

1. They give birth only every five years.
2. She has done very well in her studies.
3. She was born two months early.
4. He had done everything he could for the patient.
5. She had never eaten Thai food before.
6. He had no one to turn to for help.
7. They are extremely hard and nearly indestructible.
8. They are able to crawl into very small places.

a. Marta didn't know what to expect when she went to the restaurant for dinner.
b. Mice can hide in almost any part of a house.
c. Sayid was forced to work out the problem by himself.
d. The doctor left to attend other people.
e. Nancy expects to be hired by a top company after graduation.
f. Diamonds are used extensively in industry to cut other hard minerals.
✓ g. Female elephants do not have many offspring.
h. Monique needed special care for the first few weeks of her life.

EXERCISE 11 ▸ Looking at grammar. (Charts 18-1 → 18-4)

Check (✓) the sentences that are grammatically correct. Rewrite the incorrect sentences.

Out and About

1. _____ After leaving the theater, Tom's car wouldn't start, so we had to take a taxi home.
   → *After we left the theater, Tom's car wouldn't start, so we had to take a taxi home.*
   → *After leaving the theater, we discovered that Tom's car wouldn't start, so we took a taxi home.*

2. __✓__ After leaving work late, we stopped at a coffee shop for a late-night snack.

3. _____ While walking across the street at a busy intersection, a truck nearly hit me.

4. _____ Not wanting to miss the last bus, I yelled for it to wait as I ran along the sidewalk.

5. _____ After arriving at a picnic with my cousins, it began to rain quite hard.

6. _____ While waiting for my husband at the mall, a friend from high school called out my name.

7. _____ When asked for directions by a pair of tourists, I stopped to help them.

8. _____ Being from out of town, two streets that had the exact same name confused visitors.

9. _____ Hearing the siren, drivers pulled over and stopped to let the ambulance pass.

10. _____ Honking the horn, the ambulance driver carefully entered each intersection.

EXERCISE 12 ▸ Reading and grammar. (Charts 18-1 → 18-4)

Read the blog entry by author Stacy Hagen. <u>Underline</u> each modifying adverbial phrase and change it to an adverbial clause.

 BlueBookBlog Learning Strategies

There is a lot of interesting research that addresses how students can become more successful learners. In this blog, I'd like to highlight a few strategies for you to think about. While reading them, ask yourself if these strategies would be helpful to you.

1. **Space your practice**: When deciding whether to cram for a test or spread the review out over several days or weeks, you will benefit more by doing the latter, according to researchers. Cramming is very popular with students, but one problem is that it takes more energy to stay focused as the hours pass by. This energy is better used for learning. More important, cramming uses short-term memory. When you space out the practice over time, you activate your long-term memory and learn the material more deeply.

2. **Take a test**: Before beginning to learn new material, test your existing knowledge. For example, take a pretest like the one that opens each chapter of this book. You may get all the answers wrong, but interestingly enough, this doesn't matter. Many scientists believe that pretests help prepare the brain to take in new information. One theory is that our thinking somehow adjusts so that we better know what to look for when learning new material.

   You can also benefit from self-testing. There are many ways to do this, but here are a few common ones. After reading a passage, try to recall the key points from memory. Or, make your own practice questions to answer. Another helpful technique is to quiz yourself frequently with flashcards that you create. These types of self-quizzing force you to use your long-term memory and help you remember better.

3. **Handwrite, rather than type, your notes**. A study at Princeton and UCLA found that students who wrote out their lecture notes were better able to understand concepts and retain information than students who used a laptop. When writing out notes in longhand, students have to think more. They can't write every single word, so they have to comprehend and summarize as they write. With typing, it can become more of an automatic task, and all the words can be included without students' really thinking about them.

EXERCISE 13 ▸ Warm-up. (Chart 18-5)

Which sentences have the same meaning?

1. When Sharon heard the news of her friend's death, she began to cry.
2. Upon hearing the news of her friend's death, Sharon began to cry.
3. On hearing the news of her friend's death, Sharon began to cry.

18-5 Using *Upon* + *-ing* in Modifying Adverbial Phrases

(a) *Upon reaching* the age of 18, I can get my driver's license.	Modifying adverbial phrases beginning with *upon* + *-ing* can have the same meaning as adverb clauses introduced by *when*.
(b) *When I reach* the age of 18, I can get my driver's license.	Examples (a) and (b) have the same meaning.
(c) *On reaching* the age of 18, I can get my driver's license.	*Upon* can be shortened to *on*. Examples (a), (b), and (c) all have the same meaning.

EXERCISE 14 ▸ Looking at grammar. (Chart 18-5)
Make sentences using *upon + -ing* where possible.

1. a. When Carl saw his wife cross the marathon finish line, he broke into a big smile.
   → *Upon seeing his wife cross the marathon finish line, Carl broke into a big smile.*
   b. When Tina crossed the marathon finish line, she collapsed in exhaustion.

2. a. When I looked in my wallet, I saw I didn't have enough money to pay my restaurant bill.
   b. Sam found that the waiter had made a math error when he brought the bill.

3. a. When you finish the examination, bring your paper to the front of the room.
   b. When I finished the exam, I decided to check all my answers again.

4. a. When the kids heard the good news, they jumped up and down with joy.
   b. The kids couldn't contain their excitement when their mom announced the news.

EXERCISE 15 ▸ Looking at grammar. (Chapter 18 Review)
Change the adverb clause in each sentence to a modifying adverbial phrase if possible. Change punctuation, capitalization, and word order as necessary.

1. a. After it spends some time in a cocoon, a caterpillar will emerge as a butterfly.
   → *After spending some time in a cocoon, a caterpillar will emerge as a butterfly.*
   b. When the butterfly emerged from the cocoon, the children became very quiet. (*no change*)

2. a. When we entered the room for the exam, we showed the teacher our ID.
   → *Upon entering the room for the exam, we showed the teacher our ID.*
   b. Because I was unprepared for the test, I didn't do well.
   → *Being unprepared for the test, I didn't do well.* OR *Unprepared for the test, I didn't do well.*

3. a. Jane's family has only received a few text messages since she arrived in Kenya two weeks ago.
   b. Before Jane left on her trip, she worked two jobs to earn enough money for a three-week stay.

4. a. My parents reluctantly agreed to let me attend the concert after they talked it over.
   b. Because I hadn't checked if I had my ticket with me, I arrived at the concert empty-handed.

5. a. Because the forest area is so dry this summer, it is prohibited to light campfires.
   b. Because the forest campsites are very popular, they are often all taken by mid-morning.

6. a. After we had to wait for more than half an hour, we were finally seated at the restaurant.
   b. When I discovered that I had left my wallet in the car, I told my friends to order without me while I went to get it.

EXERCISE 16 ▸ Let's talk. (Chapter 18 Review)
Work in small groups. Imagine your friend is traveling to a foreign country and has never been abroad before. Give advice by making several suggestions for each item.

Advice Before Going Abroad

1. Before leaving on your trip, …
   → *you'll need to get a visa.*
   → *you should find out if you need immunizations.*
   → *give a friend or family member your itinerary.*
   → *don't forget to have someone pick up your mail.*

2. Upon arriving at the airport, ...
3. After getting to your destination, ...
4. When talking with the local people, ...
5. While visiting tourist sites, ...
6. Before leaving for home, ...
7. In general, when traveling to a foreign country, . . .

 EXERCISE 17 ▶ **Listening.** (Chapter 18 Review)
Listen to each conversation. Choose the sentence that has the same meaning.

Example: You will hear: A: William, don't forget to pick up some groceries after work.
                                 B: Oh yeah, thanks. That's the first thing I'll do when I leave the office.

          You will choose: (a.) After leaving work, William will stop at the grocery store.
                                 b.   Before leaving work, William will pick up some groceries.

1. a. Fearing people will laugh at her if she plays the piano, Rose doesn't want to play at the family gathering.
   b. Knowing she plays beautifully, Rose is happy to play the piano at the family gathering.

2. a. Not wanting to upset him, Jan isn't going to talk to Thomas this afternoon.
   b. Hoping to change Thomas's work behavior, Jan is going to talk to him this afternoon.

3. a. Upon finding her wedding ring, Susan hid it in a box.
   b. On finding her wedding ring, Susan felt relieved.

4. a. Never having voted in an election, Sam is taking it very seriously.
   b. Having done a lot of research before choosing a candidate, Sam voted in the presidential election.

EXERCISE 18 ▶ **Reading and grammar.** (Chapter 18 Review)
Modifying adverbial phrases are useful when summarizing information. First, read the passage about the invention of the telephone. It has no modifying adverbial phrases. Then read the summary on the next page and underline the modifying adverbial phrases. How do these phrases allow the ideas to be expressed more briefly yet still clearly?

The First Telephone

Alexander Graham Bell, a teacher of the deaf in Boston, invented the first telephone. One day in 1875, while he was running a test on his latest attempt to create a machine that could carry voices, he accidentally spilled acid on his coat. Naturally, he called for his assistant, Thomas A. Watson, who was in another room. Bell said, "Mr. Watson, come here. I want you." When he heard words coming from the machine, Watson immediately realized that their experiments had at last been successful. He rushed excitedly into the other room to tell Bell that he had heard his words over the machine.

   After he successfully tested the new machine again and again, Bell confidently announced his invention to the world. For the most part, scientists appreciated his accomplishment, but the general public did not understand the revolutionary nature of Bell's invention. Most people believed the telephone was a toy with little practical application, and they paid little attention to Bell's announcement.

Summary

A small accident helped Alexandar Graham Bell with his invention of the telephone. While running a test to create a machine for voices, Bell spilled acid on his coat. He called to Mr. Watson, his assistant, who was in a different room. Watson heard Bell's words coming out of their new machine. Upon realizing what had happened, Watson and Bell knew that the invention was successful. Bell told the world about his discovery after testing the machine multiple times. Scientists understood the value of his work, but the general public, believing the phone was more of a toy, paid little attention to his announcement.

EXERCISE 19 ▸ Reading and writing. (Chapter 18)
Part I. Read the passage.

The QWERTY Keyboard

The letters on an English keyboard have a rather strange placement. If you look at the first row of letters on the keyboard shown, you'll notice that Q-W-E-R-T-Y are the first six letters. At first glance, this design doesn't seem to make a lot of sense, but it turns out there is a logical reason for it.

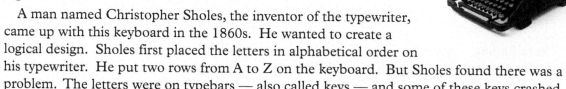

A man named Christopher Sholes, the inventor of the typewriter, came up with this keyboard in the 1860s. He wanted to create a logical design. Sholes first placed the letters in alphabetical order on his typewriter. He put two rows from A to Z on the keyboard. But Sholes found there was a problem. The letters were on typebars — also called keys — and some of these keys crashed into one another. This happened when letters that often occur together in words, like "s" and "l," were near each other on the keyboard. The keys hit each other and got stuck, and the typist had to stop and pull them apart.

Sholes tried to figure out a way to keep the keys from hitting one another. He made a list of letters commonly used together in English, like "s" and "l," or "q" and "u." He then rearranged these letters so they would be on opposite sides of the keyboard. If you look at a keyboard, "q" is on the left side and "u" is on the right side. He put the keys that were most likely to be hit in succession on opposite sides of the keyboard. This keyboard became known as QWERTY.

When we use computers, we don't have to worry about keys crashing into one another, so QWERTY is not necessarily the fastest and most efficient keyboard. People have come up with alternative keyboard patterns, but so far, none has gained much popularity. Since it has survived since the 1860s, QWERTY has demonstrated its longevity. It does not appear that it is going to be replaced any time soon by a faster, more efficient keyboard.

Part II. Write a summary of the passage. You can use the summary in Exercise 17 as a model.*
You may want to work in groups or with a partner first to list the essential information. Include at
least three modifying adverbial phrases in your writing.

> **WRITING TIP**
>
> Good writers avoid wordiness; they edit until they have only the necessary words to express
> their ideas. The use of modifying adverbial phrases is one way to make writing more concise.
> Since sentence variety is important, however, it is important not to reduce every possible
> sentence to a modifying adverbial phrase. A mix of both reduced and non-reduced sentences
> is more interesting.

Part III. Edit your writing. Check for the following:

1. ☐ only essential information in the summary
2. ☐ use of modifying adverbial phrases in some sentences
3. ☐ subjects of the adverb clause and the main clause are the same when modifying adverbial
   phrases are used
4. ☐ subjects omitted in modifying phrases
5. ☐ a comma used when modifying phrase is first in sentence
6. ☐ correct spelling (use a dictionary or spell-check)

---

*See Chapter 10, Exercise 53, p. 214, for more information on how to write a summary.

PRETEST: What do I already know?

Write "C" if a sentence has the correct connecting words and punctuation. Write "I" for incorrect. Check your answers below. After you complete each chart listed, make any necessary corrections.

1. _____ The clinic received complaints about its care, so it began sending out surveys to its patients. (19-1)

2. _____ Because of the roof was leaking, the living room had water on the floor. (19-2)

3. _____ The restaurant offers delicious Indian food. Consequently, there is often a line out the door. (19-3)

4. _____ Because most large grocery stores have delis we have been cooking less. (19-4)

5. _____ Liza got a raise at work; therefore, she celebrated with her husband. (19-4)

6. _____ The waiter was such helpful that I tipped him extra. (19-5)

7. _____ The color of your shirt is so bright that I need to put on my sunglasses! (19-5)

8. _____ Jill exercises at 5:00 A.M. every day so that she can fit it into her day. (19-6)

9. _____ The weather was sunny and warm. Nevertheless, we went to the beach. (19-7)

10. _____ Despite that Andreas is a hard worker, he can't seem to keep a job for more than a few months. (19-7)

11. _____ Malea is loud and funny; her twin sister, on the other hand, is quiet and reserved. (19-8)

12. _____ We need to hurry. Otherwise, we'll catch our plane. (19-9)

Incorrect sentences: 2, 4, 6, 9, 10, 12

EXERCISE 1 ▶ Warm-up. (Chart 19-1)

<u>Underline</u> the connecting words.

1. Even though Tracey is afraid of heights, she decided to take a ride in a hot-air balloon.
2. Tracey was afraid to go by herself, so she invited a friend.
3. The balloon traveled over mountains; consequently, the passengers had stunning views.

19-1 Introduction

Connectives can express cause/effect, contrast, and condition. They can be adverb-clause words, transitions, conjunctions, or prepositions. In Chapter 17 you studied adverb-clause words to express these ideas. In this chapter you will also look at transitions, conjunctions, and prepositions.

(a) *Because* Julian felt sick, he left work early. (b) *Even though* Julian is afraid of doctors, he decided to make an appointment.	The connectives in (a) and (b) are adverb-clause words.
(c) Julian had a rash and fever. *Consequently,* the doctor ran tests. (d) The doctor ran tests. *However,* she found nothing serious.	The connectives in (c) and (d) are transitions.
(e) Julian wasn't seriously ill, *but* his doctor told him to rest anyway. (f) Julian wasn't well, *so* his doctor told him to rest.	The connectives in (e) and (f) are conjunctions.
(g) *Due to* his illness, Julian missed several days of work. (h) He stayed home from work *because of* his illness.	The connectives in (g) and (h) are prepositions.

	Adverb-Clause Words		Transitions	Conjunctions	Prepositions
CAUSE AND EFFECT	because since now that	so (that)	therefore consequently	so	because of due to
CONTRAST	even though although though	while	however nevertheless nonetheless on the other hand	but (... anyway) yet (... still)	despite in spite of
CONDITION	if unless only if even if whether or not	in case	otherwise	or (else)	

EXERCISE 2 ▶ Reading and grammar. (Chart 19-1)

Read the passage and <u>underline</u> the connecting words from Chart 19-1.

A Distracted Driver

Even though Richard was driving the speed limit, he had an accident. The weather was clear; nevertheless, he glanced briefly at a text message. He took his eyes off the road just long enough to lose control and drive over the edge of the road. Fortunately, his car landed upright. Although he wasn't seriously hurt, he was quite shaken up.

This is Richard's second accident this year, so he knows his insurance rates will go up. Now that he's had two accidents, he's upset with himself. However, he knows his wife will be even more upset. He's not looking forward to telling her.

EXERCISE 3 ▸ Warm-up. (Chart 19-2)
Which sentences express the same meaning as the situation and result?

SITUATION: Monday was a holiday.
RESULT: All schools were closed.

1. All schools were closed on Monday because it was a holiday.
2. Because of the holiday, all schools were closed on Monday.
3. Due to the holiday, all schools were closed on Monday.
4. Due to the fact that it was a holiday, all schools were closed on Monday.
5. Because all schools were closed on Monday, it was a holiday.

19-2	Using *Because Of* and *Due To*	
(a)	*Because the weather was cold,* we stayed home.	*Because* introduces an adverb clause; it is followed by a subject and a verb, as in (a).
(b)	*Because of the cold weather,* we stayed home.	*Because of* and *due to* are phrasal prepositions; they are followed by a noun object, as in (b) and (c).
(c)	*Due to the cold weather,* we stayed home.	
(d)	*Due to the fact that* the weather was cold, we stayed home.	Sometimes (usually in more formal writing) *due to* is followed by a noun clause introduced by *the fact that.*
(e)	We stayed home *because of the cold weather.* We stayed home *due to the cold weather.* We stayed home *due to the fact that the weather was cold.*	Like adverb clauses, these phrases can also follow the main clause, as in (e).

EXERCISE 4 ▸ Looking at grammar. (Charts 17-3 and 19-2)
Identify the cause and effect in each pair of sentences. Write "C" for cause and "E" for effect. Then combine the sentences with *because*.

Accomplishments

1. Jon quit smoking. Jon has breathing problems.
   E   *C*
   → *Because Jon has breathing problems, he quit smoking.*

2. Martina feels homesick. Martina moved to a new town.

3. Vivian worked very hard. Vivian won a scholarship.

4. Viktor has lost weight. Viktor reduced his sugar intake.

5. Sanae increased her department's profits. Sanae was promoted to manager.

EXERCISE 5 ▸ Looking at grammar. (Charts 17-3 and 19-2)
Choose <u>all</u> the correct sentences.

1. a. My cell phone doesn't work because the battery is dead.
   b. Because my cell phone doesn't work, the battery is dead.
   c. Because the battery is dead, my cell phone doesn't work.
   d. The battery is dead because my cell phone doesn't work.

2. a. Because Pat doesn't want to return to the Yukon to live, the winters are too severe.
   b. Pat doesn't want to return to the Yukon to live because the winters are too severe.
   c. Because the winters are too severe, Pat doesn't want to return to the Yukon to live.
   d. The winters are too severe because Pat doesn't want to return to the Yukon to live.

EXERCISE 6 ▸ Looking at grammar. (Charts 17-3 and 19-2)
Complete the sentences with *because* or *because of/due to*.

Problems

1. We postponed our trip _____ the bad driving conditions.

2. Sue's eyes were red _____ she had been swimming in a chlorinated pool.

3. We can't visit the museum tomorrow _____ it isn't open.

4. _____ heavy fog at the airport, our plane was delayed

   for several hours.

5. _____ the elevator was broken, we had to walk up six

   flights of stairs.

6. Jim had to stop jogging _____ his sprained ankle.

EXERCISE 7 ▸ Looking at grammar. (Chart 19-2)
Complete the sentences with the ideas in parentheses.

News Reports

1. (*The traffic was heavy.*) Due to _____ *heavy traffic* _____, alternate routes are

   advised into the city.

2. (*Students have the flu.*) Many schools in the district have high absentee rates because of

   _____.

3. (*There are loud noises at the beach.*) Police are investigating reports of illegal fireworks because of

   _____.

4. (*Circumstances are beyond their control.*) Due to _____,

   all City Hall offices are closed today.

5. (*The donors are generous.*) Due to _____, the foods banks

   have enough food for the holidays.

EXERCISE 8 ▸ Warm-up. (Chart 19-3)
Check (✓) the sentences that logically complete the idea of the given sentence.

Nadia likes fresh vegetables.

1. _____ Therefore, she has a vegetable garden in her yard.
2. _____ As a result, she doesn't grow her own vegetables.
3. _____ Therefore, she buys canned vegetables at the store.
4. _____ As a result, she buys produce from local farmers.
5. _____ She eats a lot of frozen vegetables, therefore.
6. _____ Consequently, she eats produce from her garden.

19-3	Cause and Effect: Using *Therefore, Consequently,* and *So*
(a) Al failed the test because he didn't study. (b) Al didn't study. *Therefore,* he failed the test. (c) Al didn't study. *Consequently,* he failed the test.	Examples (a), (b), and (c) have the same meaning. **Therefore** and **consequently** mean "as a result." In grammar, they are called *transitions* (or *conjunctive adverbs*). Transitions connect the ideas between two sentences. They are used most commonly in formal written English and rarely in spoken English.

(d) Al didn't study. *Therefore,* he failed the test.
(e) Al didn't study. He, *therefore,* failed the test.
(f) Al didn't study. He failed the test, *therefore.*
 	
POSITIONS OF A TRANSITION:
 	
transition + **S** + **V** (+ rest of sentence)
   S + **transition** + **V** (+ rest of sentence)
   S + **V** (+ rest of sentence) + **transition**
	A transition occurs in the second of two related sentences.
	
	Notice the patterns and punctuation in the examples. A period (NOT a comma) is used at the end of the first sentence.*
	
	The transition has several positions in the second sentence. It is separated from the rest of the sentence by commas.

(g) Al didn't study, *so* he failed the test.	In (g): *So* is used as a *conjunction* between two independent clauses. It has the same meaning as **therefore**. **So** is common in both formal written and spoken English. A comma usually precedes **so** when it connects two sentences, as in (g).

*A semicolon is also possible in this situation: *Al didn't study; therefore, he failed the test.* See the footnote to Chart 19-4.

EXERCISE 9 ▸ Looking at grammar. (Chart 19-3)
Rewrite the sentence with the given words. Punctuate carefully.

The runner can compete in races because he wears a special blade attached at his knee.

1. therefore _____
   _____

2. consequently _____
   _____

3. so _____
   _____

EXERCISE 10 ▶ Looking at grammar. (Charts 17-3, 19-2, and 19-3)
Punctuate the sentences. Add capital letters as necessary. NOTE: Two sentences need no changes.

1. *adverb clause:*   Because it was cold she wore a coat.

2. *adverb clause:*   She wore a coat because it was cold.

3. *prepositional phrase:*   Because of the cold weather she wore a coat.

4. *prepositional phrase:*   She wore a coat because of the cold weather.

5. *transition:*   The weather was cold therefore she wore a coat.

6. *transition:*   The weather was cold she wore a coat therefore.

7. *conjunction:*   The weather was cold so she wore a coat.

EXERCISE 11 ▶ Looking at grammar. (Charts 17-3, 19-2, and 19-3)
Punctuate the sentences. Add capital letters as necessary.

A Storm

1. Freezing rain fell on the city it was unsafe to walk outside because of slippery streets and falling branches.

2. Due to improvements in weather forecasting people knew about the storm well in advance.

3. The storm damaged the power lines consequently the town was without electricity.

4. Due to the snowstorm only two students came to class the teacher therefore canceled the class.

EXERCISE 12 ▶ Warm-up. (Chart 19-4)
Check (✓) the sentences that have the correct punctuation.

1. _____ Some doctors recommend yoga for their patients. Because it can lower stress.

2. _____ Because yoga can lower stress some doctors recommend it for their patients.

3. _____ Yoga can lower stress. Some doctors, therefore, recommend it for their patients.

4. _____ Yoga can lower stress, so some doctors recommend it for their patients.

19-4 Summary of Patterns and Punctuation

ADVERB CLAUSES	(a) *Because it was hot,* we went swimming. (b) We went swimming *because it was hot.*	An *adverb clause* may precede or follow an independent clause. PUNCTUATION: A comma is used if the adverb clause comes first.
PREPOSITIONS	(c) *Because of the hot weather,* we went swimming. (d) We went swimming *because of the hot weather.*	A *preposition* is followed by a noun object, not by a subject and verb. PUNCTUATION: A comma is usually used if the prepositional phrase precedes the subject and verb of the independent clause.
TRANSITIONS	(e) It was hot. *Therefore,* we went swimming. (f) It was hot. We, *therefore,* went swimming. (g) It was hot. We went swimming, *therefore.* (h) It was hot; *therefore,* we went swimming.	A *transition* is used with the second sentence of a pair. It shows the relationship of the second idea to the first idea. A transition is movable within the second sentence. PUNCTUATION: A semicolon (;) may be used in place of a period, as in (h).* NOTE: A period is used between the two independent clauses in (e)–(g); a comma is not possible. Commas are usually used to set the transition off from the rest of the sentence.
CONJUNCTIONS	(i) It was hot, *so we went swimming.*	A conjunction comes between two independent clauses. PUNCTUATION: Usually a comma is used immediately in front of a conjunction.

* In general, a semicolon can be used instead of a period between any two sentences that are closely related in meaning: *Peanuts are not nuts; they are beans.* Notice that a small letter, NOT a capital letter, immediately follows a semicolon.

EXERCISE 13 ▸ Looking at grammar. (Charts 17-3 and 19-4)
Choose all the correct sentences.

1. a. It is important to wear a hat on cold days, since we lose 60% of our body heat through our head.
   b. Since we lose about 60% of our body heat through our head, it is important to wear a hat on cold days.
   c. It is important to wear a hat on cold days since we lose about 60% of our body heat through our head.

2. a. Bill's car wouldn't start; therefore, he couldn't pick us up after the concert.
   b. Bill's car wouldn't start. Therefore, he couldn't pick us up after the concert.
   c. Bill's car wouldn't start, therefore, he couldn't pick us up after the concert.

3. a. When I was in my teens and twenties, it was easy for me to get into an argument with my father because both of us can be stubborn and opinionated.
   b. When I was in my teens and twenties, it was easy for me to get into an argument with my father. Because both of us can be stubborn and opinionated.
   c. When I was in my teens and twenties, it was easy for me to get into an argument with my father, because both of us can be stubborn and opinionated.

4. a. Robert got some new business software that didn't work; so he emailed the software company for technical support.

   b. Robert got some new business software that didn't work, so he emailed the software company for technical support.

   c. Robert got some new business software that didn't work so he emailed the software company for technical support.

EXERCISE 14 ▸ Looking at grammar. (Charts 17-3 and 19-4)
Combine the sentences using the given words. Discuss correct punctuation.

We postponed our trip. The weather was bad.

Example: because → *We postponed our trip **because** the weather was bad.*
        → ***Because** the weather was bad, we postponed our trip.*

1. therefore	3. so	5. consequently
2. since	4. because of	6. due to the fact that

EXERCISE 15 ▸ Looking at grammar. (Charts 17-2 and 19-4)
Combine each pair of ideas with the words in parentheses.

Did you know ... ?

1. A camel can go completely without water for eight to ten days. It is an ideal animal for desert areas. (*due to the fact that*)

2. A tomato is classified as a fruit, but most people consider it a vegetable. It is often eaten in salads along with lettuce, onions, cucumbers, and other vegetables. (*since*)

3. There is a consumer demand for ivory. Many African elephants are being slaughtered ruthlessly. Many people who care about saving these animals from extinction refuse to buy any item made from ivory. (*due to, consequently*)

4. Most 15th-century Europeans believed the world was flat and that a ship could conceivably sail off the end of the earth. Many sailors of the time refused to venture forth with explorers into unknown waters. (*because*)

EXERCISE 16 ▸ Warm-up. (Chart 19-5)
Create humorous sayings by matching a phrase on the left with one on the right.

1. It's such a hot day that I could _____
2. I'm so hungry that I could _____
3. He is such a rich man that he _____
4. She is so sick that she _____

a. buys a new boat when one gets wet.
b. needs two beds.
c. eat a horse.
d. fry an egg on the sidewalk.

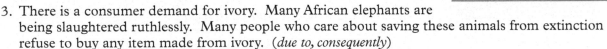

19-5 Other Ways of Expressing Cause and Effect: *Such ... That* and *So ... That*

(a) Because the weather was nice, we went to the zoo. (b) It was *such nice weather that* we went to the zoo. (c) The weather was *so nice that* we went to the zoo.	Examples (a), (b), and (c) have the same meaning.
(d) It was *such good coffee that* I had another cup. (e) It was *such a foggy day that* we couldn't see the road.	*Such ... that* encloses a modified noun: *such + adjective + noun + that*
(f) The coffee is *so hot that* I can't drink it. (g) I'm *so hungry that* I could eat a horse. (h) She speaks *so fast that* I can't understand her. (i) He walked *so quickly that* I couldn't keep up with him.	*So ... that* encloses an adjective or adverb: *so +* $\left\{\begin{array}{c} adjective \\ or \\ adverb \end{array}\right\}$ *+ that*
(j) She made *so many mistakes that* she failed the exam. (k) He has *so few friends that* he is always lonely. (l) She has *so much money that* she can buy whatever she wants. (m) He had *so little trouble* with the test *that* he left 20 minutes early.	*So ... that* is used with *many, few, much,* and *little.*
(n) It was *such a good book (that)* I couldn't put it down. (o) I was *so hungry (that)* I didn't wait for dinner to eat something.	Sometimes, primarily in speaking, *that* is omitted.

EXERCISE 17 ▶ Looking at grammar. (Chart 19-5)

Complete the sentences with *so* or *such*.

1. a. It was _____*such*_____ an enjoyable party that no one wanted to leave.

   b. The party was _____*so*_____ enjoyable that no one wanted to leave.

   c. We had _____*so*_____ much fun that no one wanted to leave.

2. a. Leta is _____ afraid of flying that she traveled by train across Canada.

   b. She was gone for _____ a long time that she got homesick.

   c. People on the train were _____ kind that she will always remember them.

3. a. My elderly aunt has _____ few friends that I am beginning to worry about her.

   b. She's not poor, but she spends _____ little money that I'm not sure she's eating right.

   c. I've wanted to visit _____ many times, but she always says no.

4. a. The movie was _____ scary that none of us could sleep last night.

   b. We were _____ scared that we held hands when we walked home.

   c. I was afraid of having _____ bad dreams that I didn't sleep well for a week.

EXERCISE 18 ▶ Let's talk. (Chart 19-5)

Work in small groups. Take turns making sentences using *so/such ... that.* Try to exaggerate your answers. Share your favorite sentences with the class.

Example: I'm hungry. In fact, I'm ... → *I'm **so** hungry (**that**) I could eat a horse.*

Exaggerations

1. I'm really tired. In fact, I'm ....
2. I didn't expect it! I was really surprised. In fact, I was ...
3. I took a very slow bus to town. In fact, it was ...
4. We watched a very exciting movie. In fact, it was ...
5. The weather was really, really hot. In fact, it was ...
6. My wallet fell out of my pocket and I lost a lot of money. In fact, I lost ...
7. I ordered an expensive meal at a restaurant. The server brought a small plate with a tiny amount of food to my table. In fact, it was ...
8. I saw a shark while I was swimming in the ocean. I was frightened. In fact, I was ...

EXERCISE 19 ▶ Looking at grammar. (Chart 19-5)

Make new sentences using **so** or **such** by combining each sentence on the left with the appropriate sentence on the right. Make all necessary changes.

Example: 1. There are many pine cones on that tree.
   → *There are **so** many pine cones on that tree that it is impossible to count them.*

a pine cone

1. There are many pine cones on that tree.
2. The radio was too loud.
3. Olga did poor work.
4. The food was too hot.
5. The wind was strong.
6. The tornado struck with great force.
7. Few students showed up for class.
8. Charles used too much paper when he wrote his report.

a. It burned my tongue.
b. She was fired from her job.
c. It blew my hat off my head.
d. The teacher postponed the test.
✓ e. It is impossible to count them.
f. It lifted cars off the ground.
g. I couldn't hear what Michael was saying.
h. The printer ran out of ink.

EXERCISE 20 ▶ Warm-up. (Chart 19-6)

Check (✓) the sentences that correctly complete the given sentence.

Kay got a new job so that ...

1. _____ she could be closer to home.
2. _____ she is very excited.
3. _____ her husband is taking her out to dinner to celebrate.
4. _____ she could earn more money.

19-6	**Expressing Purpose: Using *So That***

| (a) I turned off the TV ***in order to*** enable my roommate to study in peace and quiet. | ***In order to*** expresses *purpose*. (See Chart 15-1, p. 335.) |
| (b) I turned off the TV ***so*** (***that***) my roommate could study in peace and quiet. | In (a): I turned off the TV for a purpose. The purpose was to make it possible for my roommate to study in peace and quiet. Examples (a) and (b) have the same meaning. |

So That + Can or Could

(c) I'm going to cash a check ***so that I can*** buy my textbooks.	***So that*** also expresses *purpose*.* It expresses the same meaning as ***in order to***. The word *that* is often omitted, especially in speaking.
(d) I cashed a check ***so that I could*** buy my textbooks.	***So that*** is often used instead of ***in order to*** when the idea of ability is being expressed. ***Can*** is used in the adverb clause for a present/future meaning.
	In (c): ***so that I can buy*** = *in order to be able to buy*
	Could is used after ***so that*** in past sentences, as in (d).**

So That + Will / Would or Simple Present

(e) I'll take my umbrella ***so that I won't*** get wet.	In (e): ***so that I won't get wet*** = *in order to make sure that I won't get wet*
(f) Yesterday I took my umbrella ***so that I wouldn't*** get wet.	***Would*** is used in past sentences, as in (f).
(g) I'll take my umbrella ***so that I don't*** get wet.	In (g): It is sometimes possible to use the simple present after ***so that*** in place of ***will***; the simple present expresses a future meaning.

*NOTE: *In order that* has the same meaning as *so that* but is less commonly used.
   Example: *I turned off the TV **in order that** my roommate could study in peace and quiet.*
Both *so that* and *in order that* introduce adverb clauses. It is unusual but possible to put these adverb clauses at the beginning of a sentence: ***So that** my roommate could study in peace and quiet, I turned off the TV.*

Also possible but less common: the use of ***may* or ***might*** in place of ***can*** or ***could*** (e.g., *I cashed a check **so that I might** buy my textbooks.*).

EXERCISE 21 ▶ Looking at grammar. (Chart 19-6)

Combine the sentences by using ***so*** (***that***).

1. a. Please turn down your music. I want to be able to get to sleep.
      → *Please turn down your music so (that) I can get to sleep.*
   b. My wife turned down her music. I wanted to be able to get to sleep.
      → *My wife turned down her music so (that) I could get to sleep.*

2. a. Put the milk in the refrigerator. We want to make sure it won't/doesn't spoil.
   → *Put the milk in the refrigerator so (that) it won't/doesn't spoil.*

   b. I put the milk in the refrigerator. I wanted to make sure it didn't spoil.
   → *I put the milk in the refrigerator so (that) it wouldn't spoil.*

3. a. Please be quiet. I want to be able to hear what Sharon is saying.
   b. I asked the children to be quiet. I wanted to be able to hear what Sharon was saying.

4. a. I'm going to go to a cash machine. I want to make sure that I have enough money to go to the store.
   b. I went to a cash machine yesterday. I wanted to make sure that I had enough money to go to the store.

5. a. Ann and Larry have a six-year-old child. Tonight they're going to hire a babysitter. They want to be able to go out with some friends.
   b. Last week Ann and Larry hired a babysitter. They wanted to be able to go to a dinner party at the home of Larry's boss.

6. a. Yesterday I put the meat in the oven at 5:00. I wanted it to be ready to eat by 6:30.
   b. Be sure to put the meat in the oven at 5:00. You want to be sure that it will be (OR is) ready to eat by 6:30.

7. a. I'm going to leave the party early. I want to be able to get a good night's sleep tonight.
   b. I'm not going to look at any messages on my phone or computer before I go to sleep. I want to be sure that my mind is free of distractions.

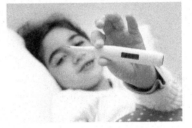

8. a. Tommy pretended to be sick. He wanted to stay home from school.
   b. He held a thermometer under hot water. He wanted it to show a high temperature.

EXERCISE 22 ▸ Looking at grammar. (Charts 19-4 and 19-6)

Add *that* to the sentence if *so* means *in order that*. If *so* means *therefore*, add a comma.

Needs

1. I need to borrow some money so _^ I can pay my rent. *[that inserted above]*

2. I didn't have enough money for the movie, so I asked my friend to buy my ticket.

3. I need a visa so I can travel overseas.

4. I needed a visa so I went to the embassy to apply for one.

5. Marta is trying to improve her English so she can become a tour guide.

6. Olga wants to improve her English so she has hired a tutor.

7. Tarek borrowed money from his parents so he could start his own business.

8. I turned off my phone so I can concentrate on my paperwork.

EXERCISE 23 ▶ Warm-up. (Chart 19-7)

Usually when someone breaks an arm, he/she goes to a doctor. That is expected behavior. Answer the same question about expected behavior for each statement. Circle *yes* or *no*.

	EXPECTED BEHAVIOR?

1. Ron broke his arm, but he didn't go to the doctor.   yes   no
2. Joe went to the doctor because he broke his arm.   yes   no
3. Sue broke her arm, so she went to the doctor.   yes   no
4. Amy broke her arm; nevertheless, she didn't go to the doctor.   yes   no
5. Despite having a broken arm, Rick didn't go to the doctor.   yes   no
6. Jeff broke his arm; therefore, he went to the doctor.   yes   no

19-7 Showing Contrast (Unexpected Result)

All of these sentences have the same meaning. The idea of cold weather is contrasted with the idea of going swimming. Usually if the weather is cold, one does not go swimming, so going swimming in cold weather is an "unexpected result." It is surprising that the speaker went swimming in cold weather.

ADVERB CLAUSES	*even though*	(a) *Even though* it was cold, I went swimming.
	although	(b) *Although* it was cold, I went swimming.
	though	(c) *Though* it was cold, I went swimming.*
CONJUNCTIONS	*but ... anyway*	(d) It was cold, *but* I went swimming (*anyway*).
	but ... still	(e) It was cold, *but* I (*still*) went swimming.
	yet ... still	(f) It was cold, *yet* I (*still*) went swimming.
TRANSITIONS	*nevertheless*	(g) It was cold. *Nevertheless,* I went swimming.
	nonetheless	(h) It was cold; *nonetheless,* I went swimming.
	however ... still	(i) It was cold. *However,* I (*still*) went swimming.
PREPOSITIONS	*despite*	(j) I went swimming *despite* the cold weather.
	in spite of	(k) I went swimming *in spite of* the cold weather.
	despite the fact that	(l) I went swimming *despite the fact that* the weather was cold.
	in spite of the fact that	(m) I went swimming *in spite of the fact that* the weather was cold.

* Another way to show contrast is to put *though* at the end of the sentence: *It was cold. I went swimming, though.* The meaning is similar to *but* (e.g., *It was cold, but I went swimming.*); however, *though* is softer. This usage is very common in spoken English.

EXERCISE 24 ▶ Looking at grammar. (Charts 19-3 and 19-7)

Complete the sentences with *inside* or *outside* to make logical statements.

1. It rained, but we had our wedding _____ anyway.
2. It rained, so we had our wedding _____.
3. It rained; nevertheless, we had our wedding _____.
4. Though it rained, we had our wedding _____.
5. Even though it rained, we had our wedding _____.
6. Although it rained, we had our wedding _____.
7. Despite the fact that it rained, we had our wedding _____.
8. It rained; therefore, we had our wedding _____.

EXERCISE 25 ▸ Looking at grammar. (Chart 19-7)
Complete the sentences with **was** or **wasn't** to make logical statements.

1. Hans had worked a 24-hour shift; nevertheless, he _____ wide-awake.

2. Though he had worked a 24-hour shift, he _____ sleepy.

3. Even though he had worked a 24-hour shift, he _____ wide-awake.

4. Hans _____ wide-awake although he had worked a 24-hour shift.

5. He had worked a 24-hour shift, yet he _____ wide-awake.

6. Despite the fact that he had worked a 24-hour shift, Hans _____ sleepy.

7. In spite of working a 24-hour shift, Hans _____ wide-awake.

EXERCISE 26 ▸ Looking at grammar. (Chart 19-7)
Part I. Complete the sentences with **but, even though,** or **nevertheless**. Notice the use of punctuation and capitalization.

1. a. Bob ate a large dinner. _____, he is still hungry.

   b. Bob ate a large dinner, _____ he is still hungry.

   c. Bob is still hungry _____ he ate a large dinner.

2. a. I had a lot of studying to do, _____ I went to a movie anyway.

   b. I had a lot of studying to do. _____, I went to a movie.

   c. _____ I had a lot of studying to do, I went to a movie.

3. a. I finished all of my work _____ I was very sleepy.

   b. I was very sleepy, _____ I finished all of my work anyway.

   c. I was very sleepy. _____, I finished all of my work.

Part II. Complete the sentences with **yet, although,** or **however**.

4. a. I washed my hands. _____, they still looked dirty.

   b. I washed my hands, _____ they still looked dirty.

   c. _____ I washed my hands, they still looked dirty.

5. a. Diana didn't know how to swim, _____ she jumped into the pool.

   b. _____ Diana didn't know how to swim, she jumped into the pool.

   c. Diana didn't know how to swim. _____, she jumped into the pool.

EXERCISE 27 ▸ Looking at grammar. (Chart 19-7)
Add commas, periods, and capital letters as necessary. Do not add, omit, or change any words.

1. a. Anna's father gave her some good advice nevertheless she did not follow it.
      → *Anna's father gave her some good advice. Nevertheless, she did not follow it.*

   b. Anna's father gave her some good advice though she didn't follow it.

   c. Even though Anna's father gave her some good advice she didn't follow it.

   d. Anna's father gave her some good advice she did not follow it however.

2. a. Thomas has been broke* for months I offered him some money he refused it.

b. Thomas refused the money although he has been broke for months.

c. Thomas has been broke for months nevertheless he refused the money that I offered him.

d. Thomas has been broke for months yet he still refused the money that I offered him.

EXERCISE 28 ▸ Looking at grammar. (Chart 19-7)

Work in pairs or small groups. Combine the sentences using the given words. Discuss correct punctuation. Use the negative if necessary to make a logical statement.

His grades were low. He was admitted to the university.

1. even though	3. yet ... still	5. despite
2. but ... anyway	4. nonetheless	6. despite the fact that

EXERCISE 29 ▸ Warm-up. (Chart 19-8)

Read the question and the answers. Which answers express "direct contrast," i.e., the idea that "this" is the opposite of "that"?

What is the difference between hurricanes and tornadoes?

a hurricane

1. Hurricanes develop over warm oceans while tornadoes form over land.
2. Hurricanes develop while they are traveling over warm ocean water.
3. Hurricanes develop over warm oceans, but tornadoes form over land.
4. Hurricanes develop over warm oceans; however, tornadoes form over land.
5. Hurricanes develop over warm oceans; on the other hand, tornadoes form over land.

19-8 Showing Direct Contrast

All of the sentences have the same meaning: "This" is the opposite of "that."

ADVERB CLAUSES	while	(a) Mary is rich, **while** John is poor.*
		(b) John is poor, **while** Mary is rich.
CONJUNCTIONS	but	(c) Mary is rich, **but** John is poor.
		(d) John is poor, **but** Mary is rich.
TRANSITIONS	however	(e) Mary is rich; **however**, John is poor.
		(f) John is poor; Mary is rich, **however**.
	on the other hand	(g) Mary is rich. John, **on the other hand**, is poor.
		(h) John is poor. Mary, **on the other hand**, is rich.

*Sometimes a comma precedes a *while*-clause that shows direct contrast. A comma helps clarify that *while* is being used to express contrast rather than time. The use of a comma in this instance is a stylistic choice by the writer.

---

be broke = have no money

EXERCISE 30 ▶ Looking at grammar. (Chart 19-8)

For each sentence, make two sentences with the same meaning using **however** and **on the other hand**. Punctuate carefully. Write your sentences on a separate piece of paper.

1. My grandfather is quite active, while my grandmother is often in bed.
2. While my grandmother has a sunny personality, my grandfather is more negative.
3. Elderly people in my country usually live with their children, but the elderly in the United States often live by themselves.

EXERCISE 31 ▶ Looking at grammar. (Chart 19-8)

Complete the sentences with your own words.

Customs

1. In some countries, people greet each other by shaking hands, while in other countries … *people kiss one another on the cheek.*
2. In the United States, people drive on the right-hand side of the road while people in …
3. While in Japan people must take off their shoes before entering a house, in some countries …
4. In some cultures, it is considered impolite to look directly at another person, while in others …

EXERCISE 32 ▶ Speaking or writing. (Chart 19-8)

Extroverts and Introverts

Part I. Read the information below about extroverts and introverts. Make several sentences with the words in the lists either orally or in writing using the words **but, however, on the other hand,** or **while**.

Examples:
→ *Extroverts like to talk more than listen,* **while** *introverts like to listen more than talk.*
→ *Introverts like to listen more than talk. Extroverts,* **however,** *like to talk more than listen.*

Extroverts …
    like to be the center of attention.
    like to talk more than listen.
    enjoy meeting people.
    prefer being active.
    like to work in groups.
    don't always think before speaking.
    don't mind noise.
    like crowds.
    are energized by being with others.

Introverts …
    are uncomfortable being the center of attention.
    like to listen more than talk.
    are reserved when meeting people.
    like to spend time alone.
    don't like to work in groups.
    think carefully before speaking.
    prefer the quiet.
    avoid crowds.
    can find it tiring to spend time with others.

Part II. Are you an extrovert or introvert? Compare yourself to someone you know who is different from you. Make several sentences.

EXERCISE 33 ▸ Let's talk. (Chart 19-8)

Think of two different countries you are familiar with. How are they different? Use **while, however, on the other hand,** and **but.** Work in pairs, in small groups, or as a class.

1. size
2. population
3. food
4. time of meals
5. economic system
6. educational system
7. role of women
8. language
9. cost of education
10. medical care
11. public transportation
12. dating customs

EXERCISE 34 ▸ Warm-up. (Chart 19-9)

Choose the logical verb for each sentence: **can** or **can't.**

SITUATION: Daniel needs coffee every morning. It wakes him up.

1. If Daniel drinks coffee in the morning, he   can / can't wake up quickly.

2. Unless Daniel drinks coffee in the morning, he   can / can't wake up quickly.

3. Daniel needs coffee every morning; otherwise, he   can / can't wake up quickly.

4. Daniel needs coffee in the morning, or else he   can / can't wake up quickly.

19-9 Expressing Conditions: Using *Otherwise* and *Or (Else)*

ADVERB CLAUSES	(a) *If I don't eat breakfast,* I get hungry. (b) You'll be late *if you don't hurry.* (c) You'll get wet *unless you take your umbrella.*	*If* and *unless* state conditions that produce certain results. (See Charts 17-6 and 17-10, pp. 382 and 387.)
TRANSITIONS	(d) I always eat breakfast. *Otherwise,* I get hungry during class. (e) You'd better hurry. *Otherwise,* you'll be late. (f) Take your umbrella. *Otherwise,* you'll get wet.	*Otherwise* expresses the idea "if the opposite is true, then there will be a certain result." In (d): *otherwise = if I don't eat breakfast*
CONJUNCTIONS	(g) I always eat breakfast, *or (else)* I get hungry during class. (h) You'd better hurry, *or (else)* you'll be late. (i) Take your umbrella, *or (else)* you'll get wet.	*Or else* and *otherwise* have the same meaning.

EXERCISE 35 ▸ Looking at grammar. (Chart 19-9)

Make sentences with the same meaning as the given sentence. Use **otherwise.**

Chores

1. If I don't clean the fridge, my roommate will start complaining about how messy I am.
   → *I need to / should / had better / have to / clean the fridge. Otherwise, my roommate will start complaining about how messy I am.*

2. If I don't wash my clothes tonight, I won't have any clean clothes to wear tomorrow.

3. If we don't start cooking dinner now, it won't be ready in time.

4. I won't be able to sleep unless I change my sheets.

5. Only if you help me get ready for the party will I have one.*
6. Unless we clear the snow from the walkway, people could slip and fall.
7. I'll get everything done only if I begin as soon as I get home.
8. If you don't start soon, the weekend will be over!

EXERCISE 36 ▸ Looking at grammar. (Chapter 19 Review)
Using the two ideas of "to study" and "to pass or fail the exam," complete the sentences. Punctuate and capitalize as necessary.

1. Because I did not study ___, *I failed the exam.* _____
2. I failed the exam because _____
3. Although I studied _____
4. I did not study therefore _____
5. I did not study however _____
6. I studied nevertheless _____
7. Even though I did not study _____
8. I did not study so _____
9. Since I did not study _____
10. If I study for the exam _____
11. Unless I study for the exam _____
12. I must study otherwise _____
13. Even if I study _____
14. I did not study consequently _____
15. I did not study nonetheless _____
16. I will probably fail the exam whether _____
17. Only if I study _____
18. I studied hard yet _____
19. You'd better study or else _____

EXERCISE 37 ▸ Listening. (Chapter 19 Review)
Listen to each sentence and choose the logical completion.

Example: You will hear: I was exhausted when I got home, but …
      You will choose: (a.) I didn't take a nap.   b. I took a nap.

1. a. my back gets sore.   b. my back doesn't get sore.
2. a. my old one works fine.   b. my old one doesn't work.

*Notice that the subject and verb in the main clause are inverted because the sentence begins with *Only if.* See Chart 17-11, p. 388.

3. a. I hurry.   b. I don't hurry.

4. a. I hurried.   b. I didn't hurry.

5. a. our offices are hot.   b. our offices aren't hot.

6. a. the noise bothers me.   b. the noise doesn't bother me.

7. a. I fell asleep during dinner.   b. I didn't fall asleep during dinner.

EXERCISE 38 ▸ Game. (Chapter 19 Review)

Work in teams. Combine these two ideas using the words below the example. The time is now, so use present and future tenses. The team with the most correct sentences wins.

to go (or not to go) to the beach \ hot, cold, nice weather

Example: because
> → **Because** *the weather is cold, we aren't going to go to the beach.*
> → *We're going to go to the beach* **because** *the weather is hot.*

1. so … that
2. so
3. nevertheless
4. despite
5. now that
6. once
7. although

8. because of
9. consequently
10. as soon as
11. such … that
12. since
13. but … anyway
14. unless

15. therefore
16. only if
17. nonetheless
18. in spite of
19. even if
20. yet … still
21. whether … or not

 ## EXERCISE 39 ▸ Grammar, reading, and listening. (Chapter 19 Review)

Complete the lecture with the words in the box. Then listen and check your answers. One word is used two times.

however	if	therefore
so that	while	since

Why We Yawn

Have you ever noticed that when a person near you yawns, you may start yawning too? This is called contagious yawning. *Contagious* in this sense means that the behavior spreads: in the case of yawning, when one person yawns, it can cause others to do the same thing.

There are various theories about why people yawn. One popular idea is that yawning brings more oxygen into the brain _____ people will wake up. Is that what you have thought?

_____, in 2007, researchers at a university in New York came up with a new idea:
yawning helps cool the brain. When people's brains are warm, they yawn more frequently; yawning brings cooler air into the body and, _____, cools the brain. This is important because cooler brains work better than warmer ones.

This may also help explain why yawning is contagious. People are more awake when their brains are cooler; _____, contagious yawning helps people be more alert. As people evolved, this was important in times of danger. _____ they yawned, they could have been signaling to others to stay awake.

_____ it can be annoying to have a person yawn when you are talking, perhaps you can tell yourself that he or she actually wants to stay awake, not go to sleep.

EXERCISE 40 ▶ Check your knowledge. (Chapter 19 Review)
Correct the errors

1. The hotel had a mistake on its website. The price was very low so that many people wanted rooms.
2. Due to medical care costs a lot in the U.S., people need to have insurance.
3. The dorm room I was assigned to has a broken heater, therefore, I have complained to the office.
4. Because Jamal's visa has expired, he waited too long to renew it.
5. Jenn had surprisingly low test scores. However, the college she chose didn't admit her.
6. Despite the weather is freezing today, I'm going to take a run in the park.
7. It was such a hard test no one finished on time.
8. We should leave now, otherwise, we will get stuck in traffic.
9. The electric bill was months overdue; nevertheless, the power company turned off the power to the home.
10. Please talk more quietly so that we could hear the speaker.
11. You should apply for a scholarship soon unless you don't want to miss the deadline.
12. Since you should change your password, many people know it.
13. My parents bought a house in our neighborhood so that they are going to be closer to their grandchildren.

Part I. Read the passage comparing optimists and pessimists.

Optimists **vs.** Pessimists

How do you see the glass in the picture? Is it half empty or half full? People who say it is half empty are called pessimists, while people who say it is half full are called optimists. In simple terms, optimists see the best in the world, while pessimists see the worst.

One of the clearest ways to see the differences between the two is to look at the way optimists and pessimists explain events. When something bad happens, optimists tend to see the event as a single occurrence that does not affect other areas of their lives.

For example, Sarah is an optimistic person. When she gets a low grade on a test, she will say something like this to herself: "Oh well, that was one test I didn't do well on. I wasn't feeling well that day. I have another test in a few weeks. I'll do better on that one."

Pessimists, on the other hand, will feel that an event is just one of a string of bad events that affects their lives, and somehow they are the cause of it. Let's take a look at Susan. She is a pessimist. When she gets a low grade on a test, she might say: "I failed again. I never do well on tests. I'm stupid. Why even try?" And when something does go well for Susan, she may say: "I was just lucky that time." She doesn't expect to do well again. While optimists don't see themselves as failures, pessimists do.

Research has shown that optimism can be a learned trait and that, despite their upbringing, people can train themselves to respond to events in more positive terms. For example, Paul has a tendency to react negatively to events. The first thing he has to do is become conscious of that behavior. Once he identifies his reaction, he can reframe his thoughts in more positive terms, as Sarah did when she failed the test. As Paul begins to do more of this, he forms new patterns of responses, and over time these responses become more automatic. Gradually he can develop a more positive outlook on life.

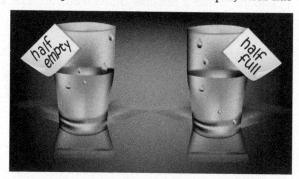

Part II. Complete the sentences with information from the passage.

1. Optimists think positively about life, while ...

2. An optimist may do poorly on a test; nevertheless, ...

3. Things sometimes go well for a pessimist; however, ...

4. Pessimists see themselves as failures; on the other hand, ...

5. Optimists see the best in the world; therefore, ...

6. Optimists see the best in the world; however, ...

7. Although people may have been raised as pessimists, ...

8. Optimism can be a learned trait; consequently, ...

9. If a pessimist wants to change how he reacts, ...

Part III. Are you an optimist, a pessimist, or a combination of both? Write about your personality, and provide some specific examples that support your ideas. Use connecting words from this chapter.

WRITING TIP

Reread the passage "Optimists vs. Pessimists." Note that there is a variety of longer and shorter sentences.

It is important to remember to vary your own sentence style to make your writing more interesting. Good writers use a combination of shorter and longer, more complex sentences. For example, you can use a transition word with a period to create a shorter sentence, but a semicolon to create a longer one.

While it is desirable to use sentence connectors, make sure that not all of your sentences become long and elaborate. Too many connecting words can make your writing seem repetitious. And remember that not all sentences need connecting words!

Part IV. Edit your writing. Check for the following:

1. ☐ a period, not a comma, between two complete sentences
2. ☐ correct meanings of transition words
3. ☐ correct use of adjective and nouns with *so* and *such*:
   so   + *adjective* + *that*
   such + *noun*   + *that*
4. ☐ use of nouns after *because of* and *due to*
5. ☐ use of nouns after *despite* and *in spite of*
6. ☐ correct punctuation (period or semicolon) with transition words
7. ☐ sentence variety by using a combination of shorter and longer sentences
8. ☐ correct spelling (use a dictionary or spell-check)

Conditional Sentences and Wishes

PRETEST: What do I already know?

Write "C" if a sentence has the correct verb forms and "I" for incorrect. Check your answers below. After you complete each chart listed, make any necessary corrections.

1. _____ If I had more money right now, I will lend you some. (20-1)

2. _____ If the lake freezes, neighborhood teens like to skate on it. (20-2)

3. _____ If the plane should take off late, we'll miss our connecting flight. (20-2)

4. _____ I would apply for a scholarship if I was you. (20-3)

5. _____ School would be easy for me if I have your memory. (20-3)

6. _____ If I had taken more math classes, I could have gotten a better job. (20-4)

7. _____ If we had been thinking, we would have picked up your package at the post office on our way home. (20-5)

8. _____ If our team had won the game last night, the town would be celebrating today. (20-6)

9. _____ Had the police known the reason for the decision, would it have made a difference? (20-7)

10. _____ The subway was late. Otherwise, I am here an hour ago. (20-8)

11. _____ Lawrence wishes he had chosen a more interesting college major. (20-9)

12. _____ I wish you will stop complaining. (20-10)

Incorrect sentences: 1, 4, 5, 10, 12

EXERCISE 1 ▶ Warm-up. (Chart 20-1)

Which sentence represents a real or true situation? Which sentence represents an unreal or impossible situation?

1. If I lived underwater, I would see colorful marine life every day.

2. If I am vacationing in the Caribbean, I like to explore coral reefs.

20-1 Overview of Basic Verb Forms Used in Conditional Sentences

Conditional sentences express the idea of *if ... , then ...* . These sentences can talk about real situations — facts, regularly occurring events, etc. — and unreal situations — imaginary or impossible ones.

Situation	*If*-Clause	Result Clause	Examples
REAL IN THE PRESENT	simple present	*simple form of the verb*	If I *have* enough time, I *watch* TV every evening.
REAL IN THE FUTURE		*will* + *simple form*	If I *have* enough time, I *will watch* TV later on tonight.
UNREAL IN THE PRESENT / FUTURE	simple past	*would* + *simple form*	If I *had* enough time, I *would watch* TV now or later on.
UNREAL IN THE PAST	past perfect	*would have* + *past participle*	If I *had had* enough time, I *would have watched* TV yesterday.

EXERCISE 2 ▸ Looking at grammar. (Chart 20-1)

Write "R" next to the sentences that express a real condition and "U" next to the sentences that express an unreal condition.

1. _____ If I have time on weekends, I volunteer at an animal shelter.

2. _____ If I have time, I will volunteer next weekend.

3. _____ If I had time, I would volunteer next weekend.

4. _____ If I had had time, I would have volunteered last weekend.

EXERCISE 3 ▸ Looking at grammar. (Chart 20-1)

Complete the sentences with the words in the box.

> would do   will do   would have done

1. Rita believes in hard work and wants her children to work hard. She always tells them, "If you work hard every day, you _____ well."

2. Scott is smart, but he doesn't work very hard. As a result, he is not good at his job. His co-workers often tell him, "If you worked hard every day, you _____ well."

3. Mark planned to study hard for a test yesterday, but some friends called, and he decided to go out with them. He didn't study at all, and he didn't do well on his test the next day. His teacher told him, "If you had studied yesterday, you _____ well on the test."

EXERCISE 4 ▸ Warm-up. (Chart 20-2)
Which sentence expresses a habitual meaning? Which sentence or sentences express a future meaning?

1. If the baby wakes up in the middle of the night, she'll cry.
2. If the baby wakes up in the middle of the night, she cries.
3. Should the baby wake up in the middle of the night, she'll cry.

20-2	Expressing Real Conditions in the Present or Future
(a) If I *don't eat* breakfast, I always *get* hungry during class. (b) If I *don't eat* breakfast tomorrow morning, I *will get* hungry during class. (c) Water *freezes* if the temperature *reaches* 32°F/0°C. (d) Water *will freeze* if the temperature *reaches* 32°F/0°C.	In conditional sentences that express real or true, factual ideas in the present/future, the *simple present* (not the simple future) is used in the *if*-clause. The result clause has various possible verb forms. A result-clause verb can be: • the *simple present,* to express a habitual activity or situation, as in (a). • the *simple future,* to express a particular activity or situation in the future, as in (b). • the *simple present* or the *simple future,* to express an established, predictable fact or general truth, as in (c) and (d).
(e) If it *rains,* we *should stay* home. If it *rains,* I *might decide* to stay home. If it *rains,* we *can't go.* If it *rains,* we *'re going to stay* home.	The result clause can also include *modals* and *phrasal modals* such as ***should***, ***might***, ***can***, ***be going to***, as in (e).
(f) If anyone *calls,* please *take* a message. (g) If anyone *should call,* please take a message.	An imperative verb can be used in the result clause, as in (f). Sometimes ***should*** is used in an *if*-clause, as in (g). It indicates a little more uncertainty than the use of the simple present, but basically the meaning of examples (f) and (g) is the same.

EXERCISE 5 ▸ Looking at grammar. (Chart 20-2)
Decide if each sentence expresses a habitual or future meaning.

1. a. If it rains, the streets get wet.   habitual   future
   b. If it rains, the streets will get wet.   habitual   future
2. a. If it should rain, we'll take the bus   habitual   future
   b. If it rains, we take the bus.   habitual   future
3. a. If the meetings run late, I leave early.   habitual   future
   b. Should the meetings run late, I will leave early.   habitual   future

EXERCISE 6 ▸ Looking at grammar. (Chart 20-2)
Choose the correct verb for the result clauses. In some cases, both answers are correct.

1. If there is a bike race, the road   is / will be   closed.
2. If I find out the answer, I   will let / let   you know.
3. If you run up a hill, your heart   beats / will beat   fast.
4. If I have extra time, I   tutor / am going to tutor   students in math.

5. If it should rain tomorrow, we   might change / will change   our plans.

6. If my cell phone battery goes dead, I   will recharge / am recharging   it.

EXERCISE 7 ▸ Let's talk. (Chart 20-2)

Read the three superstitions. Do you agree? Then answer the questions with *if* to express other common superstitions. Work in pairs, groups, or as a class.

Superstitions

- If I cross my fingers, it will bring good luck.
- If I open an umbrella indoors, bad luck will "rain" down on me.
- If I have an itchy palm, I may get or lose money soon.

1. Friday the 13th is an unlucky day in many cultures. What may happen on Friday the 13th?

2. Many hotels don't have a 13th floor. Why do you think this is? What do people think will happen?

3. What happens if you walk under a ladder?

4. What happens if you find the end of a rainbow?

5. What happens if you see a black cat?

6. What happens if you step on a crack in the sidewalk?

7. What happens if you find a four-leaf clover?

EXERCISE 8 ▸ Listening. (Chart 20-2)

If + *pronoun* can be difficult to hear at the beginning of sentences because these words are generally unstressed. Additionally, *if* at the beginning of a sentence is often reduced to /f/. Listen to the sentences spoken in casual, relaxed English. Complete the sentences with the non-reduced forms of the words you hear.

Example: You will hear: If I hear anything, I'll tell you.

You will write: _____ *If I hear* _____ anything, I'll tell you.

1. _____ too fast, please tell me.

2. _____ married, everyone will be shocked.

3. _____ OK, I'll ask for some advice.

4. _____ to quit, I hope he lets us know soon.

5. _____, we'll need to try something else.

6. _____ harder, I'm sure she'll succeed.

7. _____ the job, I'll call you right away.

EXERCISE 9 ▸ Warm-up. (Chart 20-3)

Choose the correct completions.

1. If Tom were a teacher, he would teach law.

   a. Tom   is / isn't   a teacher.

   b. Tom   teaches / doesn't teach   law.

2. If he had enough money for tuition, he would be in graduate school.

   a. He   has / doesn't have   enough money.

   b. He   is / isn't   in graduate school.

20-3 Unreal (Contrary to Fact) in the Present or Future

(a) If I *taught* this class, I *wouldn't give* tests.	In (a): Actually, I don't teach this class.
(b) If he *were* here right now, he *would help* us.	In (b): Actually, he is not here right now.
(c) If I *were* you, I *would accept* their invitation.	In (c): Actually, I am not you.
	NOTE: *Were* is used for both singular and plural subjects. *Was* (with *I, he, she, it*) is sometimes used in very informal speech: *If I **was** you, I'd accept their invitation.*
COMPARE: (d) If I had enough money, I *would buy* a car. (e) If I had enough money, I *could buy* a car.	In (d): The speaker wants a car but doesn't have enough money. **Would** expresses desired or predictable results. In (e): The speaker is expressing one possible result. **could** = *would be able to*; **could** expresses possible options.

EXERCISE 10 ▸ Looking at grammar. (Charts 20-2 and 20-3)
Decide if each sentence expresses a real or unreal idea.

1. a. If I had more money, I would buy a new car. real   unreal
   b. If I have enough money, I will buy a car real   unreal
2. a. If the shirts are on sale, I will get a few. real   unreal
   b. If the shirt were on sale, I would get a few. real   unreal
3. a. If you were a teacher, you could help me. real   unreal
   b. If you are a teacher, you can help me. real   unreal

EXERCISE 11 ▸ Looking at grammar. (Chart 20-3)
Choose the correct completions by looking at the pictures. Then make sentences with the given words.

1. Grandpa (is)/ isn't   allergic to flowers.

   If Grandpa weren't allergic to flowers, he would bring Grandma flowers more often.

   (if \ Grandpa \ be \ allergic to flowers \ he \ bring \ Grandma flowers more often)

2. Your roommates   spend / don't spend   a lot of time shopping.

   _____

   (If \ they \ spend \ so much time shopping \ they \ save \ a lot of money)

3. The boy   likes / doesn't like   peas.

   _____

   (If \ the boy \ like peas \ he \ eat \ them)

EXERCISE 12 ▸ Looking at grammar. (Charts 20-2 and 20-3)

Complete the sentences with the verbs in parentheses.

1. a. If I have enough apples, I (*bake*) _____*will bake*_____ an apple pie this afternoon.

   b. If I had enough apples, I (*bake*) ___*would bake / could bake*___ an apple pie.

2. a. I will fix your bike if I (*have*) _____ the right screwdriver.

   b. I would fix your bike if I (*have*) _____ the right screwdriver.

3. a. I (*go*) _____ to a movie tonight if I don't have any homework to do.

   b. I (*go*) _____ to a movie tonight if I didn't have any homework to do.

4. a. I turn off my phone when I (*be*) _____ in meetings.

   b. I would turn on my phone if I (*be, not*) _____ in a meeting right now.

EXERCISE 13 ▸ Let's talk: interview. (Chart 20-3)

Interview your classmates. Share some of the most interesting answers with the class.

1. If you had the choice of any job in the world, what would it be?
2. If someone famous invited you to dinner, who would you want it to be?
3. If you were in an accident and had to lose one of your five senses*, which one would it be?
4. If you saw someone shoplift something at a jewelry store, what would you do?
5. If you were given a million dollars, what would you do with it?
6. If you knew you only had a week to live, what would you do?
7. If someone were following you on the street at night, what would you do?
8. If you found out that you were going to be the parent of septuplets**, what would you do?
9. If you were lost on a desert island with only three items, what three items would they be?
10. If you spoke five languages fluently, which ones would they be?

EXERCISE 14 ▸ Looking at grammar. (Charts 20-2 and 20-3)

Complete the sentences with the verbs in parentheses.

Science and Nature

1. Oil floats on water. If you pour oil on water, it (*float*) _____ .

2. If there (*be*) _____ no trees on earth, there (*be, not*) _____ _____ enough oxygen. Life as we know it (*exist, not*) _____ _____ .

3. If you boil water, it (*disappear*) _____ into the atmosphere as vapor.

4. Many animals hibernate in the winter. One reason is because of food. If animals (*hibernate, not*) _____ , they (*need*) _____ to find food at a time when food is scarce.

---

*five senses = sight, hearing, feel, touch, smell
**septuplets = seven babies born at the same time

5. If people (*have*) _____ paws instead of hands with fingers

and opposable thumbs, the machines we use in everyday life (*have to*)

_____ be constructed very differently. We

(*be, not*) _____ able to turn knobs, push small

buttons, or hold tools and utensils securely.

EXERCISE 15 ▸ Warm-up. (Chart 20-4)
Choose the correct time word.

1. If Ann were available, she would help us.   now   yesterday
2. If Ann had been available, she would have helped us.   now   yesterday

20-4	Unreal (Contrary to Fact) in the Past
(a) If you *had told* me about the problem, I *would have helped* you.	In (a): Actually, you did not tell me about it.
(b) If they *had studied*, they *would have passed* the exam.	In (b): Actually, they did not study. Therefore, they failed the exam.
(c) If I *hadn't slipped* on the stairs, I *wouldn't have broken* my arm.	In (c): Actually, I slipped on the stairs. I broke my arm.
	NOTE: The auxiliary verbs are often reduced in speech. "If you'd told me, I would've helped you (or I-*duv* helped you)."*
COMPARE:	In (d): *would* expresses a desired or predictable result.
(d) If I had had enough money, I *would* have bought a car.	In (e): *could* expresses a possible option.
(e) If I had had enough money, I *could* have bought a car.	*could have bought* = would have been able to buy

*In casual, informal speech, some native speakers sometimes use *would have* in an *if*-clause: *If you would've told me about the problem, I would've helped you.* This verb form usage is generally considered to be grammatically incorrect in standard English, but it occurs fairly commonly.

EXERCISE 16 ▸ Looking at grammar. (Chart 20-4)
Write the correct form of the verb in parentheses. Then complete the sentence with a phrase from the right.

1. If Reya had (*go*) _____ to the hospital,
she __d__ .

2. If Tim hadn't (*lose*) _____ his passport,
he ____ .

3. If you hadn't (*stay*) _____ out all night,
you ____ .

4. If you had (*help*) _____ us move, we ____ .

5. If the waiter had (*be*) _____ friendlier,
I ____ .

6. If we had (*have*) _____ chains in the car,
we ____ .

a. wouldn't have slept all day

b. would have left a bigger tip

c. would have finished already

d. would have gotten better more quickly

e. wouldn't have gotten stuck in the snow

f. wouldn't have missed the flight home

tire chains

EXERCISE 17 ▸ Looking at grammar. (Chart 20-4)
Complete the sentences with past conditionals.

Getting Lost

1. If the map on my phone (*be, not*) __hadn't been__ wrong, we (*get, not*) __wouldn't__
   __have gotten__ lost.

2. If you (*follow*) _____ my directions, we (*spend, not*) _____
   _____ the last two hours driving around.

3. If I (*be, not*) _____ so tired, I (*pay*) _____
   closer attention.

4. If we (*rent*) _____ a car with GPS, we (*find*) _____
   _____ the hotel by now.

5. If you (*listen*) _____ to me, we (*drive, not*) _____
   _____ around in circles.

6. If we (*take*) _____ the train, we (*be*) _____
   there an hour ago.

EXERCISE 18 ▸ Let's talk: pairwork. (Chart 20-4)
Work with a partner. Take turns making statements with *If I had known*.

Example: I didn't know it was your birthday.
> *If I had known it was your birthday, I would have brought you a gift.*

PARTNER A	PARTNER B
1. I didn't know your dad was in the hospital.	1. I didn't know you were sick for a month.
2. I didn't know you broke your arm and needed help.	2. I didn't know you were broke and couldn't pay your bills.
3. I didn't know you had a graduation party and invited me.	3. I didn't know someone stole your bike and you had trouble getting to school.
4. I didn't know you were allergic to nuts. I put them in the salad.	4. I didn't know you had free tickets to the soccer game and you wanted me to go.

EXERCISE 19 ▸ Listening. (Chart 20-4)
In conditional sentences, /h/ is often dropped in the auxiliary verbs *have* and *had*. *Would have* can sound like "would-a" or "would-uv." Listen to the sentences spoken in casual, relaxed English. Complete the sentences with the non-reduced forms of the words you hear.

SITUATION: Jon told several good friends a lie, and they recently found out. Here are their reactions:

Example: You will hear: If he had been truthful, he wouldn't have lost my trust.
> You will write: ___If he had been___ truthful, ___he wouldn't have lost___ my trust.

1. _____ the truth sooner, _____ differently.

2. _____ him, _____ so foolish.

3. _____ me what a great guy Jon was, _____

   _____ him so easily.

4. _____ another person, _____ so shocked.

5. _____ , _____ more respect for him.

EXERCISE 20 ▶ Looking at grammar. (Charts 20-3 and 20-4)

Answer the questions.

1. If I had gone to the movie with you, I would have enjoyed it.

   a. Did I go with you? _____*no*_____

   b. Did I enjoy the movie? _____*no*_____

   c. Is the meaning present or past? _____*past*_____

2. If I had brought my ID, I could have gotten a student discount.

   a. Did I bring my ID? _____

   b. Did I get a discount? _____

   c. Is the meaning present or past? _____

3. If Dad had his ID, he would get a senior citizen discount.

   a. Does he have his ID? _____

   b. Is he going to get a discount? _____

   c. Is the meaning present or past? _____

4. If I felt better, I would go to work.

   a. Do I feel better? _____

   b. Am I going to work? _____

   c. Is the meaning present or past? _____

5. If I didn't have any friends, I would be lonely.

   a. Am I lonely? _____

   b. Do I have friends? _____

   c. Is the meaning present or past? _____

6. Jackson would have made it to class on time this morning if the bus hadn't been late.

   a. Was the bus late? _____

   b. Did Jackson make it to class on time? _____

   c. Is the meaning present or past? _____

7. If I had more time, I would stay longer and talk.

   a. Do I have more time? _____

   b. Will I stay longer? _____

   c. Is the meaning present or past? _____

EXERCISE 21 ▸ Looking at grammar. (Charts 20-1 → 20-4)

Underline the clause that expresses a condition. Write "R" if the condition is a real condition. Write "U" if the condition is unreal. Then decide if the sentence refers to present/future or past time.

1. a. __R__ If the weather is warm, we'll eat outdoors.   (present/future)   past

   b. __U__ If the weather were warm, we would eat outdoors.   (present/future)   past

   c. _____ If the weather had been warm, we would have eaten   present/future   past
         outdoors.

2. a. _____ If I had more money, I would work less.   present/future   past

   b. _____ If I had had more money, I would have worked less.   present/future   past

3. a. _____ If I don't have to work, I can visit you.   present/future   past

   b. _____ If I hadn't had to work, I could have visited you.   present/future   past

   c. _____ If I didn't have to work, I could visit you.   present/future   past

EXERCISE 22 ▸ Looking at grammar. (Charts 20-1 → 20-4)

Draw a line to each correct completion.

1. a. If I have enough money,   I would have bought it.
   b. If I had enough money,   I will buy it.
   c. If I had had enough money,   I would buy it.

2. a. If they arrive early,   they would call.
   b. If they arrived early,   they would have called.
   c. If they had arrived early,   they will call.

3. a. If he had needed help,   he will ask.
   b. If he needs help,   he would have asked.
   c. If he needed help,   he would ask.

4. a. I would buy the coat   if it had fit.
   b. I would have bought the coat   if it fit.
   c. I will buy the coat   if it fits.

5. a. We will stop by   if we had extra time.
   b. We would have stopped by   if we had had extra time.
   c. We would stop by   if we have extra time.

EXERCISE 23 ▸ Looking at grammar. (Charts 20-1 → 20-4)

Complete the sentences with the verbs in parentheses.

1. a. If I (*have*) _____ time, I will go with you.

   b. If I (*have*) _____ time, I would go with you.

   c. If I (*have*) _____ time, I would have gone with you.

2. a. If the weather were nice today, we (*go*) _____ to the zoo.

   b. If the weather had been nice yesterday, we (*go*) _____ to the zoo.

   c. If the weather is nice tomorrow, we (*go*) _____ to the zoo.

3. a. Linda wasn't at home yesterday. If she (be) _____ at home yesterday,

   I (visit) _____ her.

   b. If Sally (be) _____ at home tomorrow, I (visit) _____ her.

   c. Jim isn't home right now. If he (be) _____ at home right now, I (visit)

   _____ him.

EXERCISE 24 ▶ Looking at grammar. (Charts 20-1 → 20-4)

Complete the sentences with the verbs in parentheses.

Conversations

1. A: You should tell your father exactly what happened. If I (be) _____

   you, I (tell) _____ him the truth as soon as possible.

   B: You're right. I'll do it.

2. A: If I (have) _____ my camera with me yesterday, I

   (take) _____ a picture of Alex standing on his head.

   B: He's good at yoga. He can do a lot of different poses.

3. A: I'm almost ready to plant my garden. I have a lot of seeds. Maybe

   I have more than I need. If I (have) _____ more seeds than I need, I

   (give) _____ some to my neighbor.

   B: She would really appreciate it.

4. A: George has only two pairs of socks. If he (have) _____ more than two pairs of

   socks, he (have to, not) _____ wash his socks so often.

   B: I'm not sure that he washes them that often!

5. A: Since I broke my foot, I haven't been able to clean my apartment.

   B: Why didn't you say something? I (come) _____ over and

   (help) _____ you if you (tell) _____ me.

   A: I know you (come) _____ right away if I (call) _____

   _____ you, but I didn't want to bother you.

   B: It wouldn't have been a bother. What are friends for?

6. A: It's been a long drought. It hasn't rained for over a month. If it (rain, not) _____

   _____ soon, a lot of crops (die) _____ . If the crops

   (die) _____, many people (go) _____ hungry this coming winter.

   B: I'm very worried about our water supply.

7. A: Shhh! Your father is taking a nap. Uh-oh. You woke him up.

   B: Sorry. If I (realize) _____ he was sleeping, I (make, not) _____

   _____ so much noise when I came in.

8. A: What (*we, use*) _____ to look at ourselves when we comb our hair if

we (*have, not*) _____ mirrors?

B: It would be very strange to live without mirrors.

🎧 **EXERCISE 25 ▸ Listening.** (Charts 20-1 → 20-4)
Listen to the statements and answer the questions.

Example: You will hear: If Bob had asked me to keep the news about his marriage a secret, I
wouldn't have told anybody. I know how to keep a secret.

      You will answer: a. Did I tell anybody the news? _____*yes*_____

                  b. Did Bob ask me to keep it a secret? _____*no*_____

1. a. Am I going to go to the art museum? _____

  b. Do I have enough time? _____

2. a. Did Mrs. Jones receive immediate medical attention? _____

  b. Did she die? _____

3. a. Am I a carpenter? _____

  b. Do I want to build my own house? _____

  c. Am I going to build my own house? _____

4. a. Was the hotel built to withstand an earthquake? _____

  b. Did the hotel collapse? _____

EXERCISE 26 ▸ Looking at grammar. (Charts 20-1 → 20-4)
If-clauses can be shortened by the use of an auxiliary verb. Study the examples and then complete
the sentences.

Examples: Ella isn't patient, but if she **were**, she would be a better teacher.
           I don't live in the city, but if I **did**, I wouldn't need to take the subway to work.
           I didn't go to bed early last night, but if I **had**, I would have gotten up earlier.

1. I don't have a pen, but if I _____*did*_____, I would lend it to you.

2. He is busy right now, but if he _____*weren't*_____, he would help us.

3. I didn't vote in the election, but if I _____*had*_____, I would have voted for Senator Todd.

4. I don't have enough money, but if I _____, I would buy that book.

5. The weather is cold today, but if it _____, I'd go swimming.

6. She didn't come, but if she _____, she would have met my brother.

7. Helium is lighter than air. If it _____, a helium
blimp wouldn't float upward.

8. I'm not a good cook, but if I _____, I would
make all of my own meals.

9. He didn't go to a doctor, but if he _____, the cut
on his hand wouldn't have gotten infected.

10. I always pay my bills. If I _____, I'd get in a lot of trouble.

11. I called my husband to tell him I would be late. If I _____, he would have gotten worried about me.

EXERCISE 27 ▶ Warm-up. (Chart 20-5)
Read the statements and answer the questions.

OLGA: If I hadn't been painting my apartment, I would have gone to a movie with my friends.
YOKO: If I weren't painting my apartment, I would go to a movie with my friends.

1. Who is busy painting her apartment now?
2. Who was busy painting her apartment earlier?

20-5	Using Progressive Verb Forms in Conditional Sentences

Notice the use of progressive verb forms in these examples. Even in conditional sentences, progressive verb forms are used in progressive situations.

(a) Real Situation:	It *is raining* right now, so I *will not go* for a walk.
(b) Conditional Statement:	If it *were not raining* right now, I *would go* for a walk.
(c) Real Situation:	It *was raining* yesterday afternoon, so I *did not go* for a walk.
(d) Conditional Statement:	If it *had not been raining*, I *would have gone* for a walk.

EXERCISE 28 ▶ Looking at grammar. (Chart 20-5)
Make conditional sentences.

1. a. I'm working. If I _____*weren't*_____ working, I would be at home.

   b. I'm not working. If I _____ working, I wouldn't be at home.

2. a. Fortunately, the copy machine was working. If it _____ working, we wouldn't have finished our presentation.

   b. The copy machine wasn't working. If it _____ working, we _____ finished our presentation.

3. a. The elevators weren't working. If they _____ working, I _____ walked up to the top floor.

   b. The elevators were working. If they _____ working, I _____ walked up to the top floor.

EXERCISE 29 ▸ Looking at grammar. (Chart 20-5)
Change the statements to conditional sentences.

1. You weren't listening, so you didn't understand the directions. But …
   → *if you had been listening, you would have understood the directions.*
2. You aren't wearing a coat, so you're cold. But …
3. Joe got a ticket because he was driving too fast. But …
4. I'm enjoying myself, so I won't leave. But …
5. You were sleeping, so I didn't tell you the news as soon as I heard it. But …

EXERCISE 30 ▸ Looking at grammar. (Chart 20-5)
Complete the sentences with the verbs in parentheses. Make conditional statements.

1. It's snowing. We can't go to the park.

   If it (*snow*) _____*weren't snowing*_____, we could go to the park.

2. It wasn't snowing. We went to the park.

   If it (*snow*) _____*had been snowing*_____, we wouldn't have gone to the park.

3. Elena just got out of the shower. She's drying her hair with a hair dryer, so she can't hear
   the doorbell.

   If Elena (*dry*) _____ her hair, she could hear the doorbell.

4. Elena was waiting for a package to come, but as it happened, she was drying her hair when it
   arrived, and she couldn't hear the doorbell.

   If Elena (*dry*) _____ her hair when the package arrived, she could have

   heard the doorbell.

5. Max is at a party at his friend's apartment, but he's not having any fun. He wants to leave.
   Max wouldn't want to leave early if he (*have*) _____ fun.

6. My sister was reading a text message while she was driving and wasn't paying enough attention
   to traffic. When the car in front of her stopped, she rear-ended it.

   If my sister (*read*) _____ a text message, she wouldn't have rear-ended

   the car in front of her.

7. Simon is vacuuming the car. When he vacuums, he can't
   hear his phone.

   If Simon (*vacuum*) _____ the car,
   he could hear his phone ring.

EXERCISE 31 ▸ Warm-up. (Chart 20-6)

Choose the correct time words.

1. If I had done my homework   now / earlier,   I would know the answers   now / earlier.
2. Anita wouldn't be sick   now / earlier   if she had followed the doctor's orders   now / earlier.

20-6 Using "Mixed Time" in Conditional Sentences

Frequently the time in the *if*-clause and the time in the result clause are different: one clause may be in the present and the other in the past. Notice that past and present times are mixed in these sentences.

		past	present
(a)	Real Situation:	I *did not eat* breakfast *several hours ago*,	so I *am* hungry *now*.
		past	present
(b)	Conditional Statement:	If I *had eaten* breakfast *several hours ago*,	I *would not be* hungry *now*.
		present	past
(c)	Real Situation:	He *is not* a good student.	He *did not study* for the test *yesterday*.
		present	past
(d)	Conditional Statement:	If he *were* a good student,	he *would have studied* for the test *yesterday*.

EXERCISE 32 ▸ Looking at grammar. (Chart 20-6)

Choose the correct time frames for each sentence.

1. If I hadn't eaten so much at dinner   now / earlier,   I would feel better   now / earlier.
2. Lynn would be in Egypt   now / earlier   if she had renewed her passport   now / earlier.
3. Professor Azeri would be happier   now / earlier in the semester   if she had been given a different teaching assignment   now / earlier in the semester.
4. Had you told me the truth   now / in the past,   I would trust you more   now / in the past.
5. If you were a more organized person   now / yesterday,   you wouldn't have misplaced your keys, glasses, and phone   now / an hour ago.
6. If my mom weren't in bed with the flu   today / yesterday,   she would have come shopping with us   now / this morning.
7. You wouldn't be paying a fine   right now / yesterday   if you had returned the library book now / yesterday.

EXERCISE 33 ▸ Looking at grammar. (Chart 20-6)

Put one line under the present clause. Put two lines under the past clause. Then restate the sentences as conditional statements.

1. I'm hungry now because I didn't eat dinner earlier.
    → *If I'd eaten dinner earlier, I wouldn't be hungry now.*
2. The room is full of flies because you left the door open.
3. You are tired this morning because you didn't go to bed at a reasonable hour last night.
4. I didn't finish my report yesterday, so I can't begin a new project today.
5. I'm not you, so I didn't tell him the truth.
6. I don't know anything about plumbing, so I didn't fix the leak in the sink myself.

EXERCISE 34 ▸ Reading and grammar. (Chart 20-4 → 20-6)
Read the passage. Then choose the correct completions in the sentences that follow.

Why Did Dinosaurs Become Extinct?

There are several scientific theories as to why dinosaurs became extinct. One theory has to do with asteroids. Asteroids are rocky objects that orbit the sun. According to this theory, an asteroid collided with the earth millions of years ago, causing disastrous changes in the earth's climate, such as tsunamis, high winds, and dust in the atmosphere that blocked the sun. As a result, dinosaurs could no longer survive. Some scientists believe that if this asteroid had not collided with the earth, dinosaurs would not have become extinct.

1. According to one theory, if an asteroid   had collided / hadn't collided   with the earth, several disastrous changes in the earth's climate would not have taken place.
2. If an asteroid   had hit / hadn't hit   the earth, there wouldn't have been catastrophic changes in the earth's climate.
3. If dust   had blocked / hadn't blocked   the sun, the earth would have been warmer.
4. If an asteroid   had collided / hadn't collided   with the earth, dinosaurs might still exist.
5. If dinosaurs   had survived / hadn't survived,   the earth would be a very different place.

EXERCISE 35 ▸ Warm-up. (Chart 20-7)
Check (✓) all the correct sentences.

1. a. _____ Were I more adventurous, I would hike in the Australian Outback.

   b. _____ If I were more adventurous, I would hike in the Australian Outback.

2. a. _____ If my friends had known about my trip, they would have told me to go there.

   b. _____ Had my friends known about my trip, they would have told me to go there.

3. a. _____ Should anyone ask, I'll be gone for another month.

   b. _____ If anyone should ask, I'll be gone for another month.

Pinnacles Desert, Australian Outback

20-7	Omitting *If*
(a) *Were I* you, I wouldn't do that. (b) *Had I known,* I would have told you. (c) *Should anyone call,* please take a message.	With *were, had* (past perfect), and *should,* sometimes *if* is omitted, and the subject and verb are inverted. In (a): *Were I you* = *if I were you* In (b): *Had I known* = *if I had known* In (c): *Should anyone call* = *if anyone should call*

EXERCISE 36 ▸ Looking at grammar. (Chart 20-7)
Make sentences with the same meaning by omitting *if*.

FYI (For Your Information)

1. If you should need more money, I'll lend it to you.
   → *Should you need more money, I'll lend it to you.*
2. If I were you, I would let someone know where you'll be.
3. If I were your teacher, I would insist you do more careful work.
4. If I should change my mind, I'll let you know.
5. She would have gotten the job if she had been better prepared.
6. It's just my opinion, but I think your boss is awful. If I had a choice, I would look for another job.
7. I'll be out of the office until June 12th. If you should need to reach me, I'll be at our company headquarters in Seoul.
8. If I had known what would happen, I would have done things differently.

EXERCISE 37 ▸ Looking at grammar. (Charts 20-3 → 20-7)
Work with a partner. Choose all the sentences that best express the meaning of the given sentence.

1. If I hadn't been driving so fast, I wouldn't have gotten a speeding ticket.
   a. I get a lot of speeding tickets.
   b. I was driving too fast.
   c. I like to drive fast.
   d. I was given a ticket.

2. Should you need help, I'll be in the room next door.
   a. I'll be helping others in the room.
   b. I'm available to help you.
   c. You shouldn't ask me for help.
   d. Do you need help from me?

3. Had you told us sooner, we could have helped you.
   a. We're glad you told us.
   b. We were happy that we helped you.
   c. We needed to know earlier.
   d. We didn't help you.

4. If there had been a faster way to get to the theater, I would have taken it.
   a. I took the fastest way to the theater.
   b. I didn't take the fastest way.
   c. The theater was too far away.
   d. I took several different routes.

5. Should you have questions, give me a call on my cell.
   a. I'm available by cell phone.
   b. Did you have questions?
   c. Call me soon.
   d. Call me if you have questions.

6. Had anyone warned us about the situation, we would have stayed home.
   a. We stayed home.
   b. We didn't stay home.
   c. No one warned us.
   d. Someone warned us.

7. Were we rich, we would live in a house overlooking the ocean.
   a. Are we rich?
   b. Rich people live in houses overlooking the ocean.
   c. We aren't rich.
   d. We don't live in a house overlooking the ocean.

EXERCISE 38 ▸ Warm-up. (Chart 20-8)

Read the paragraph. Check (✓) the sentences that are true.

One night a fire started in Janet's apartment. A blanket on the sofa got too close to an electric heater. Janet was in a deep sleep and wasn't aware of the fire. Fortunately, her neighbors saw smoke coming out of the window and threw rocks at her bedroom window to wake her up. Janet was very grateful that she hadn't been killed or injured in the fire.

1. _____ Janet would have kept sleeping, but the neighbors woke her up.

2. _____ Janet would have awakened without her neighbors' help.

3. _____ Janet was awakened by her neighbors; otherwise, she wouldn't have woken up.

20-8 Implied Conditions

(a) I **would have gone** with you, *but I had to study*. (b) I never **would have succeeded** *without your help*.	Often the *if*-clause is implied, not stated. Conditional verbs are still used in the result clause. In (a): the implied condition = *if I hadn't had to study* In (b): the implied condition = *if you hadn't helped me*
(c) She ran; *otherwise*, she **would have missed** her bus.	Conditional verbs are frequently used following **otherwise**. In (c), the implied *if*-clause = *if she had not run*

EXERCISE 39 ▸ Looking at grammar. (Chart 20-8)

Identify the implied conditions by making sentences using *if*-clauses.

Thank goodness!

1. My phone would have died, but Gina had a charger.
   → *My phone would have died if Gina hadn't had a charger.*

2. I couldn't have paid my school tuition without your loan.
   → *I couldn't have paid my school tuition if you hadn't loaned me money.*

3. The fire would have spread quickly, but the fire trucks weren't far away.

4. I stepped on the brakes. Otherwise, I would have hit the little girl on the bike.

5. I couldn't have finished my project on time without your help.

6. My noisy party guests quieted down. Otherwise, the neighbors would have called the police.

7. I would have missed my flight, but my friend called and woke me up.

EXERCISE 40 ▸ Listening. (Chart 20-8)

Choose the statement that is true for each situation. In some cases both answers are correct.

Example: You will hear: I canceled your dentist appointment for Tuesday. Otherwise, you would have had two appointments in one day.

        You will choose: a. I thought you needed two appointments.
                         (b.) I didn't think you wanted two appointments.

1. a. If I had had your number, I would have called.
   b. I didn't have your number; otherwise, I would have called.

2. a. If my parents hadn't helped me, I wouldn't have gone to college.
   b. If I hadn't gone to college, my parents wouldn't have helped me.

3. a. I picked up your clothes.
   b. I wasn't able to pick up your clothes.

4. a. If someone had told us about the party, we would have come.
   b. We came to the party even though you didn't tell us about it.

5. a. If I'd had your advice, I would have known what to do.
   b. Because of your advice, I knew what to do.

EXERCISE 41 ▶ Looking at grammar. (Charts 20-1 → 20-8)

Complete the sentences with the verbs in parentheses. Some of the verbs are passive.

A Walk Around Town

1. If I could speak better Japanese, I (*try*) _____ to have a conversation with the group of people over there.

2. See that apartment building? We are going to move into it June 1st if it (*finish*) _____ _____ by then.

3. The rent was very reasonable. Otherwise, I (*try*) _____ to find an apartment that was already finished.

4. Thanks for waiting for me. I (*be*) _____ here sooner, but I had car trouble.

5. It's too bad that Nadia can't join us. If she (*work, not*) _____ all the time, we would see her more often.

6. Had I known we were going to walk so far, I (*wear*) _____ more comfortable shoes.

7. A: It's so hot out. It feels suffocating.
   B: I know. If there (*be*) _____ only a breeze, it (*be, not*) _____ quite so bad.

8. A: What would you be doing right now if you (*be, not*) _____ here?
   B: I (*pay*) _____ bills.

9. If I (*turn on, not*) _____ my phone just before you called, I would have missed this chance to be with you.

10. I can't remember if your birthday is this week or next week. Sorry — I have such a bad memory that I (*forget*) _____ my head if it (*be, not*) _____ attached to my body.

11. I try to walk every day. A day without exercise (*be*) _____ unthinkable for me.

12. A: Want to ride the Ferris wheel?
    B: No way! I have a fear of heights. I (*ride, not*) _____ it if you paid me a million dollars!

EXERCISE 42 ▶ Let's talk. (Charts 20-1 → 20-8)

Explain what you would do in these circumstances. Work in pairs or small groups.

Suppose ...

Example:
SPEAKER A (*book open*):   Suppose you find a wallet with money in it in a classroom.
                               What would you do?
SPEAKER B (*book closed*): I would turn it in to the lost-and-found office.

1. You are at a party. A man starts talking to you, but he is speaking so fast that you can't catch what he is saying. What would you do?
2. Ricardo went to a friend's house for dinner. His friend served a dish that he can't stand/doesn't like at all. What if you were Ricardo?
3. Suppose you went to a cash machine. The amount you got was double what you asked for. What would you do?
4. John was cheating during an exam. Suppose you were the teacher and you saw him. What would you have done?
5. Suppose there were a fire in this building right now. What would you do?
6. Suppose there were a fire in your room or apartment or house. You had time to save only one thing. What would you save?
7. Imagine that one night you were driving your car down a deserted street. You were all alone. In an attempt to avoid a dog in the road, you swerved and hit a parked car. No one saw you. What would you do?

EXERCISE 43 ▶ Warm-up. (Chart 20-9)

Which sentences are true for you? What do you notice about the words in blue?

1. I wish I were someplace else right now.   yes   no
2. I wish I had learned English when I was a child.   yes   no

---

20-9   Wishes About the Present and Past

Wish is used when the speaker wants reality to be different, to be exactly the opposite, but it isn't.

	"True" Statement	Verb Form Following *Wish*	
A WISH ABOUT THE PRESENT	(a) I *don't know* French.	I *wish* (that) I *knew* French.	*Wish* can be followed by a noun clause (see Chart 12-5, p. 257). Past verb forms, similar to those in conditional sentences, are used in the noun clause.
	(b) It *is raining* right now.	I *wish* it *weren't raining* right now.	
	(c) I *can't speak* Japanese.	I *wish* I *could speak* Japanese.	To make a wish about the present, a past verb form is used, as in (a)–(c).
A WISH ABOUT THE PAST	(d) John *didn't come*.	I *wish* John *had come*.*	In (d), the past perfect (**had come**) is used to make a wish about the past.
	(e) Mary *couldn't come*.	I *wish* Mary *could have come*.	
(f) I *wish* I *could* come. (It's not possible. I can't come.)			Note the difference between *wish* and *hope*. **Wish** is used for unreal, contrary-to-fact situations. **Hope** is used for real or possible situations.
(g) I *hope* I *can* come. (It's a possibility. Maybe I can come.)			

*You may hear *I wish Josh would have come.* This is incorrect in formal English.

EXERCISE 44 ▸ Looking at grammar. (Chart 20-9)
Complete the sentences with an appropriate verb form. You may need to add *not*.

1. Our classroom doesn't have any windows. I wish our classroom _____*had*_____ windows.

2. The sun isn't shining. I wish the sun _____ right now.

3. I didn't go shopping. I wish I _____ shopping.

4. I don't know how to dance. I wish I _____ how to dance.

5. It's cold today. I'm not wearing a coat. I wish I _____ a coat.

6. I don't have enough money to buy that book. I wish I _____ enough money.

7. You can't meet my parents. I wish you _____ them, but they're out of town.

8. Khalid didn't come to the meeting. I wish he _____ to the meeting.

9. I'm not lying on a sunny beach. I wish I _____ on a sunny beach.

10. Ingrid forgot to get Ernesto's new phone number. She wishes she _____ _____ to get his phone number.

11. I didn't eat breakfast before I came to class. I wasn't hungry, but now I am. I wish I _____ breakfast.

12. Pedro stayed up really late last night. Today he's having trouble staying awake at work. He wishes he _____ stayed up really late last night.

EXERCISE 45 ▸ Looking at grammar. (Chart 20-9)
Complete the sentences with an appropriate auxiliary verb.

1. I'm not at home, but I wish I _____*were*_____.

2. I don't know her, but I wish I _____*did*_____.

3. I can't sing well, but I wish I _____*could*_____.

4. I didn't go, but I wish I _____*had*_____.

5. I don't have a bike, but I wish I _____.

6. I didn't read that book, but I wish I _____.

7. I want to go, but I can't. I wish I _____.

8. The city won't add more parks, but I wish it _____.

9. He isn't old enough to drive a car, but he wishes he _____.

10. They didn't go to the movie, but they wish they _____.

11. I don't have a driver's license, but I wish I _____.

12. I'm not living by myself, but I wish I _____.

13. I have roommates, but I wish I _____.

14. You can't come with us, but I wish you _____.

15. He didn't buy a ticket to the game, but he wishes he _____.

EXERCISE 46 ▸ Reading and grammar. (Charts 20-1 → 20-9)

Part I. Read the blog entry by author Stacy Hagen.

Do you know these words?
- *wander*
- *brain scan*
- *nap*
- *pop into*

 **BlueBookBlog** Becoming "Unstuck"

If you were trying to write a research paper for a class and couldn't come up with any ideas, what would you do? Would you keep working away or would you stop for a while? Interestingly, research points to stopping so that your mind can wander. Instead of continuing to focus on a task, the best thing to do is to leave the task for a while and do something else that frees up your thinking.

Surprisingly, if we stop concentrating on something, we actually become more creative. Researchers have found by looking at brain scans that our minds are very active during the daydreaming stage. By not focusing on a problem, we are able to look at it in new ways when we come back to it. As our minds wander, they often find the solution.

The company 3M has known this for decades. Since 1948, they have had the 15% rule: 15% of employees' time can be spent on a hobby or project of their choice. On top of that, they are encouraged to take walks, breaks, naps — whatever their minds need to help unlock their creativity.

A Stanford University study found that walking outdoors increased creativity by an average of 60%. I decided to give this a try and was amazed at how quickly I became "unstuck." Possibilities and answers really did pop into my head. To be honest, I was surprised at how effective this was. And, it's not just walking that has helped. Sometimes all I need to do is leave my computer and start another task that lets me daydream — something as simple as getting a snack.

I wish I had known this during my college days. I'm sure it would have helped me be a more efficient and productive student. I certainly know I would have been calmer and more relaxed when I got stuck.

Part II. Identify the time frame of the ideas in the phrases (*now* or *past*). Decide if they express real or unreal conditions.

	NOW/PAST	REAL/UNREAL
1. If you were trying to write a research paper for a class and couldn't come up with any ideas, ...	*now*	*unreal*
2. ... would you keep working away?		
3. ... would you stop for a while?		
4. If we stop concentrating on something, ...		
5. It would have helped me ...		
6. I would have been calmer and more relaxed ...		

Part III. Think about challenges you have when you do homework. What slows you down? Do you ever get stuck? What helps you get unstuck? Would the techniques in this blog work for you if you tried them? Why or why not? Discuss the questions with a partner or in small groups.

EXERCISE 47 ▸ Warm-up. (Chart 20-10)

Check (✓) <u>all</u> the correct sentences.

1. _____ I wish I were going to visit you next week.   3. _____ I wish I could visit you next week.

2. _____ I wish I visited you next week.   4. _____ I wish I would visit you next week.

20-10 Wishes About the Future; Use of *Wish* + *Would*

(a) He *isn't going to be* here next week. I *wish* he *were going to be* here next week.	Wishes about the future can be expressed with **were going to**, **could**, or **would**. The speaker wants the situation to be the opposite of what it will be.
(b) She *can't come* tomorrow. I *wish* she *could come* tomorrow.	**Could**, not **would**, is used when the speaker is making a wish with *I*, as in (d).
(c) She *won't tell you*. I *wish* she *would tell you*.	
(d) I *wish* I *could go* with you.	*INCORRECT:* I wish I would go with you.
(e) It is raining. I *wish* it *would stop*.	**Wish + would** can be used when the speaker wants an action or event to change, as in (e). Note that it cannot be used for situations. *INCORRECT:* I wish you would know the answer.
(f) I *wish* you *would leave* now.	**Wish + would** can also be used to make a strong request, as in (f).

EXERCISE 48 ▸ Looking at grammar. (Chart 20-10)

Make future wishes.

1. I can't go with you tomorrow, but I wish I _____*could go*_____ .

2. My friend won't ever lend me his car. I wish he _____ me his car for my date tomorrow night.

3. Mrs. Takasawa isn't coming to dinner with us tonight. I wish she _____ to dinner with us.

4. The teacher is going to give an exam tomorrow. I wish he _____ us an exam tomorrow.

5. Jon won't tell me about his plans, but I wish he _____ me something.

6. It probably won't happen, but I wish it _____ .

EXERCISE 49 ▸ Let's talk. (Charts 20-9 and 20-10)

Work with a partner or in small groups. Read the given information. Then answer the questions with ***wish*** + ***would***.

Example:

TOM: Why are you pacing back and forth?

SUE: I'm waiting to hear from Sam. I want him to call me. I need to talk to him right now. We had an argument. I need to make sure everything's OK.

    (a) What does Sue want to happen?
        → *She **wishes** Sam would call her.*
    (b) What else does Sue wish?
        → *She **wishes** she **could** talk to Sam right now.*
           *She probably **wishes** she and Sam **hadn't had** an argument.*

1. ANNA: Can't you come to the concert? Please change your mind. I'd really like you to come.
   YOKO: Thanks for the invitation, but I don't see how I can change my work schedule.

   (a) What does Anna want Yoko to do?
   (b) What else does Anna wish?

2. Helen is a neat and orderly person. Judy, her roommate, is messy. Judy never picks up after herself. She leaves dirty dishes in the sink. She drops her clothes all over the apartment. She never makes her bed. Helen nags Judy to pick up after herself.

   (a) What does Helen want Judy to do?
   (b) What does Judy probably wish?

EXERCISE 50 ▸ Looking at grammar. (Charts 20-9 and 20-10)
Make wishes using the verbs in the box.

be	become	come	have to	✓need	tell	wear

1. I need nine hours of sleep. I wish I _____*didn't need*_____ so much sleep. I could get so much more done in a day.

2. Alice doesn't like her job as a nurse. She wishes she _____ a nurse. She wishes she _____ a doctor.

3. We had a good time in the mountains over vacation. I wish you _____ with us.

4. I know that something's bothering you. I wish you _____ me what it is. Maybe I can help.

5. A: I wish I _____ work today.

   B: So do I. I wish it _____ a holiday.

6. A: My feet are killing me! I wish I _____ shoes.

   B: Yeah, me too. I didn't know we were going to be walking on rocks.

EXERCISE 51 ▸ Let's talk: interview. (Charts 20-9 and 20-10)
Ask two classmates each question. Share some of their answers with the class.

1. What is something you can't do but you wish you could do?
2. Where do you wish you were right now? What do you wish you were doing?
3. What is something you don't have but wish you had?
4. What is something that didn't happen yesterday but that you wish had happened?
5. What is something you don't know but wish you knew?
6. What is something you have to do but wish you didn't have to do?
7. What is something you were unable to do yesterday but you wish you could have done?
8. What is something that has never happened in your life but that you wish would happen?
9. What do you wish were different about this city/town?
10. What is something in your life that you wish could be different?

EXERCISE 52 ▸ Check your knowledge. (Chapter 20 Review)
Correct the errors.

1. If I had know more about it, I would have had better advice for you.

2. If were I you, I would spend more time outdoors.

3. Should my manager needs to reach me, I'll be at the bank and post office.

4. Anyone should ask for me, tell them I'm not available.

5. If you continue to drive so fast, I would get out of the car.

6. She wishes she went to the doctor when she first had symptoms.

7. If it were not snow outside, we could walk to the mall.

8. I would have done things differently were I received the correct information.

9. They hurried; otherwise, they wouldn't have missed their train.

10. The team never will have won the game yesterday without your help.

11. I hope I could meet with you tomorrow.

12. We're really late. I wish you hurry.

13. If I had brought a lunch to work, I wouldn't have been hungry now.

14. I wish I would ask more questions when we reviewed for the exam yesterday.

EXERCISE 53 ▸ Reading and writing. (Chapter 20)
Part I. Read the passage. Which words are used to introduce hypothetical situations? Underline them.

Do you know these words?
- appealing   - throbbing
- agonizing   - untold
- suffering   - outcomes

A Life Without Pain

Can you imagine a world where people felt no pain? At first it sounds appealing. You wouldn't know the agonizing suffering that comes from pain. If you had a throbbing headache or toothache, you wouldn't even feel it. But you also wouldn't know to check if the headache or toothache indicated something more serious. Or if you had a different condition, like a broken bone, you wouldn't necessarily know that it needed to be treated.

Some people are born with an inability to feel pain. However, rather than being a positive condition, it causes untold problems. If people can't feel pain, they don't know if they are hurt. For parents of young children, this is a nightmare. How would a child know about the dangers of a hot stove or broken glass? A burn wouldn't be painful and a cut wouldn't hurt.

Parents of these children have to continually watch for injuries. Normal activities like going to the playground aren't at all normal. Suppose a child fell from the top of a slide. He or she might find this fun and try to do it again, risking further injury.

Pain turns out to be lifesaving; it helps us to know if something is wrong and requires treatment. Without it, we would go through life hurting ourselves, possibly with deadly outcomes.

As you have learned, sentence variety (changing the length and structure of your sentences) makes your writing more interesting. Remember that always using *if* to express hypothetical situations can become repetitious. As you saw in the reading passage, there are other words and expressions you can use to introduce hypothetical situations: *without, suppose, imagine, how would.*

Or, as you have learned in Chart 20-7, you can sometimes omit *if* and invert the subject and verb.

Part II. Look at the following topics. Brainstorm ideas with your classmates. Then choose one and write about it. Use conditionals in your writing.

What would life be like without ...
- a sense of smell?
- the need for sleep?
- the sun?
- trees?
- schools/education?
- the Internet?
- a cell phone?
- social media?

Part III. Edit your writing. Check for the following:

1. ☐ use of conditional sentences
2. ☐ use of correct verbs with conditional sentences
3. ☐ sentence variety by not always using *if*
4. ☐ correct spelling (use a dictionary or spell-check)

Appendix

Supplementary Grammar Charts

UNIT A: Basic Grammar Terminology

A-1 Subjects, Verbs, and Objects

(a) $\overset{S}{Birds}$ $\overset{V}{fly}$. (noun) (verb)	Almost all English sentences contain a subject (**S**) and a verb (**V**). The verb may or may not be followed by an object (**O**).
(b) The $\overset{S}{baby}$ $\overset{V}{cried}$. (noun) (verb)	VERBS: Verbs that are not followed by an object, as in (a) and (b), are called "intransitive verbs." Common intransitive verbs: *agree, arrive, come, cry, exist, go, happen, live, occur, rain, rise, sleep, stay.*
(c) The $\overset{S}{student}$ $\overset{V}{needs}$ a $\overset{O}{pen}$. (noun) (verb) (noun)	Verbs that are followed by an object, as in (c) and (d), are called "transitive verbs." Common transitive verbs: *build, cut, find, like, make, need, send, use, want.*
(d) My $\overset{S}{friend}$ $\overset{V}{enjoyed}$ the $\overset{O}{party}$. (noun) (verb) (noun)	Some verbs can be either intransitive or transitive. Intransitive: *A student studies.* Transitive: *A student studies books.*
	SUBJECTS AND OBJECTS: The subjects and objects of verbs are nouns (or pronouns). Examples of nouns: *person, place, thing, John, Asia, pen, information, appearance, amusement.*

A-2 Adjectives

(a) Ann is an *intelligent* student. (adjective) (noun)	Adjectives describe nouns. In grammar, we say that adjectives modify nouns. The word *modify* means "change a little." Adjectives give a little different meaning to a noun: *intelligent student, lazy student, good student.*
(b) The *hungry* child ate fruit. (adjective) (noun)	Examples of adjectives: *young, old, rich, beautiful, brown, French, modern.*
(c) I saw some *beautiful* pictures. INCORRECT: beautiful -s- pictures	An adjective is neither singular nor plural. A final -**s** is never added to an adjective.

A-3 Adverbs

(a) He walks *quickly*. 　　　　　(adverb)	Adverbs modify verbs. Often they answer the question "How?" In (a): *How does he walk?* Answer: *Quickly*.
(b) She opened the door *quietly*. 　　　　　　　　　　(adverb)	Adverbs are often formed by adding *-ly* to an adjective. 　Adjective: *quick* 　Adverb: 　 *quickly*
(c) I am *extremely happy*. 　　　(adverb)　(adjective)	Adverbs are also used to modify adjectives, i.e., to give information about adjectives, as in (c).
(d) Ann will come *tomorrow*. 　　　　　　　　(adverb)	Adverbs are also used to express time or frequency. Examples: *tomorrow, today, yesterday, soon, never, usually, always, yet.*
MIDSENTENCE ADVERBS: (e) Ann *always comes* on time. (f) Ann *is always* on time. (g) Ann *has always come* on time. (h) Does she *always come* on time?	Some adverbs may occur in the middle of a sentence. Midsentence adverbs have usual positions; they • come in front of simple present and simple past verbs (except *be*), as in (e); • follow *be* (simple present and simple past), as in (f); • come between a helping verb and a main verb, as in (g). In a question, a midsentence adverb comes directly after the subject, as in (h).

Common midsentence adverbs

ever	usually	generally	seldom	never	already
always	often	sometimes	rarely	not ever	finally
	frequently	occasionally	hardly ever		just
					probably

A-4 Prepositions and Prepositional Phrases

Common prepositions

about	at	beyond	into	since	up
above	before	by	like	through	upon
across	behind	despite	near	throughout	with
after	below	down	of	till	within
against	beneath	during	off	to	without
along	beside	for	on	toward(s)	
among	besides	from	out	under	
around	between	in	over	until	

S　　　V　　PREP　O of PREP (a) The student studies *in* the *library*. 　　　　　　　　　　　　　　　　(noun)	An important element of English sentences is the prepositional phrase. It consists of a preposition (**PREP**) and its object (**O**). The object of a preposition is a noun or pronoun. In (a): *in the library* is a prepositional phrase.
S　　V　　　　O　PREP　O of PREP (b) We enjoyed the party *at* your *house*. 　　　　　　　　　　　　　　　　　(noun)	
(c) We went　*to the zoo*　*in the afternoon*. 　　　　　　　　(Place)　　　　(Time) (d) *In the afternoon,* we went to the zoo.	In (c): In most English sentences, "place" comes before "time." In (d): Sometimes a prepositional phrase comes at the beginning of a sentence.

A-5 Preposition Combinations with Adjectives and Verbs

A
- *be* absent from
- *be* accused of
- *be* accustomed to
- *be* acquainted with
- *be* addicted to
- *be* afraid of
- agree with
- *be* angry at, with
- *be* annoyed with, by
- apologize for
- apply to, for
- approve of
- argue with, about
- arrive in, at
- *be* associated with
- *be* aware of

B
- believe in
- blame for
- *be* blessed with
- *be* bored with, by

C
- *be* capable of
- care about, for
- *be* cluttered with
- *be* committed to
- compare to, with
- complain about, of
- *be* composed of
- *be* concerned about
- *be* connected to
- consist of
- *be* content with
- contribute to
- *be* convinced of
- *be* coordinated with
- count (up)on
- *be* covered with
- *be* crowded with

D
- decide (up)on
- *be* dedicated to
- depend (up)on
- *be* devoted to
- *be* disappointed in, with
- *be* discriminated against
- distinguish from
- *be* divorced from
- *be* done with

- dream of, about
- *be* dressed in

E
- *be* engaged in, to
- *be* envious of
- *be* equipped with
- escape from
- excel in, at
- *be* excited about
- excuse for
- *be* exhausted from
- *be* exposed to

F
- *be* faithful to
- *be* familiar with
- feel like
- fight for
- *be* filled with
- *be* finished with
- *be* fond of
- forget about
- forgive for
- *be* friendly to, with
- *be* frightened of, by
- *be* furnished with

G
- *be* gone from
- *be* grateful to, for
- *be* guilty of

H
- hide from
- hope for

I
- *be* innocent of
- insist (up)on
- *be* interested in
- introduce to
- *be* involved in

J
- *be* jealous of

K
- keep from
- *be* known for

L
- *be* limited to
- *be* located in
- look forward to

M
- *be* made of, from
- *be* married to

O
- object to
- *be* opposed to

P
- participate in
- *be* patient with
- *be* pleased with
- *be* polite to
- pray for
- *be* prepared for
- prevent from
- prohibit from
- *be* protected from
- *be* proud of
- provide with

Q
- *be* qualified for

R
- recover from
- *be* related to
- *be* relevant to
- rely (up)on
- *be* remembered for
- rescue from
- respond to
- *be* responsible for

S
- *be* satisfied with
- *be* scared of, by
- stare at
- stop from
- subscribe to
- substitute for
- succeed in

T
- take advantage of
- take care of
- talk about, of
- *be* terrified of, by
- thank for
- think about, of
- *be* tired of, from

U
- *be* upset with
- *be* used to

V
- vote for

W
- *be* worried about

UNIT B: Questions

B-1 Forms of Yes / No and Information Questions

A yes/no question = a question that may be answered by *yes* or *no*		A: Does he live in Chicago? B: Yes, he does. OR No, he doesn't.
An information question = a question that asks for information by using a question word		A: Where does he live? B: In Chicago.

Question word order = (*Question word*) + *helping verb* + *subject* + *main verb*

Notice that the same subject-verb order is used in both *yes/no* and information questions.

(Question Word)	Helping Verb	Subject	Main Verb	(Rest of Sentence)	
(a) (b) Where	Does does	she she	live live?	there?	If the verb is in the simple present, use ***does*** (with *he, she, it*) or ***do*** (with *I, you, we, they*) in the question. If the verb is simple past, use ***did***.
(c) (d) Where	Do do	they they	live live?	there?	
(e) (f) Where	Did did	he he	live live?	there?	Notice: The main verb in the question is in its simple form; there is no final ***-s*** or ***-ed***.
(g) (h) Where	Is is	he he	living living?	there?	If the verb has an auxiliary (a helping verb), the same auxiliary is used in the question. There is no change in the form of the main verb.
(i) (j) Where	Have have	they they	lived lived?	there?	
(k) (l) Where	Can can	Mary Mary	live live?	there?	If the verb has more than one auxiliary, only the first auxiliary precedes the subject, as in (m) and (n).
(m) (n) Where	Will will	he he	be living be living?	there?	
(o) Who (p) Who	Ø can	Ø Ø	lives come?	there?	If the question word is the subject, usual question-word order is not used; ***does***, ***do***, and ***did*** are not used. The verb is in the same form in a question as it is in a statement. Statement: *Tom came.* Question: *Who came?*
(q) (r) Where	Are are	they they?	Ø Ø	there?	Main verb ***be*** in the simple present (*am, is, are*) and simple past (*was, were*) precedes the subject. It has the same position as a helping verb.
(s) (t) Where	Was was	Jim Jim?	Ø Ø	there?	

	Question	Answer	
When	(a) **When** did they arrive? **When** will you come?	Yesterday. Next Monday.	**When** is used to ask questions about *time*.
Where	(b) **Where** is she? **Where** can I find a pen?	At home. In that drawer.	**Where** is used to ask questions about *place*.
Why	(c) **Why** did he leave early? **Why** aren't you coming with us?	Because he's ill. I'm tired.	**Why** is used to ask questions about *reason*.
How	(d) **How** did you come to school? **How** does he drive?	By bus. Carefully.	**How** generally asks about *manner*.
	(e) **How much** money does it cost? **How many** people came?	Ten dollars. Fifteen.	**How** is used with **much** and **many**.
	(f) **How old** are you? **How cold** is it? **How soon** can you get here? **How fast** were you driving?	Twelve. Ten below zero. In ten minutes. 50 miles an hour.	**How** is also used with adjectives and adverbs.
	(g) **How long** has he been here? **How often** do you write home? **How far** is it to Miami from here?	Two years. Every week. 500 miles.	**How long** asks about *length of time*. **How often** asks about *frequency*. **How far** asks about *distance*.
Who	(h) **Who** can answer that question? **Who** came to visit you?	I can. Jane and Eric.	**Who** is used as the subject of a question. It refers to people.
	(i) **Who** is coming to dinner tonight? **Who** wants to come with me?	Ann, Bob, and Al. We do.	**Who** is usually followed by a singular verb even if the speaker is asking about more than one person.
Whom	(j) **Who(m)** did you see? **Who(m)** are you visiting?	I saw George. My relatives.	**Whom** is used as the object of a verb or preposition. In everyday spoken English, **whom** is rarely used; **who** is used instead. **Whom** is used only in formal questions. NOTE: **Whom**, not **who**, is used if preceded by a preposition.
	(k) **Who(m)** should I talk *to*? *To* **whom** should I talk? (formal)	The secretary.	
Whose	(l) **Whose** book did you borrow? **Whose** key is this? (**Whose** is this?)	David's. It's mine.	**Whose** asks questions about *possession*.

	Question	Answer	
What	(m) *What* made you angry? *What* went wrong?	His rudeness. Everything.	**What** is used as the subject of a question. It refers to things.
	(n) *What* do you need? *What* did Alice buy?	I need a pencil. A book.	**What** is also used as an object.
	(o) *What* did he talk *about*? *About what* did he talk? (formal)	His vacation.	
	(p) *What kind of* soup is that? *What kind of* shoes did he buy?	It's bean soup. Sandals.	**What kind of** asks about the particular variety or type of something.
	(q) *What did* you *do* last night? *What is* Mary *doing*?	I studied. Reading a book.	**What** + *a form of* **do** is used to ask questions about activities.
	(r) *What countries* did you visit? *What time* did she come? *What color* is his hair?	Italy and Spain. Seven o'clock. Dark brown.	**What** may accompany a noun.
	(s) *What is* Ed *like*?	He's kind and friendly.	**What** + **be like** asks for a general description of qualities.
	(t) *What is* the weather *like*?	Hot and humid.	
	(u) *What does* Ed *look like*?	He's tall and has dark hair.	**What** + **look like** asks for a physical description.
	(v) *What does* her house *look like*?	It's a two-story,* red brick house.	
Which	(w) I have two pens. *Which pen* do you want? *Which one* do you want? *Which do* you want?	The blue one.	**Which** is used instead of **what** when a question concerns choosing from a definite, known quantity or group.
	(x) *Which book* should I buy?	That one.	
	(y) *Which countries* did he visit? *What countries* did he visit?	Peru and Chile.	In some cases, there is little difference in meaning between **which** and **what** when they accompany a noun, as in (y) and (z).
	(z) *Which class* are you in? *What class* are you in?	This class.	

*American English: *a two-**story** house.*
British English: *a two-**storey** house.*

B-3 Shortened *Yes / No* Questions

(a) *Going to bed now?* = *Are you going to bed now?* (b) *Finish your work?* = *Did you finish your work?* (c) *Want to go to the movie with us?* = *Do you want to go to the movie with us?*	Sometimes in spoken English, the auxiliary and the subject *you* are dropped from a *yes/no* question, as in (a), (b), and (c).

B-4 Negative Questions

(a) *Doesn't she live* in the dormitory? (b) *Does she not live* in the dormitory? (very formal)	In a *yes/no* question in which the verb is negative, usually a contraction (e.g., *does + not = doesn't*) is used, as in (a). Example (b) is very formal and is usually not used in everyday speech. Negative questions are used to indicate the speaker's idea (i.e., what she/he believes is or is not true) or attitude (e.g., surprise, shock, annoyance, anger).
(c) Bob returns to his dorm room after his nine o'clock class. Matt, his roommate, is there. Bob is surprised. Bob says, *"What are you doing here? Aren't you supposed to be in class now?"*	In (c): Bob believes that Matt is supposed to be in class now. *Expected answer:* **Yes**.
(d) Alice and Mary are at home. Mary is about to leave on a trip, and Alice is going to take her to the airport. Alice says, *"It's already two o'clock. We'd better leave for the airport. Doesn't your plane leave at three?"*	In (d): Alice believes that Mary's plane leaves at three. She is asking the negative question to make sure that her information is correct. *Expected answer:* **Yes**.
(e) The teacher is talking to Jim about a test he failed. The teacher is surprised that Jim failed the test because he usually does very well. The teacher says, *"What happened? Didn't you study?"*	In (e): The teacher believes that Jim did not study. *Expected answer:* **No**.
(f) Barb and Ron are riding in a car. Ron is driving. He comes to a corner where there is a stop sign, but he does not stop the car. Barb is shocked. Barb says, *"What's the matter with you? Didn't you see that stop sign?"*	In (f): Barb believes that Ron did not see the stop sign. *Expected answer:* **No**.

B-5 Tag Questions

(a) Jack *can* come, *can't* he? (b) Fred *can't* come, *can* he?	A tag question is a question added at the end of a sentence. Speakers use tag questions mainly to make sure their information is correct or to seek agreement.*

AFFIRMATIVE SENTENCE + NEGATIVE TAG → AFFIRMATIVE ANSWER EXPECTED
Mary *is* here,   *isn't* she?   Yes, she is. You *like* tea,   *don't* you?   Yes, I do. They *have left*, *haven't* they?   Yes, they have.

NEGATIVE SENTENCE + AFFIRMATIVE TAG → NEGATIVE ANSWER EXPECTED
Mary *isn't* here,   *is* she?   No, she isn't. You *don't* like tea, *do* you?   No, I don't. They *haven't* left, *have* they?   No, they haven't.

(c) *This / That* is your book, isn't *it*? *These / Those* are yours, aren't *they*?	The tag pronoun for ***this / that*** = ***it***. The tag pronoun for ***these / those*** = ***they***.
(d) *There is* a meeting tonight, *isn't there*?	In sentences with ***there + be***, ***there*** is used in the tag.
(e) *Everything* is OK, isn't *it*? (f) *Everyone* took the test, didn't *they*?	Personal pronouns are used to refer to indefinite pronouns. ***They*** is usually used in a tag to refer to ***everyone***, ***everybody***, ***someone***, ***somebody***, ***no one***, ***nobody***.
(g) *Nothing is* wrong, *is* it? (h) *Nobody called* on the phone, *did* they? (i) You*'ve never been* there, *have* you?	Sentences with negative words take affirmative tags.
(j) *I am* supposed to be here, *am I not*? (k) *I am* supposed to be here, *aren't I*?	In (j): ***am I not***? is formal English. In (k): ***aren't I***? is common in spoken English.

*A tag question may be spoken:
   (1) with a rising intonation if the speaker is truly seeking to ascertain that his/her information, idea, belief is correct (e.g., *Ann lives in an apartment, doesn't she?*); OR
   (2) with a falling intonation if the speaker is expressing an idea with which she/he is almost certain the listener will agree (e.g., *It's a nice day today, isn't it?*).

Jim *could* use some help, *couldn't* he?

UNIT C: Contractions

C Contractions

IN SPEAKING: In everyday spoken English, certain forms of **be** and auxiliary verbs are usually contracted with pronouns, nouns, and question words.

IN WRITING: (1) In written English, contractions with pronouns are common in informal writing, but they're not generally acceptable in formal writing.

(2) Contractions with nouns and question words are, for the most part, rarely used in writing. A few of these contractions may be found in quoted dialogue in stories or in very informal writing, such as a chatty letter to a good friend, but most of them are rarely if ever written.

In the following, quotation marks indicate that the contraction is frequently spoken but rarely, if ever, written.

	With Pronouns	With Nouns	With Question Words
am	*I'm* reading a book.	Ø	*"What'm"* I supposed to do?
is	*She's* studying. *It's* going to rain.	My *"book's"* on the table. *Mary's* at home.	*Where's* Sally? *Who's* that man?
are	*You're* working hard. *They're* waiting for us.	My *"books're"* on the table. The *"teachers're"* at a meeting.	*"What're"* you doing? *"Where're"* they going?
has	*She's* been here for a year. *It's* been cold lately.	My *"book's"* been stolen! *Sally's* never met him.	*Where's* Sally been living? *What's* been going on?
have	*I've* finished my work. *They've* never met you.	The *"books've"* been sold. The *"students've"* finished the test.	*"Where've"* they been? *"How've"* you been?
had	*He'd* been waiting for us. *We'd* forgotten about it.	The *"books'd"* been sold. *"Mary'd"* never met him before.	*"Where'd"* you been before that? *"Who'd"* been there before you?
did	Ø	Ø	*"What'd"* you do last night? *"How'd"* you do on the test?
will	*I'll* come later. *She'll* help us.	The *"weather'll"* be nice tomorrow. *"John'll"* be coming soon.	*"Who'll"* be at the meeting? *"Where'll"* you be at ten?
would	*He'd* like to go there. *They'd* come if they could.	My *"friends'd"* come if they could. *"Mary'd"* like to go there too.	*"Where'd"* you like to go?

UNIT D: Negatives

D-1 Using *Not* and Other Negative Words

(a) AFFIRMATIVE: The earth is round. (b) NEGATIVE: The earth is *not* flat.		*Not* expresses a *negative* idea.

		AUX + NOT + MAIN VERB				*Not* immediately follows an auxiliary verb or *be*.

(c)	I	will	not	go	there.
	I	have	not	gone	there.
	I	am	not	going	there.
	I	was	not		there.
	I	do	not	go	there.
	He	does	not	go	there.
	I	did	not	go	there.

Not immediately follows an auxiliary verb or *be*.

NOTE: If there is more than one auxiliary, *not* comes immediately after the first auxiliary: *I will not be* going there.

Do or *does* is used with *not* to make a simple present verb (except *be*) negative.

Did is used with *not* to make a simple past verb (except *be*) negative.

Contractions of auxiliary verbs with *not*

are not = aren't*	has not = hasn't	was not = wasn't
cannot = can't	have not = haven't	were not = weren't
could not = couldn't	had not = hadn't	will not = won't
did not = didn't	is not = isn't	would not = wouldn't
does not = doesn't	must not = mustn't	
do not = don't	should not = shouldn't	

(d) I almost *never* go there.
I have *hardly ever* gone there.
	In addition to *not*, the following are negative adverbs:
	    never, rarely, seldom
	    hardly (ever), scarcely (ever), barely (ever)

(e) There's *no* chalk in the drawer.	*No* also expresses a negative idea.
COMPARE: *NOT* VS. *NO* (f) I *do not have* any money. (g) I have *no money*.	*Not* is used to make a verb negative, as in (f). *No* is used as an adjective in front of a noun (e.g., money), as in (g). NOTE: Examples (f) and (g) have the same meaning.

*Sometimes in spoken English you will hear "ain't." It means "am not," "isn't," or "aren't." *Ain't* is not considered proper English although it is frequently used for humor.

D-2 Avoiding Double Negatives

(a) INCORRECT: I ~~don't~~ have ~~no~~ money. (b) CORRECT: I *don't* have *any* money. CORRECT: I have *no* money.	Sentence (a) is an example of a "double negative," i.e., a confusing and grammatically incorrect sentence that contains two negatives in the same clause. One clause should contain only one negative.*

*Negatives in two different clauses in the same sentence cause no problems; for example:
    *A person who **doesn't** have love **can't** be truly happy.*
    *I **don't** know why he **isn't** here.*

D-3 Beginning a Sentence with a Negative Word

(a) *Never will I do* that again! (b) *Rarely have I eaten* better food. (c) *Hardly ever does he come* to class on time.	When a negative word begins a sentence, the subject and verb are inverted (i.e., question word order is used).*

*Beginning a sentence with a negative word is relatively uncommon in everyday usage; it is used when the speaker/writer wishes to emphasize the negative element of the sentence and be expressive.

UNIT E: Verbs

E-1 The Verb *Be*

(a) John *is* **a student**. (be)　(noun) (b) John *is* **intelligent**. (be)　(adjective) (c) John *was* **at the library**. (be)　(prep. phrase)	A sentence with **be** as the main verb has three basic patterns: In (a): **be** + *a noun* In (b): **be** + *an adjective* In (c): **be** + *a prepositional phrase*
(d) Mary *is* writing a letter. (e) They *were* listening to some music. (f) That letter *was* written by Alice.	**Be** is also used as an auxiliary verb in progressive verb tenses and in the passive. In (d): **is** = *auxiliary;* **writing** = *main verb*

Tense Forms of *Be*

	SIMPLE PRESENT	SIMPLE PAST	PRESENT PERFECT
SINGULAR	*I am* *you are* *he, she, it is*	*I was* *you were* *he, she, it was*	*I have been* *you have been* *he, she, it has been*
PLURAL	*we, you, they are*	*we, you, they were*	*we, you, they have been*

E-2 Spelling of *-ing* and *-ed* Verb Forms

(1)	VERBS THAT END IN A CONSONANT AND **-e**	(a) hope date injure	hoping dating injuring	hoped dated injured	*-ING* FORM: If the word ends in **-e**, drop the **-e** and add **-ing**.* *-ED* FORM: If the word ends in a consonant and **-e**, just add **-d**.
(2)	VERBS THAT END IN A VOWEL AND A CONSONANT	ONE-SYLLABLE VERBS			
		(b) stop rob	stopping robbing	stopped robbed	1 vowel → 2 consonants**
		(c) rain fool	raining fooling	rained fooled	2 vowels → 1 consonant
		TWO-SYLLABLE VERBS			
		(d) listen offer	listening offering	listened offered	1st syllable stressed → 1 consonant
		(e) begin prefer	beginning preferring	(began) preferred	2nd syllable stressed → 2 consonants
(3)	VERBS THAT END IN TWO CONSONANTS	(f) start fold demand	starting folding demanding	started folded demanded	If the word ends in two consonants, just add the ending.
(4)	VERBS THAT END IN **-y**	(g) enjoy pray	enjoying praying	enjoyed prayed	If **-y** is preceded by a vowel, keep the **-y**.
		(h) study try reply	studying trying replying	studied tried replied	If **-y** is preceded by a consonant: *-ING* FORM: keep the **-y**; add **-ing**. *-ED* FORM: change **-y** to **-i**; add **-ed**.
(5)	VERBS THAT END IN **-ie**	(i) die lie	dying lying	died lied	*-ING* FORM: Change **-ie** to **-y**; add **-ing**. *-ED* FORM: Change **-y** to **-i**; add **-ed**.

*Exception: If a verb ends in **-ee**, the final **-e** is not dropped: *seeing, agreeing, freeing.*
Exception: **-w and **-x** are not doubled: *plow → plowed; fix → fixed.*

The Simple Tenses

This basic diagram will be used in all tense descriptions.

SIMPLE PRESENT 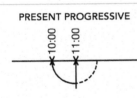	(a) It *snows* in Alaska. (b) Tom *watches* TV every day.	In general, the simple present expresses events or situations that exist *always, usually, habitually;* they exist now, have existed in the past, and probably will exist in the future.
SIMPLE PAST 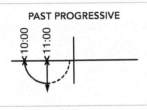	(c) It *snowed* yesterday. (d) Tom *watched* TV last night.	*At one particular time in the past,* this happened. It began and ended in the past.
SIMPLE FUTURE 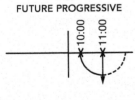	(e) It *will snow* tomorrow. It *is going to snow* tomorrow. (f) Tom *will watch* TV tonight. Tom *is going to watch* TV tonight.	*At one particular time in the future,* this will happen.

The Progressive Tenses

Form: *be + -ing* (*present participle*)

Meaning: The progressive tenses* give the idea that an action is in progress during a particular time. The tenses say that an action *begins before, is in progress during, and continues after* another time or action.

PRESENT PROGRESSIVE 10:00 11:00	(a) Tom *is sleeping* right now.	It is now 11:00. Tom went to sleep at 10:00 tonight, and he is still asleep. His sleep began in the past, *is in progress at the present time*, and probably will continue.
PAST PROGRESSIVE 10:00 11:00	(b) Tom *was sleeping* when I arrived.	Tom went to sleep at 10:00 last night. I arrived at 11:00. He was still asleep. His sleep began before and *was in progress at a particular time in the past*. It continued after I arrived.
FUTURE PROGRESSIVE 10:00 11:00	(c) Tom *will be sleeping* when we arrive.	Tom will go to sleep at 10:00 tomorrow night. We will arrive at 11:00. The action of sleeping will begin before we arrive, and it *will be in progress at a particular time in the future*. Probably his sleep will continue.

*The progressive tenses are also called the "continuous" tenses: present continuous, past continuous, and future continuous.

(continued)

The Perfect Tenses

Form: *have* + *past participle*

Meaning: The perfect tenses all give the idea that one thing *happens before* another time or event.

PRESENT PERFECT	(a) Tom *has* already *eaten*.	Tom *finished* eating *sometime before now.* The exact time is not important.

PAST PERFECT 	(b) Tom *had* already *eaten* when his friend arrived.	First Tom finished eating. Later his friend arrived. Tom's eating was completely *finished before another time in the past.*
FUTURE PERFECT	(c) Tom *will* already *have eaten* when his friend arrives.	First Tom will finish eating. Later his friend will arrive. Tom's eating will be completely *finished before another time in the future.*

The Perfect Progressive Tenses

Form: *have* + *been* + *-ing* (*present participle*)

Meaning: The perfect progressive tenses give the idea that one event is *in progress immediately before, up to, until another time or event*. The tenses are used to express the duration of the first event.

PRESENT PERFECT PROGRESSIVE	(a) Tom *has been studying* for two hours.	Event in progress: studying. When? *Before now, up to now.* How long? For two hours.
2 hrs.		
PAST PERFECT PROGRESSIVE 2 hrs.	(b) Tom *had been studying* for two hours before his friend came.	Event in progress: studying. When? *Before another event in the past.* How long? For two hours.
FUTURE PERFECT PROGRESSIVE 2 hrs.	(c) Tom *will have been studying* for two hours by the time his friend arrives.	Event in progress: studying. When? *Before another event in the future.* How long? For two hours.

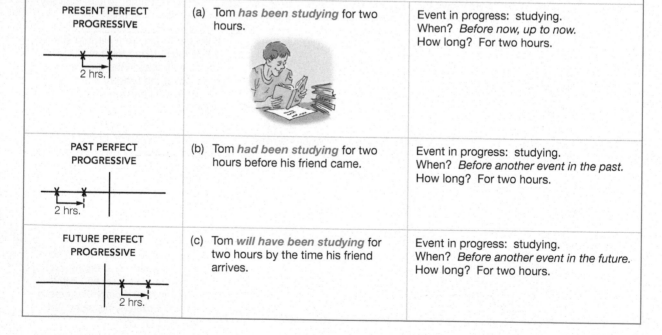

Simple Present

Tom *studies* every day.

Present Progressive

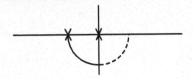

Tom *is studying* right now.

Simple Past

Tom *studied* last night.

Past Progressive

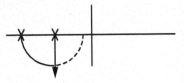

Tom *was studying* when they came.

Simple Future

Tom *will study* tomorrow.
Tom *is going to study* tomorrow.

Future Progressive

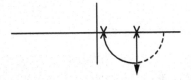

Tom *will be studying* when they come.
Tom *is going to be studying* when they come.

Present Perfect

Tom *has* already *studied* Chapter 1.

Present Perfect Progressive

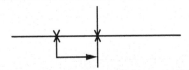

Tom *has been studying* for two hours.

Past Perfect

Tom *had* already *studied* Chapter 1 before he began studying Chapter 2.

Past Perfect Progressive

Tom *had been studying* for two hours before his friends came.

Future Perfect

Tom *will* already *have studied* Chapter 4 before he studies Chapter 5.

Future Perfect Progressive

Tom *will have been studying* for two hours by the time his roommate gets home.

E-5 Regular Verbs: Pronunciation of -ed Endings

Final **-ed** has three different pronunciations: /t/, /d/, and /əd/. The schwa /ə/ is an unstressed vowel sound. It is pronounced like *a* in *alone* in normal, rapid speech (e.g., *She lives alone.*).

(a)	looked	→	look/t/
	clapped	→	clap/t/
	missed	→	miss/t/
	watched	→	watch/t/
	finished	→	finish/t/
	laughed	→	laugh/t/

Final **-ed** is pronounced /t/ after voiceless sounds.

Voiceless sounds are made by pushing air through your mouth; no sound comes from your throat.

Examples of voiceless sounds: "k," "p," "s," "ch," "sh," "f."

(b)	smelled	→	smell/d/
	saved	→	save/d/
	cleaned	→	clean/d/
	robbed	→	rob/d/
	played	→	play/d/

Final **-ed** is pronounced /d/ after voiced sounds.

Voiced sounds come from your throat. If you touch your neck when you make a voiced sound, you can feel your voice box vibrate.

Examples of voiced sounds: "l," "v," "n," "b," and all vowel sounds.

(c)	decided	→	decide/əd/
	needed	→	need/əd/
	wanted	→	want/əd/
	invited	→	invite/əd/

Final **-ed** is pronounced /əd/ after "t" and "d" sounds. The sound /əd/ adds a whole syllable to a word.

COMPARE: looked = one syllable → look/t/
smelled = one syllable → smell/d/
needed = two syllables → need/əd/

E-6 Pronunciation of Final -s in Verbs and Nouns

Final **-s** has three different pronunciations: /s/, /z/, and /əz/.

(a)	seats	→	*seat*/s/
	ropes	→	*rope*/s/
	backs	→	*back*/s/

Final **-s** is pronounced /s/ after voiceless sounds, as in (a).

"t," "p," and "k" are examples of voiceless sounds.

(b)	seeds	→	*seed*/z/
	robes	→	*robe*/z/
	bags	→	*bag*/z/
	sees	→	*see*/z/

Final **-s** is pronounced /z/ after voiced sounds, as in (b).

"d," "b," "g," and "ee" are examples of voiced sounds.

(c)	dishes	→	*dish*/əz/
	catches	→	*catch*/əz/
	kisses	→	*kiss*/əz/
	mixes	→	*mix*/əz/
	prizes	→	*prize*/əz/
	edges	→	*edge*/əz/

Final **-s** and **-es** are pronounced /əz/ after "sh," "ch," "s," "x," "z," and "ge"/"dge" sounds.

The /əz/ ending adds a syllable.

All of the words in (c) are pronounced with two syllables.

COMPARE: All of the words in (a) and (b) are pronounced with one syllable.

E-7 Linking Verbs

(a) The soup *smells* *good*. (linking verb) (adjective) (b) This food *tastes delicious*. (c) The children *feel happy*. (d) The weather *became cold*.	Other verbs like **be** that may be followed immediately by an adjective are called "linking verbs." An adjective following a linking verb describes the subject of a sentence.* Common verbs that may be followed by an adjective: • *feel, look, smell, sound, taste* • *appear, seem* • *become* (and *get, turn, grow* when they mean "become")

*COMPARE:

   (1) *The man looks angry.* → An adjective (**angry**) follows **look**. The adjective describes the subject (**the man**). **Look** has the meaning of "appear."

   (2) *The man looked at me angrily.* → An adverb (**angrily**) follows **look at**. The adverb describes the action of the verb. **Look at** has the meaning of "regard, watch."

Ann *is at the laudromat*.
She *looks* very *busy*.

E-8 Troublesome Verbs: *Raise / Rise, Set / Sit, Lay / Lie*

Transitive	Intransitive	
(a) *raise, raised, raised* Tom **raised** his hand.	(b) *rise, rose, risen* The sun **rises** in the east.	**Raise**, **set**, and **lay** are *transitive* verbs; they are followed by an object. **Rise**, **sit**, and **lie** are intransitive; they are NOT followed by an object.*
(c) *set, set, set* I **will set** the book on the desk.	(d) *sit, sat, sat* I **sit** in the front row.	In (a): **raised** is followed by the object **hand**. In (b): **rises** is not followed by an object.

(e) *lay, laid, laid*
I **am laying** the book on the desk.
	(f) *lie,** lay, lain*
	He **is lying** on his bed.
		NOTE: **Lay** and **lie** are troublesome for native speakers too and are frequently misused.
		    lay = put
		    lie = recline

  *See Appendix Chart A-1 for information about transitive and intransitive verbs.

  ***Lie** is a regular verb (*lie, lied*) when it means "not tell the truth": **He lied** to me about his age.

NOTE: Verbs followed by a bullet (•) are defined at the end of the this list.

Simple Form	Simple Past	Past Participle	Simple Form	Simple Past	Past Participle
arise	arose	arisen	forbid	forbade	forbidden
awake	awoke	awoken	forecast•	forecast	forecast
be	was, were	been	forget	forgot	forgotten
bear	bore	borne/born	forgive	forgave	forgiven
beat	beat	beaten/beat	forsake•	forsook	forsaken
become	became	become	freeze	froze	frozen
begin	began	begun	get	got	gotten/got*
bend	bent	bent	give	gave	given
bet•	bet	bet	go	went	gone
bid•	bid	bid	grind•	ground	ground
bind•	bound	bound	grow	grew	grown
bite	bit	bitten	hang**	hung	hung
bleed	bled	bled	have	had	had
blow	blew	blown	hear	heard	heard
break	broke	broken	hide	hid	hidden
breed•	bred	bred	hit	hit	hit
bring	brought	brought	hold	held	held
broadcast•	broadcast	broadcast	hurt	hurt	hurt
build	built	built	keep	kept	kept
burn	burned/burnt	burned/burnt	kneel	kneeled/knelt	kneeled/knelt
burst•	burst	burst	know	knew	known
buy	bought	bought	lay	laid	laid
cast•	cast	cast	lead	led	led
catch	caught	caught	lean	leaned/leant	leaned/leant
choose	chose	chosen	leap	leaped/leapt	leaped/leapt
cling•	clung	clung	learn	learned/learnt	learned/learnt
come	came	come	leave	left	left
cost	cost	cost	lend	lent	lent
creep•	crept	crept	let	let	let
cut	cut	cut	lie	lay	lain
deal•	dealt	dealt	light	lighted/lit	lighted/lit
dig	dug	dug	lose	lost	lost
do	did	done	make	made	made
draw	drew	drawn	mean	meant	meant
dream	dreamed/dreamt	dreamed/dreamt	meet	met	met
drink	drank	drunk	mislay	mislaid	mislaid
drive	drove	driven	mistake	mistook	mistaken
eat	ate	eaten	pay	paid	paid
fall	fell	fallen	prove	proved	proven/proved
feed	fed	fed	put	put	put
feel	felt	felt	quit***	quit	quit
fight	fought	fought	read	read	read
find	found	found	rid	rid	rid
fit	fit/fitted	fit/fitted	ride	rode	ridden
flee•	fled	fled	ring	rang	rung
fling•	flung	flung	rise	rose	risen
fly	flew	flown			

*In British English: *get–got–got.* In American English: *get–got–gotten/got.*

**Hang* is a regular verb when it means to kill someone with a rope around his/her neck.

COMPARE: *I **hung** my clothes in the closet. They **hanged** the murderer by the neck until he was dead.*

***Also possible in British English: *quit–quitted–quitted.*

Simple Form	Simple Past	Past Participle	Simple Form	Simple Past	Past Participle
run	ran	run	spring•	sprang/sprung	sprung
say	said	said	stand	stood	stood
see	saw	seen	steal	stole	stolen
seek•	sought	sought	stick	stuck	stuck
sell	sold	sold	sting•	stung	stung
send	sent	sent	stink•	stank/stunk	stunk
set	set	set	strike•	struck	struck/stricken
shake	shook	shaken	strive•	strove/strived	striven/strived
shed•	shed	shed	string	strung	strung
shine	shone/shined	shone/shined	swear	swore	sworn
shoot	shot	shot	sweep	swept	swept
show	showed	shown/showed	swell	swelled	swelled/swollen
shrink•	shrank/shrunk	shrunk	swim	swam	swum
shut	shut	shut	swing•	swung	swung
sing	sang	sung	take	took	taken
sink•	sank	sunk	teach	taught	taught
sit	sat	sat	tear	tore	torn
sleep	slept	slept	tell	told	told
slide•	slid	slid	think	thought	thought
slit•	slit	slit	throw	threw	thrown
smell	smelled/smelt	smelled/smelt	thrust•	thrust	thrust
sneak	sneaked/snuck	sneaked/snuck	understand	understood	understood
speak	spoke	spoken	undertake	undertook	undertaken
speed	sped/speeded	sped/speeded	upset	upset	upset
spell	spelled/spelt	spelled/spelt	wake	woke/waked	woken
spend	spent	spent	wear	wore	worn
spill	spilled/spilt	spilled/spilt	weave•	wove	woven
spin•	spun	spun	weep•	wept	wept
spit	spit/spat	spit/spat	win	won	won
split•	split	split	wind•	wound	wound
spoil	spoiled/spoilt	spoiled/spoilt	withdraw	withdrew	withdrawn
spread•	spread	spread	write	wrote	written

•Definitions of some of the less frequently used irregular verbs:

bet . . . . . wager; offer to pay money if one loses

bid . . . . . make an offer of money, usually at a public sale

bind . . . . . fasten or secure

breed . . . . . bring animals together to produce young

broadcast . . . . . send information by radio waves; announce

burst . . . . . explode; break suddenly

cast . . . . . throw

cling . . . . . hold on tightly

creep . . . . . crawl close to the ground; move slowly and quietly

deal . . . . . distribute playing cards to each person; give attention to (deal with)

flee . . . . . escape; run away

fling . . . . . throw with force

forecast . . . . . predict a future occurrence

forsake . . . . . abandon or desert

grind . . . . . crush, reduce to small pieces

seek . . . . . look for

shed . . . . . drop off or get rid of

shrink . . . . . become smaller

sink . . . . . move downward, often under water

slide . . . . . glide smoothly; slip or skid

slit . . . . . cut a narrow opening

spin . . . . . turn rapidly around a central point

split . . . . . divide into two or more parts

spread . . . . . push out in all directions (e.g., butter on bread, news)

spring . . . . . jump or rise suddenly from a still position

sting . . . . . cause pain with a sharp object (e.g., pin) or bite (e.g., by an insect)

stink . . . . . have a bad or foul smell

strike . . . . . hit something with force

strive . . . . . try hard to achieve a goal

swing . . . . . move back and forth

thrust . . . . . push forcibly; shove

weave . . . . . form by passing pieces of material over and under each other (as in making baskets, cloth)

weep . . . . . cry

wind . . . . . (sounds like *find*) turn around and around

Listening Script

Chapter 12: Noun Clauses

Exercise 38, p. 265.
1. I'm not going to the personnel meeting because I have to finish a report.
2. I can't lend Marta any money because my wallet is in my coat pocket back at home.
3. Someone in this room is wearing very strong perfume. It's giving me a headache.
4. Hi, Emma. I'll meet you at the coffee shop at 9:00. I promise not to be late.
5. I'm considering looking for a new job. What do you think I should do?
6. We are going to be late for the concert. My wife has to attend a business function after work.

Chapter 13: Adjective Clauses

Exercise 5, p. 274.
Part I
1. He has a friend who'll help him.
2. He has a friend who's helping him.
3. He has a friend who's helped him.
4. He has friends who're helping him.
5. He has friends who've helped him.
6. He has a friend who'd helped him.
7. He has a friend who'd like to help him.
8. He has a friend who's been helping him.

Part II
1. We know a person who'll be great for the job.
2. We know a person who'd like to apply for the job.
3. That's the man who's moving to our department.
4. I know of three people who've asked to transfer to another location.
5. I'd like to talk to the people who're asking to move.
6. There are two people at this company who've worked here all their adult lives.
7. The manager who'd been stealing from the company quit.

Exercise 22, p. 281.
1. I met the professor who's going to be my advisor.
2. I know someone who's famous in the music industry.
3. I talked to the man whose wife was in the car accident on Fifth Street yesterday. She's in the hospital, but she's going to be OK.
4. I forget the name of the woman who's going to call you later — Mrs. Green or Mrs. White or something like that.
5. I need to hurry. The neighbor whose bike I borrowed is waiting for me to return it.
6. I got an email from a friend who's studying in Malaysia. It was really good to hear from her.
7. I recently heard from a friend who's overseas. He finally sent me an email.
8. I'm thinking about getting a pet. There's a woman at work whose dog just had puppies. I might adopt one.

Exercise 23, p. 282.
1. That's the person who's going to help us.
2. That's the person whose help we need.
3. I'd like to introduce you to a teacher who's spent time in Africa.
4. I'd like to introduce you to the teacher whose husband is from Africa.
5. The company is looking for a person who's bilingual.
6. The company is looking for a person whose native language is Arabic.
7. The company is looking for a person who's had a lot of experience in sales.
8. They want to hire a person who's familiar with their sales territory.

Exercise 32, p. 285.
1. The man who gave the news interview is a friend of mine.
2. Two people died in an accident that blocked all lanes of the highway for two hours.
3. The small town where I was born is now a large city.
4. The music teacher who gave me music lessons a long time ago became a rock star.
5. The phone that I got from my parents takes excellent pictures.
6. My neighbor often drops in for a visit about the time when we would like to sit down to dinner.

Exercise 42, p. 290.
1. My mother looked in the fruit basket and threw away the apples that were rotten.
2. My mother looked in the fruit basket and threw away the apples, which were rotten.
3. The students who had done well on the test were excused from class early.
4. The students, who had done well on the test, were excused from class early.

Exercise 54, p. 296.

1. The fence surrounding our house is made of wood.
2. The children attending that school receive a good education.
3. Dr. Stanton, the president of the university, will give a speech at the commencement ceremonies.
4. Our solar system is in a galaxy called the Milky Way.

Chapter 14: Gerunds and Infinitives, Part 1

Exercise 8, p. 306.

1. A: What should we do tomorrow night?
   B: Let's watch a movie. That's what I like doing on weekends.
   A: Same here.
2. A: I was really looking forward to the hike in the mountains this weekend, but I guess we're not going to get there.
   B: It doesn't look like it. I don't think there's any hope. It's supposed to rain for the next two weeks.
3. A: Do you want to take a break?
   B: No, we have to finish this report by 5:00. We don't have time for a break.
4. A: Let's go into the city this weekend. There's a free concert at the park.
   B: That sounds like fun. Who's playing?
5. A: I'd really like to go out this evening, but I have all this work to do. I have three assignments, and I haven't begun to write any of them.
   B: I know how you feel. I'm way behind in my homework too.
6. A: I just heard that there's an accident on the freeway and nothing's moving.
   B: Let's stay here for another couple of hours. We can get caught up on our work.
   A: Good idea. I have so much to do.

Exercise 21, p. 313.

1. Joan remembered to call her husband before she left work yesterday.
2. Rita remembered going to the farmers' market with her grandmother.
3. Roger stopped smoking when the doctor told him he had heart disease.
4. Mr. and Mrs. Olson stopped to eat before the movie.
5. I regret leaving school before I graduated.

Exercise 30, p. 319.

1. A: I'm sorry I'm late.
   B: No problem. We have lots of time.
2. A: I finished the project early.
   B: That's great you got it done so quickly.
3. A: I hate to do housework.
   B: I know. I do too. It's a lot of work.
4. A: You were a big help. Thanks.
   B: Sure. I was happy to help out.
5. A: Your report isn't finished. What's your excuse?
   B: Uh, well, sorry. I don't really have one.

6. A: How do you like the food here?
   B: It's too spicy. I can't eat much of it.
7. A: How was your weekend? Did you go away for the holiday?
   B: No. I got the flu and spent the whole weekend in bed.

Exercise 41, p. 325.

1. I have a terrible memory. I can't even remember my children's birthdays.
2. My teenage son tried to hide his report card, but I caught him.
3. I'm in a hurry in the mornings. I always stand at the kitchen counter and eat my breakfast.
4. Foreign languages are hard for me to learn.
5. I sat in traffic for two hours. It was a waste of time.
6. We sang songs on the bus trip. It was fun.
7. I looked all over for Tom. He was studying in the library.
8. There was a line to buy movie tickets. I had to wait for an hour.

Chapter 15: Gerunds and Infinitives, Part 2

Exercise 13, p. 340.

1. Benjamin is too old to have a driver's license.
2. Our daughter isn't old enough to stay home alone yet.
3. The test results are too good to believe.
4. This room seems big enough for an office.
5. You will have time enough to take a tour of the city.
6. The leftovers look too old to eat.

Exercise 17, p. 342.

An Issue in Health Care: Illiteracy

According to some estimates, well over half of the people in the world are functionally illiterate. This means that they are unable to perform everyday tasks because they can't read, understand, and respond appropriately to information. One of the problems this creates in health care is that millions of people are not able to read directions on medicine bottles or packages. Imagine being a parent with a sick child and being unable to read the directions on a medicine bottle. We all know that it is important for medical directions to be understood clearly. One solution is pictures. Many medical professionals are working today to solve this problem by using pictures to convey health-care information.

Chapter 16: Coordinating Conjunctions

Exercise 19, p. 365.

1. Ben will call either Mary or Bob.
2. Both my mother and father talked to my teacher.
3. Simon saw not only a whale but also a dolphin.
4. Our neighborhood had neither electricity nor water after the storm.

5. Either Mr. Anderson or Ms. Wiggins is going to teach our class today.

Exercise 21, p. 367.

Bats

What do people in your country think of bats? Are they mean and scary creatures, or are they symbols of both happiness and luck?

In Western countries, many people have an unreasoned fear of bats. According to scientist Dr. Sharon Horowitz, bats are not only harmless but also beneficial mammals. "When I was a child, I believed that a bat would attack me and tangle itself in my hair. Now I know better," said Dr. Horowitz.

Contrary to popular Western myths, bats do not attack humans. Although a few bats may have diseases, they are not major carriers of rabies or other frightening diseases. Bats help natural plant life by pollinating plants, spreading seeds, and eating insects. If you get rid of bats that eat overripe fruit, then fruit flies can flourish and destroy the fruit industry.

According to Dr. Horowitz, bats are both gentle and trainable pets. Not many people, however, own or train bats, and bats themselves prefer to avoid people.

Chapter 18: Reduction of Adverb Clauses to Modifying Adverbial Phrases

Exercise 17, p. 401.

1. A: I don't want to play the piano at the family gathering. I don't play well enough. People will laugh at me.
   B: Rose, I know you're nervous, but you play beautifully. Everyone will love hearing you.
2. A: Jan, are you going to tell Thomas that he needs to do more work on the project? He hasn't done his share. He's being really lazy.
   B: Well, he'll probably get upset, but I'm going to talk with him about it this afternoon.
3. A: I'm so relieved that I found my wedding ring. It'd been missing for a month. The next time I take it off, I'm going to put it in a box on top of my dresser.
   B: That sounds like a wise thing to do, Susan. It'd be terrible to lose your wedding ring again.
4. A: This is the first year I'm eligible to vote in the presidential election. I'm going to research all the candidates extensively.
   B: They have very different positions, Sam. It's good to get as much information as you can.

Chapter 19: Connectives That Express Cause and Effect, Contrast, and Condition

Exercise 37, p. 421.

1. Because I lift heavy boxes at work, ...
2. I bought a new TV even though ...
3. Even if I'm late for work, ...
4. I was late for work this morning; nevertheless, ...
5. The air-conditioning has been broken; therefore, ...
6. Although I live in a noisy city, ...
7. I was so tired last night that ...

Exercise 39, p. 422.

Why We Yawn

Have you ever noticed that when a person near you yawns, you may start yawning too? This is called contagious yawning. *Contagious* in this sense means that the behavior spreads: in the case of yawning, when one person yawns, it can cause others to do the same thing.

There are various theories about why people yawn. One popular idea is that yawning brings more oxygen into the brain so that people will wake up. Is that what you have thought?

However, in 2007, researchers at a university in New York came up with a new idea: yawning helps cool the brain. When people's brains are warm, they yawn more frequently; yawning brings cooler air into the body and, therefore, cools the brain. This is important because cooler brains work better than warmer ones.

This may also help explain why yawning is contagious. People are more awake when their brains are cooler; therefore, contagious yawning helps people be more alert. As people evolved, this was important in times of danger. If they yawned, they could have been signaling to others to stay awake.

While it can be annoying to have a person yawn when you are talking, perhaps you can tell yourself that he or she actually wants to stay awake, not go to sleep.

Chapter 20: Conditional Sentences and Wishes

Exercise 8, p. 429.

1. If I'm talking too fast, please tell me.
2. If we get married, everyone will be shocked.
3. If it's OK, I'll ask for some advice.
4. If he's planning to quit, I hope he lets us know soon.
5. If it's not working, we'll need to try something else.

6. If she works harder, I'm sure she'll succeed.
7. If I should get the job, I'll call you right away.

Exercise 19, p. 433.

1. If I had known the truth sooner, I would have acted differently.
2. If we hadn't believed him, we wouldn't have felt so foolish.
3. If you hadn't told me what a great guy Jon was, I wouldn't have believed him so easily.
4. If it had been another person, I wouldn't have been so shocked.
5. If he hadn't lied, I would have had more respect for him.

Exercise 25, p. 437.

1. If I had enough time, I'd go to the art museum this afternoon. I love going to art museums.

2. Mrs. Jones is really lucky. If she hadn't received immediate medical attention, she would have died.
3. If I were a carpenter, I'd build my own house. I'd really enjoy that.
4. So many people died unnecessarily in the earthquake. If the hotel had been built to withstand an earthquake, it wouldn't have collapsed.

Exercise 40, p. 443.

1. I would have called, but I left your number at home.
2. I couldn't have gone to college without my parents' financial help.
3. I ran out of time. Otherwise, I would have picked up your clothes from the cleaners.
4. We would have come to the party, but no one told us about it.
5. Without your advice, I wouldn't have known what to do.

Index

Able to, 202, 205 (*Look on pages 202 and 205.*)	The numbers following the words listed in the index refer to page numbers in the text.
Continuous tenses, 3*fn.* (*Look at the footnote on page 3.*)	The letters *fn.* mean "footnote." Footnotes appear beneath some charts and readings or at the bottom of some pages.

When:
    in adjective clauses, 284
    in adverb clauses, 373
    in adverbial phrases, 394
    meaning *upon,* 394*fn.*
    in questions, 456
Whenever, 373
Where:
    in adjective clauses, 282
    in questions, 456
Whereas, 381*fn.*
Whether, 253
Whether or not, 384, 405
Which:
    in adjective clauses, 273, 273*fn.*, 276,
        287*fn.*, 293
    in questions, 457
While:
    in adverb clauses, 373, 381, 405, 418, 418*fn.*
    in adverbial phrases, 394, 395
    vs. *whereas,* 381*fn.*
Whose, 280, 456
Who/whom:
    in adjective clauses, 273, 276
    in questions, 456
    vs. *whose,* 280
Why, 456

Will:
    in conditional sentences, 427
    contractions with, 460
    after *so that,* 414
Wish, 445, 448
Word order:
    in adjective phrases, 295*fn.*
    after negatives, 461
    in noun clauses, 249
    after *only if,* 388
    in questions, 252*fn.*, 455
Would:
    in conditional sentences, 427, 430, 432
    contractions with, 460
    in reported speech, 264
    after *so that,* 414
    with *wish,* 448
Would have, 427, 432*fn.*, 445*fn.*

Y

-Y, final, spelling:
    with *-ed, -ing,* 462
Yes/no questions, 455, 458
Yet, 405, 416
You:
    vs. *your,* 320*fn.*

Credits

Photo Credits

NOTES

NOTES

NOTES

NOTES

NOTES

NOTES